Coaching and Mentoring at Work

Coaching and Mentoring at Work

Developing Effective Practice

Third Edition

Mary Connor and Julia Pokora

 Open University Press

Open University Press
McGraw-Hill Education
8th Floor, 338 Euston Road
London
England
NW1 3BH

email: enquiries@openup.co.uk
world wide web: www.openup.co.uk

and Two Penn Plaza, New York, NY 10121-2289, USA

First published 2007
Second edition published 2012
First published in this third edition 2017

A catalogue record of this book is available from the British Library

ISBN-13: 978-0-335-22692-4
ISBN-10: 0-33-5226922
eISBN: 978-0-335-22693-1

Library of Congress Cataloging-in-Publication Data
CIP data applied for

Typeset by Transforma Pvt. Ltd., Chennai, India

Printed and bound by CPI Group (UK) Ltd, Croydon, CR0 4YY

Praise page

"So many people think that mentoring is simple – you just pass on what you know from the pinnacle of your wisdom and experience. In fact when well done it is the art that conceals art. Similarly there is an art in making what is not simple sound accessible and do-able, which is exactly what this book does. It breaks the news very gently and very clearly that successful mentoring and coaching is nothing like as easy as it looks, either to be a good mentor or to be a good mentee. Throughout the book the message is clear: being a coach or mentor is very different from the expert helper role familiar to most managers – a lot more difficult and a lot more effective and here is how to do it."

Jenny Rogers, Executive Coach and author of
*Coaching Skills: The Definitive Guide
to Being a Coach, Fourth Edition*
(Open University Press, 2016), UK

"The third edition of Coaching & Mentoring at Work *has been revised and updated. There are two new chapters: 'Coaching & Mentoring Approaches and Models', and 'Glimpses of Coaches and Mentors at Work'. Readers of the previous editions have valued the focus on effective and ethical practice as well as the clear links between principles, approaches, skills, tools, techniques and interactive case examples. This latest edition continues to be an excellent resource for coaching and mentoring purchasers, providers and students."*

Gerard Egan, Professor Emeritus,
Loyola University, Chicago, USA

"It is great to see this new updated edition of Mary Connor and Julia Pokora's book, which shows how much is developing and changing in this fast moving field."

Peter Hawkins, Professor of Leadership,
Henley Business School,
Chairman of Renewal Associates,
author of many books including
Creating a Coaching Culture
(Open University Press, 2012) and
Leadership Team Coaching (2014), UK

"This new edition from Connor and Pokora has some new and interesting additions. In the ten years since the first edition, much has happened in the coaching and mentoring world. The highlighting of ethical issues in Part 1 of the book recognises that the coaching and mentoring worlds have become much more aware of ethical concerns. The addition of insights into the variety of models for coaching and mentoring and the practical nature of Part 2 of the book is welcome and the shift of focus in Part 3 to Coach and Mentor Development reflects contemporary debate. Written in a practical and accessible style, this book is a must for those working with coaching and mentoring."

Professor Bob Garvey, Managing Partner,
The Lio Partnership, UK

"When this book was first published in 2007 it immediately became an invaluable reference and source of guidance for the part of my work involved with the development mentoring of engineers and engineering project management professionals. The restructured content and additional material provided by the third edition make the book an even more valuable resource for coaches, mentors and their clients in all work sectors. I have always liked the practical exercises, examples and checklists that are to be found throughout the content and I find the glimpses into the experiences of current coaching and mentoring practitioners contained within the new Chapter 12 particularly interesting and useful."

Tony Maplesden, Project Management Consultant, UK

"Still my favourite coaching and mentoring book – this new edition is better than ever! For the coach/mentor there are plenty of additional resources including a helpful chapter giving insightful reflections on real examples of coaching practice and developing coaching schemes. What I really like about this book is how useful it is for people at different stages in their coaching and mentorship practice – and there's plenty for coachees and mentees too which helps maximise the benefit of the coaching relationship."

Sue Covill, Former HR Director, UK

"This book illustrates the importance of skills, personal qualities and ethical understanding in promoting healthy and meaning relationships, and this work may also be relevant in other helping professions. However, this book also helps anyone who wants to improve their conversations with those around them (co-workers, family and friends)."

Assoc. Prof. Dr Ruhani Mat Min,
Universiti Malaysia Terengganu, Malaysia

Contents

List of illustrations

Figures

Tables

Authors and Contributors

Mary Connor is co-founder of Coaching & Mentoring Consultants. She has been providing coaching, mentoring, training, supervision and research to both public and private sector organizations for more than 25 years. Previously, she was Head of Individual and Organization Development Studies at the University College of York St John and an honorary fellow at the Centre for Leadership Development at the University of York. She has considerable experience of working with Professor Gerard Egan, of Chicago, author of The Skilled Helper model. She has a particular interest in ethical practice and professional development, and she has served for 15 years on NHS research ethics committees as well as having been Chair of Governors in a school.

Julia Pokora. Following an early career with BP and Exxon, Julia established an independent organization and management development consultancy, and at that time was an associate with the Teamworking Services unit at Ashridge Management College. She has over 30 years' experience of consultancy and has worked in both the private and public sectors, with organizations, teams and individuals. In recent years, she has focused on developing the mentoring and coaching capability of doctors, dentists and other professionals in the Health Service. She holds an MSc in occupational psychology and a Graduate Diploma in counselling.

Wendy Briner is a Leadership Coach and Researcher at Ashridge Executive Education, Hult International Business School. She was Director of Leadership Coaching for the Ashridge Leadership Process, introducing coaching as an integrated part of leadership development. She is a Qualified Systemic Family Therapist. Her main activities are designing, participating in and introducing appreciative action research in health settings, especially in the Middle East.

David Harrison has spent 30 years in education, the last 15 years in a leadership role, as Headteacher of an outstanding school. He is currently the Executive Headteacher of three schools in North Yorkshire. David is also a National Leader in Education and he leads a Teaching School Alliance.

Martin Hill is a solicitor and is a senior consultant for the British School of Coaching. He is the Programme Director for their ILM7 Executive Coaching and Mentoring course. He coaches and supervises across both public and private sectors in the UK and the Middle East.

Malcolm Hurrell is Director of New Mindsets Ltd. He was previously Vice President of HR UK at AstraZeneca. He is a passionate advocate of coaching, believing it to be one of the most critical development interventions for senior leaders and an essential capability for organizations seeking to create a high performance culture.

Shaun Lincoln is a Leadership and Management Coach working primarily with leaders and senior leadership teams in Further Education colleges, creative enterprises and charities, as well as more widely in the public and private sectors. He uses a solution-focused approach to enable leaders and teams to do more of what works, and to become high performing teams.

Arti Maini is a GP and Coaching Lead for the Department of Primary Care and Public Health at Imperial College, London. She works with Health Education England, NHS London Leadership Academy and Coaching Supervision Academy. She co-authored *Coaching for Health: Why it Works and How To Do it.*

Sarah Montgomery. As a Head of Learning and Organizational Development within the NHS, Sarah has successfully established a coaching culture within her current organization, demonstrating real evidence of the difference coaching makes to staff and organizational performance. Sarah's coaching style balances support with challenge to enable people to maximize their potential and ultimately improve services.

Nancy Redfern is a Consultant Anaesthetist and the Honorary Membership Secretary of the Association of Anaesthetists of Great Britain and Ireland. She has established mentoring programmes and schemes at the AAGBI, and in Royal Colleges and Hospitals throughout the UK, changing culture so that mentoring in seen as part of professional development.

Kam Urwin is Mentoring Manager at Housing Diversity Network. She believes that mentoring can provide an opportunity for mentees and mentors to focus on achieving their personal goals. She has delivered the Housing Diversity Network Mentoring Programme since 2007. In 2016, the programme won the CIPD People Management Award for 'Best Coaching & Mentoring Initiative'.

Preface to the third edition

In the ten years since the first edition of this book was published, coaching and mentoring have flourished. Studies have highlighted the positive impacts of coaching and mentoring on individuals and organizations in both the public and private sectors. Research continues to shed light on the age-old question of which factors in coaching and mentoring can best predict successful outcomes. Advances in neuroscience have greatly increased understanding of how the brain works and this has led to discussion of which are the most productive coaching and mentoring approaches and interventions. In the context of developments such as these, this third edition revises, updates and supplements the previous editions. We have added two new chapters. One discusses a range of approaches and models and the other comprises first-hand glimpses from coaches and mentors as they reflect on their own experiences of coaching and mentoring at work. In response to reader feedback, we have reorganized the book so that Part 1 addresses the foundations of effective practice, Part 2 focuses on models, approaches and techniques, and Part 3 on coach and mentor development.

We hope that the book will be a source of encouragement and stimulation, whether you are a client, a coach, a mentor, a sponsor or someone who may one day be one of these.

Acknowledgements

This third edition has been produced with the support and encouragement of our families and friends, and our editor Monika Lee. Many valued colleagues, too numerous to mention individually, have contributed to the development of our ideas, and we thank Professor Gerard Egan for inspiring our thinking and practice.

We appreciate the enthusiasm and commitment of all the sponsors, facilitators and participants with whom we work. We thank our clients, and all those who have coached and mentored us, whether knowingly or otherwise. Learning with you, and from you, has informed and encouraged us.

We are grateful to Cengage Learning for permission to reproduce Figures 3.1 and 3.2 from Egan. *The Skilled Helper, International Edition*, 9E. © 2010 South-Western, a part of Cengage Learning, Inc. Reproduced by permission. www.cengage.com/permissions.

Introduction

For more than 25 years we have been involved in coaching, mentoring and supervision at work, both informally and in more structured settings. We have designed and delivered coach and mentor training throughout the UK. We have written this book to address, practically, all the aspects of coaching and mentoring at work that seemed important to us. Feedback from colleagues and participants was that they wanted a text which encapsulated the learning from training programmes and sustained them when they were on their own, back at work, trying to be effective coaches and mentors. So we have written this book partly for them.

We also wanted to write a book which could be read by clients. Much is said about the partnership nature of coaching and mentoring, yet most of the literature and most training programmes focus on only half of that partnership. The book is written, therefore, for the other half also – the clients – to help them get the best out of coaching and mentoring.

In addition, we noticed the ongoing debate about coaching versus mentoring, and in our everyday experience we found that these activities had much in common. Conversations with colleagues in both the public and private sectors revealed that while terminology differs, there is considerable overlap in what many coaches and mentors actually do. So, this book seeks to identify the common ground, and to explain the key principles that underpin both effective coaching and effective mentoring.

Another reason for writing this book was to answer frequently asked questions. We wanted to write a book that was accessible to busy people. A book that was full of practical examples and exercises, with ideas that could be used in everyday life and work. The chapters address the topics that are often raised by clients, coaches or mentors and the penultimate chapter specifically addresses frequently asked questions.

Anyone who has tried to coach or mentor knows just how demanding the work can be. It seems straightforward enough to suggest that someone can be helped to help themselves, rather than being told or advised what to do. However, it can be hard work and it is certainly not commonplace. Spend a few minutes listening to the conversations around you in the workplace and you will see what we mean. Nevertheless, when we have experienced skilful coaching and mentoring from friends, colleagues and professionals, it has made a world of difference. So we hope that this book will support the reader in developing their skills and making a difference.

We are concerned about maintaining high standards in coaching and mentoring. The serendipity that was historically evident in the provision of coaching and mentoring services has been rightly challenged by the current focus on competent, ethical and professional practice. In this book we aim to make the connection between everyday practice and ongoing professional development.

Both of us have benefited from wise mentors and coaches, some formal and some informal, some qualified and some not. We hope in this book to share something of their wisdom, which we have found to be more easily 'caught' than 'taught'. It is not easy to capture the essence of wisdom, but we experience a wholeness and a sense of deep integrity in those coaches and mentors who have, in brief moments as well as over many sessions, transformed aspects of our lives.

The structure of the book

Part 1 sets out the foundations of effective coaching and mentoring at work. In Chapter 1, we define what it is and outline the key principles which support effective practice in coaching and mentoring. We also introduce ideas which have informed our approach. Chapters 2 and 3 consider the coaching and mentoring relationship from each partner's perspective, describing how the reader can develop as an effective coach or mentor and also as a client or mentee. In Chapter 4, we discuss some of the important ethical issues underpinning safe and effective practice.

Part 2 focuses upon approaches, models, tools and techniques. Chapter 5 is new. We introduce several approaches and models which can be used to enhance the learning relationship between coach, mentor and client, and which help clients to take charge of their own development, release potential and achieve results which they value. Chapters 6 and 7 are chapters on The Skilled Helper model. In Chapter 6, we explore the model in detail. We get consistent feedback that, when used wisely, it provides a valuable framework for the coaching and mentoring process. In Chapter 7, we show how the model can be used in practice with an interactive example that invites you to be the coach. The case example illustrates the development of a learning relationship and how you might use the stages of the framework and key skills. Chapter 8 presents a range of tools and techniques which can support coaching and mentoring, with a discussion of their advantages and disadvantages.

Part 3 focuses upon coach and mentor development. We highlight the importance of developing reflective practice and supervision, alongside training, accreditation and professional networking. In Chapter 9, we consider coach and mentor development. Chapter 10 is an interactive case study exploring aspects of reflective practice and issues to take to supervision. Chapter 11 offers responses to questions which are frequently asked when we run coach and mentor training. Finally, a new addition to the book, Chapter 12 gives glimpses of the work of nine coaches and mentors. Each reflects upon the approaches they use, the projects which they undertake, high points and low points in their coaching and mentoring experience, lessons learned, rewards, and their vision for the future of coaching and mentoring.

A note about examples used in the book

We have tried to make this book as practical and relevant as possible, so you will find that it is full of examples, many of which are interactive. Confidentiality in coaching and mentoring is key. For this reason, throughout the book we have constructed the examples rather than use client case material.

PART 1
Effective Coaching and Mentoring

1 What is effective coaching and mentoring at work?

- Introduction
- What is coaching and mentoring?
- Key principles for effective practice
- Influences on our practice
- Summary

Introduction

Our aim in writing this book is to capture the essence of coaching and mentoring, and to energize and equip the reader, whether as coach, mentor or client, and whether coaching or mentoring formally or informally.

It is addressed to all those who want to find out more about what makes for effective coaching and mentoring, whether or not already involved in these activities. It is for those who:

- are a coach or mentor;
- want to become a coach or mentor;
- are looking for a coach or mentor;
- use coaching or mentoring skills at work;
- are participants on coaching or mentoring training programmes;
- train or supervise coaches and mentors;
- want to establish or review the provision of coaching and mentoring in their organization or profession;
- see coaching or mentoring as part of leadership, management or professional development.

There is plenty of evidence that, since writing the first edition of this book, coaching and mentoring have become integrated into many organizations. Rather than being only for exceptional performers or underperformers, coaching and mentoring are now increasingly widely available and seen as part of the culture in many organizations. Particularly in larger institutions, the development of internal resources to deliver coaching and mentoring means that the activities are coming to be viewed as the 'way we do things around here'. We have noticed this change as we train and develop coaches and mentors. In the past, some participants were uncertain as to the relevance of coaching and mentoring to their everyday world of work, whether as manager, doctor, nurse, educator or other professional. Some participants were unfamiliar with the terms and had little idea of what to expect in practice. Nowadays, mostly, participants arrive already convinced of the benefits and are eager to learn the skills to help them do their jobs better. Unlike in the past, many participants now have first-hand experience of being a coach or mentor or client, either formally or informally, and are keen to develop their capabilities.

Survey results provide evidence of the increasing prevalence of coaching and mentoring. One survey (CIPD 2015b: 12) found that coaching and mentoring were offered by just over 75% of responding organizations, with this figure rising to 89% in the public sector. Henley Business School (2016) reported individual coaching as the learning and development method most likely to be used by respondents, ahead of education programmes or online learning, and also the preferred learning and development method for senior staff and high flyers. Recognition of the value of coaching has given a strong message that successful leaders are also clients who benefit from working regularly with a coach. It seems that coaching and mentoring are replacing (or being used alongside) formal training as mechanisms for developing talent. Of course, many successful leaders and managers are also coaches and mentors. Research (Boyatzis et al. 2006) has highlighted the benefits for a leader of being a coach: coaching others and experiencing compassion serves to balance at a physiological level the effects of the stresses of the leadership role.

While external coaches continue to have a role in executive coaching, internal coaches and mentors are becoming increasingly important. Coaching and mentoring are not only for senior people and many organizations expect that leaders, managers and supervisors at all levels will use coaching and mentoring skills to enhance individuals' learning and development and increase productivity. Coaching and mentoring by line managers and peers are seen as one of the most effective forms of learning and development and coaching by line managers or peers is a method likely to grow (CIPD 2015b: 10). Coaching and mentoring are often used alongside appraisal, work planning, training and development, and performance review. The increasing importance of coaching and mentoring can be seen too in the health and education sectors. Mentoring is now included in the UK General Medical Council good medical practice guidelines. The guidelines state that doctors should be 'willing to take on a mentoring role for more junior doctors and other healthcare professionals'

(General Medical Council 2013: 15). In education, the development of coaching and mentoring skills is seen as a key aspect of continuing professional development and required professional standards for teachers. Research has demonstrated the positive impact of coaching and mentoring both on staff and on the development of a culture of learning and collaboration, and there is now a national framework for coaching and mentoring in education (CUREE: online).

Terminology can be problematic and so in this book we generally use the term 'client' or 'mentee' to refer to the person with whom the coach or mentor is working.

There is debate in the literature about the differences and similarities between coaching and mentoring. Some authors assert that there is an important distinction between the activities, some say that there is overlap and the differences are unclear, and others that they are simply different names for the same thing. We see some truth in each of these perspectives. Yes, coaching and mentoring encompass a range of helping activities which can be differentiated. Yes, the distinction is not always clear. And, yes, what is described as mentoring in one organization is sometimes called coaching in another. We say more about this debate in the next section.

In this book, we take the view that there is common ground, expressed as underlying principles, which underpins both coaching and mentoring. In this chapter we will describe these principles and the ways in which they support effective practice. We define coaching and mentoring as: 'learning relationships which help people to take charge of their own development, to release their potential and to achieve results which they value' (see Figure 1.1).

We believe that the learning relationship is central to both coaching and mentoring, which are more than just a set of activities or skills. The coaching

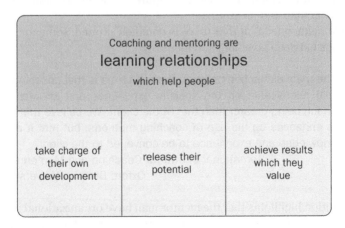

Figure 1.1   Definition of coaching and mentoring

or mentoring relationship facilitates insight, learning and change. Through this relationship, potential is identified, possibilities become reality and tangible results are delivered. Coaching and mentoring help a person to see the present as a springboard to the future, and to be strategic about their development. Whether they seek help with a specific current work issue, or a longer-term career question, the coach or mentor can facilitate exploration, help in the formulation of goals, and provide support while action is implemented.

What is coaching and mentoring?

As has been noted, opinions vary about whether coaching is different from mentoring. In practice, the terms are often used alongside each other or interchangeably, and to add to the confusion there are numerous definitions of the terms.

Many academic and professional bodies share the view that the activities are similar, but not identical, with a common set of approaches and methodologies and underpinning values.

Some of these similarities have been identified by Zeus and Skiffington (2000). Both coaching and mentoring assume basic values and beliefs: that humans have the ability to change; that they make the best choices available to them; that helping is not a quick fix: 'it is a journey where the process of learning is as important as the knowledge and skills gained' (Zeus and Skiffington 2000: xv). They describe coaching and mentoring as essentially a conversation where learning takes place through asking the right questions rather than providing answers. This leads to personal and professional transformation and reinventing of oneself. Figure 1.2 describes some similarities between coaching and mentoring.

While acknowledging that there is common ground, some authors draw distinctions between coaching and mentoring:

> The main distinction between the two terms is that coaching does not rely necessarily on the specific experience and knowledge of the coach being greater than that of the client. We believe that mentoring is enhanced by the use of coaching methods, but that it also allows knowledge and experience to be conveyed to the client.
>
> (International Centre for Coaching and Mentoring Studies,
> Oxford Brookes University: online)

This definition highlights that the mentor may have organizational or context-specific experience and expertise to help their client's development. Indeed, traditionally mentoring is carried out by a more experienced person in an

- There is a non-directive helping relationship
- There is a relationship of trust
- There are agreed confidentiality boundaries
- The coach or mentor has developed helping skills, including active listening, supporting and challenging
- Client or mentee learning and development are accelerated
- The focus is work and career-related issues
- The coach or mentor understands the client or mentee organization or context
- There are valued outcomes for the client or mentee related to work or career
- The client or mentee becomes more productive in their work and life
- Client or mentee autonomy is encouraged and dependency discouraged
- There is ongoing review of the helping process

Figure 1.2 Some similarities between coaching and mentoring

organization or profession helping a more junior or less experienced colleague. A coach, in contrast, may not have a similar background or experience.

The National College for Teaching and Leadership (2013) takes a similar view and notes that an important distinction between coaching and mentoring is that a mentor shares their knowledge and experience whereas a coach may or may not have such knowledge.

A charter (European Economic and Social Committee 2011: online), signed by leading coaching and mentoring professional bodies, offers much the same perspective. It describes how mentoring 'may involve a transfer of skill or knowledge from a more experienced to a less experienced person through learning dialogue and role modeling, and may also be a learning partnership between peers'. Coaching is seen as the facilitation of learning to reach client goals and as a creative partnership through which the client maximizes their potential.

Another distinction made between coaching and mentoring is that coaching is more likely to be shorter term and focused on specific issues, whereas mentoring may be longer term and with a broader perspective.

Table 1.1 summarizes some differences between coaching and mentoring. If the distinction between coaching and mentoring is accepted, then a question arises. It is generally accepted that giving advice in coaching and mentoring is often unhelpful, unproductive and sometimes positively harmful. We wonder, then, how a mentor in practice uses their workplace knowledge and expertise without straying into becoming overly prescriptive and giving advice, and we

Coaching	Mentoring
Often short term or fixed duration	Can be longer-term relationship
Coach may or may not have similar background	Mentor often has similar professional background
Coach focuses on client resources/ self-development	Mentor shares experience and knowledge when appropriate
Addresses specific issues	Addresses ongoing career development
Coach may be peer, external or different profession	Mentor often more senior internal role model
Person being helped is often referred to as client	Person being helped is often referred to as mentee

Table 1.1   Some differences between coaching and mentoring

would welcome more research in this area. Rogers (2016: 18) notes this difficulty; 'In practice, mentoring does have the overtones of implying that the older and wiser person will be passing on their advice. Where this is so, mentoring is a different activity from coaching.'

One public sector mentee, newly appointed in his role, describes how his mentor managed to tread the difficult path of remaining non-directive while giving her views, and who offered perspectives without being seen as directive:

> She was a great mentor. She was interested in me and I was listened to. I found myself sharing more and more about the issues on my mind. The process of talking things through left me feeling that the tasks that I had to achieve were manageable and it clarified my priorities. She asked very few but very pertinent questions. Sometimes she made some suggestions, based on her knowledge of the organization, and I was grateful for that, because she had experience and organizational know-how that I lacked. I saw her ideas as useful perspectives rather than advice that I had to follow, and I valued what she had to say.

Distinguishing between coaching and mentoring can become more complicated when we look at the various ways in which the term 'mentoring' is used.

In some sectors, mentoring has historically been equated to patronage, where a senior person actively champions the career and professional success of a junior colleague. This can be the case with, for example, graduate trainees. Megginson et al. (2006) call this 'sponsorship mentoring' and contrast it with 'developmental mentoring'. In the latter, the mentor aims to facilitate learning rather than smooth a career path. Much mentoring nowadays emphasizes the developmental aspect, with mentoring being used to support the development of staff, or as a means of identifying and sustaining talent at different levels of an organization.

Peer mentoring and reverse mentoring are found too. In reverse mentoring, a younger and probably more junior employee might help an older one, for example, to stay abreast of technology and social media and current trends. Learning can be two-way, with the younger colleague gaining insights into the senior management role.

In healthcare settings, mentoring for doctors and dentists is often similar to if not coterminous with coaching. However, for nursing and many health professions, the term mentor is often used with a different meaning. It can refer to the educational role of a nurse, midwife, health visitor or allied health professional in supervising and facilitating the learning of students in a practice setting. The mentor role can involve education, supervision, monitoring of learning, assessment of progress and assessment of fitness to practise.

In the education sector, teachers are expected to mentor other staff in their department or team as part of the role of 'subject' or 'pastoral' leader. As part of this mentoring role, coaching will be offered for more specific problems or concerns about performance.

In summarizing this discussion of what coaching and mentoring are, we note that while coaches and mentors may have different roles and responsibilities in organizations, there is considerable overlap in the underlying values, processes used and skills required. We understand the distinction made between coaching as shorter term and performance-focused versus mentoring as longer term and focused on career and professional development. However, we are aware that, in real life, specific performance development issues and broader professional development are often inextricably linked. Our view is that:

1 In practice, coaching and mentoring often overlap.
2 What an activity is called is often determined more by the organization or professional context or culture than the activity itself.
3 Both coaching and mentoring may encompass the transmission of knowledge or skills and this should be accomplished in a facilitative, rather than a directive manner.
4 Our definition of coaching and mentoring and our nine principles for effective practice apply equally to both activities.

5   In considering what makes for effective coaching or mentoring, we find it more helpful to focus on the principles and how they operate in practice rather than being overly concerned about whether the activity is called coaching or mentoring.

Key principles for effective practice

Effective coaching and mentoring are underpinned by nine key principles (summarized in Figure 1.3). These principles, derived from our experience, have informed and guided our coaching and mentoring. We introduce them here. In subsequent chapters, they are explored in greater depth and linked to case examples and interactive exercises.

1   LEARNING RELATIONSHIP is at the heart of change.
2   CLIENT sets the agenda and is resourceful.
3   COACH OR MENTOR facilitates learning and development.
4   CONTEXT is work.
5   OUTCOME is change and action.
6   APPROACH OR MODEL provides movement and direction.

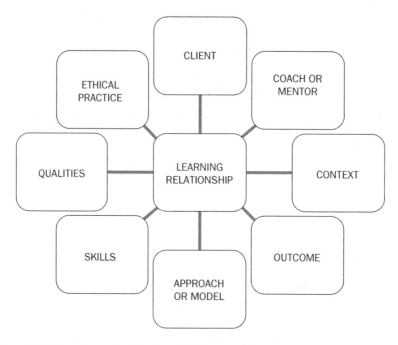

Figure 1.3   Nine key principles for effective practice

7   SKILLS develop insight, release potential and deliver results.
8   QUALITIES of the coach or mentor affirm, enable and sustain the client.
9   ETHICAL PRACTICE safeguards and enhances coaching and mentoring.

1   The learning relationship is at the heart of change

The central principle is that learning, change and transformation occur through the relationship with a coach or mentor. Numerous studies have high-lighted the quality of the relationship, as perceived by the client, as more important for effective helping than, for example, the use of any particular model or framework. Coaching and mentoring are not just an interaction or a transaction. They involve conversation and dialogue rather than merely dis-cussion. In dialogue, there is listening with an open mind and asking questions which build shared understanding. This is different from discussion which is, literally, about the breaking apart of ideas and about debating, persuading and convincing. In coaching and mentoring, two people engage with one another, they relate to one another and if the coaching and mentoring are effective, they connect with one another. Dialogue is important in establishing and maintaining the connection. In a learning dialogue there is, on both sides, a willingness to share perspectives, to listen, to understand, to be open to new ideas and to take joint responsibility for the conversation and the outcomes. Dialogue sustains the connection and it follows, therefore, that the learning relationship is a partnership, and not an activity imposed by one person on another.

2   The client sets the agenda and is resourceful

Centre stage in the learning relationship is the client and their agenda. The effective coach or mentor works with the client to help them to clarify what they want and how they will achieve their aims. Being centre stage and being the focus of attention can be both challenging and empowering for the client. Some clients have clear goals, some only vague ideas. Some clients are eager, some are reluctant. Sometimes when a client is referred, they may have little interest or belief in creating their own agenda, and this first step may be one of the most demanding tasks of the coaching and mentoring relationship. However, it may also be one of the most rewarding. When the client actively engages and becomes a partner in the learning relationship, with a sense of purpose, it is much more likely to be successful.

Once the agenda is clear, the task of the coach or mentor is to help the client to identify and use the resources, both internal and external, which will enable them to change and develop. Internal resources may include the client's strengths, their successes and their learning from past experience. External resources may include colleagues, friends and organizational factors. Affirming the client's resourcefulness, and communicating this affirmation to the client, is an important role. The coach or mentor can communicate hope and possibility when the client seems to lack energy or focus, or ideas, or direction. They can enable a client by believing in them, especially at times when the client's self-belief falters. This communication of hope and setting of positive expectations has been shown to be a significant factor in achieving successful outcomes.

3   The coach or mentor facilitates learning and development

The coach or mentor is a facilitator, not an instructor. This means starting with the client's perspective, not the coach's or mentor's. They need to be flexible enough to follow the client story rather than impose too rigid a structure. They support and challenge the client to learn and to develop. The client learns by acquiring new awareness, insight, skills, ideas and knowledge. Development involves integrating this learning into their everyday working and way of being. It is important that the facilitator asks questions which provoke new perspectives and change in the client, rather than giving them answers.

The effective facilitator reviews the learning relationship and the learning process, and does not take these for granted. They ask the client about what is helping their learning and development and what is getting in the way. They find learning methods that suit the client. They help the client to clarify how they learn best, and how to make coaching or mentoring work for them.

4   The context is work

This book is about coaching and mentoring at work. While the effective coach or mentor values the client as a whole person, they understand that the context is work. They are sensitive to boundaries and are aware that coaching and mentoring are not career patronage or counselling or therapy. They are able to talk with clients about these boundaries, and are aware of other resources and networks which may be needed. Because coaching and mentoring are not therapy, they keep the focus on the client's present and future experience, and encourage them to use past experience and learning to inform their future opportunities and development.

Within the work context, the client may want or need to improve their work performance in the short term, or they may be concerned with broader issues of personal, professional and career development. Short- and long-term issues are often interrelated, and the coach or mentor appreciates this. They know enough about the work context to be able to facilitate exploration of issues and are aware that opportunities and resources in the workplace differ from person to person and from organization to organization.

5   The outcome is change and action

Coaching and mentoring enable reflection leading to change which produces valued outcomes. The client achieves something that they care about, that makes a positive difference in their working life or career. The real significance of change should be judged in relation to the client's agenda and their goal. A minor change in attitude for one client may be just as transforming as a major job promotion for another. Insight and understanding are important in coaching and mentoring in so far as they lead to change. Of course, change is hard work. Change can provoke resistance, a normal reaction to facing up to difficult issues. Effective coaches and mentors work with client resistance, rather than try to overcome it. Through dialogue, they help the client to explore any resistance and look at what will help or hinder them in making changes.

In addition, the effective coach or mentor understands the importance of what happens between sessions. They know that coaching and mentoring sessions should be a catalyst for action in the real world, not a substitute. They build an expectation of change into the coaching dialogue. An example of this is when the coach or mentor starts a session by asking about what has happened since the last meeting and what the client has been doing, rather than assuming the conversation will continue on from the previous session.

6   The approach or model used for the change process provides movement and direction

The effective coach or mentor is clear about the theories, models or frameworks which influence the way they work. They integrate theory into practice and into their way of working, rather than applying it impersonally. They use approaches and models wisely. There is no conclusive evidence that any one approach or model works better than another in coaching and mentoring; however, consistency and transparency do seem to be important. So the effective coach or mentor is clear with clients about their approach and can share this with them. However, any approach, model or framework should be used with a light touch, or even set aside, if that is what would be most helpful for the client. It should not be used to unhelpfully constrain or limit the conversation. We find that having a model, even if only in one's back pocket, so to speak, helps us to feel confident in working in a flexible way, so that we can follow our clients' narratives rather than leading or overly structuring conversations.

One way of thinking about approaches or models is that they can provide a map for the coaching journey. Just as when two people go for a walk in the countryside, a map does not dictate the route or prevent them from slowing down or speeding up or taking shortcuts or meandering away from the path. Both can look at the map. It can help them to know where they are and to judge the best route for that day, given the time available and how they are feeling. And they can return another day, map in hand, with a clearer sense of the terrain, to choose which direction they will then take.

7   The skills develop insight, release potential and deliver results

The effective coach or mentor pays attention to learning and developing their skills and to using these appropriately to enable the client to develop insight and release potential. They understand that the skills of listening and supporting and challenging are fundamentally important. They develop these skills and seek feedback on their effect. They use the skills in an integrated way within the learning relationship, working with their client rather than merely applying a set of competences to the client. The skills communicate the coach or mentor belief in, and valuing of, the client. Wise and judicious use of the skills ensures a balance of support and challenge, of reflection and action. The effective coach or mentor has a repertoire of tools and techniques which they offer appropriately to the client to support their learning and development.

8   The qualities of the coach or mentor affirm, enable and sustain the client

The distinctive style, personality, values, and experiences of the coach or mentor are shared as 'self'. Moreover, when the chemistry between coach or mentor and client really works, there is a sense of deep connection. The paradox of this connection is that it is not tangible and yet it is powerfully present and effective in bringing about the client's self-belief, hope, courage and action.

Effective coaches and mentors are not only smart, but also wise. They have the wisdom to make sound judgements on what they see, hear and experience in the learning relationship. They communicate caring, valuing, respect and empathy. They model a way of being which is both human and professional. This is not deliberately taught but is often 'caught'. Learning is not just from the coach or mentor, but also with and through them. Learning through the coach or mentor, from their way of being, is often overlooked, yet it may be the most powerful learning of all.

9 Ethical practice safeguards and enhances coaching and mentoring

Both the client and the coach or mentor are safeguarded when ethical principles inform and guide practice. Such principles might include: respecting the client's autonomy; keeping promises and honouring commitments; acting in ways which are beneficial to the client; not doing harm; and acting fairly. When these principles are in operation there is an openness and transparency in the coaching and mentoring relationship. This not only safeguards the interests of both parties, but also enhances the quality of their work together. The effective coach or mentor discusses expectations, boundaries and safeguards with the client, and reviews these as necessary. Working within agreed limits and boundaries helps the client to feel secure, for example, in relation to issues of confidentiality or conflicts of interest. Effective coaches and mentors are aware of legal requirements, organizational policies and professional codes of practice, and understand how to contract with clients and sponsors.

Influences on our practice

We have found that the most important thing we bring to our work is ourselves. In this section, we discuss approaches which have particularly influenced us and which we have incorporated into the way we work. These approaches have been experienced by us as clients and as helpers in both formal and informal coaching and mentoring contexts.

A significant influence on our work is that of humanistic approaches and particularly the work of Carl Rogers (1961, 1983). He emphasized the importance of psychological contact between helper and client, and particularly the communication by the helper of what have become known as the 'core conditions' of respect, empathy and genuineness. Humanistic or person-centred approaches describe the innate tendency of people, given these conditions, to grow and to develop and to fulfil their potential. Maslow's research (1970) highlighted the importance of the core conditions. He found that basic needs for acceptance, respect and trust needed to be met in order for higher-order needs, such as achievement and self-actualization to be realized. Many studies (for example, Asay and Lambert 1999) have confirmed the importance of the core conditions. They show that an important factor in predicting positive outcomes is the client's perception of the core conditions and of a positive relationship with their helper. Page and de Haan's (2014) research on executive coaching found that the strength of the relationship between coach and client was the best predictor of coaching effectiveness, and more important than factors such as personality or coaching approach. While few coaching and mentoring approaches nowadays would agree with Carl Rogers that the core conditions are both necessary and sufficient for change to occur, most would agree that they are the cornerstones upon which to build effective practice.

We see the relationship and the communication of warm genuine respect as central to coaching and mentoring. What we value from the person-centred approach is the emphasis on relationship and connection between two people, and on the intrinsic human capacity for growth. We experience again and again in our work the transforming power of being fully present with, and listening to, a person, and in so doing enabling them to access their own resourcefulness.

The humanistic view of the individual as growth-oriented and resourceful is found too in the field of Positive Psychology, with the emphasis on using client strengths and resources to enhance well-being (Seligman 2002, 2011). Positive psychology encourages clients to identify and apply their strengths to achieve their goals. It uses interventions to help clients to build their resourcefulness and lead more fulfilled lives. We find such interventions are particularly useful in helping clients to access resources and creativity at times when, if they are stuck with a problem, they may not feel very creative or resourceful. A simple prompt, for example, 'How can you use your strengths in this situation?' may be enough to stimulate client thinking and action.

Appreciative Enquiry (Cooperrider et al. 2003) and Brief or Solution-Focused therapy (Berg and Szabo 2005) employ some similar approaches, with an emphasis on exploring the client's preferred future and identifying any parts of that future that are already happening. Associated with these approaches is the so-called miracle question: 'If you were to wake up tomorrow morning and a miracle had occurred and the problem was sorted, what would things look like, what would be different?' We find it valuable to ask clients to think about the future and about their goals. As coaches and mentors, we have experienced the powerful impact for clients of identifying personally meaningful, realistic goals. Research by Gail Mathews (undated) indicates that when goals are written down, and shared with a trusted person, they are more likely to be achieved, and we notice that this simple intervention can increase the probability of client success. Goal setting helps the client to focus on positive goals, rather than negative ones. So, for example, a client who states their goal 'I will stop feeling anxious in meetings' can be asked to reframe it positively, such as 'I will feel confident and assertive in meetings'. Positively stated goals are more likely to be achieved. Similarly, some clients get stuck going round and round analysing and dwelling on their problems. Because difficulties in the present absorb their energy and attention, they are unwilling or unable to think about the future. Techniques such as brainstorming a preferred future, or even a gentle prompt, 'So what would this look like if it were just a bit better?' can enable clients to move forward. We realize, however, that goal setting is neither simple nor straightforward for many clients. Our experience has been that some clients are not ready or able to set substantial goals, even after more than one session. However, after each session we expect that a client will act in some way, whether that is a significant change, simply reflecting on the session, or taking a small step.

We have been influenced by Cognitive-Behavioural Coaching (CBC) which asserts that the way a person thinks about events influences the way that they feel, and how they behave (Neenan and Dryden 2002). We find these ideas particularly useful in enabling clients to self-challenge. A client can ask themselves whether their thoughts and beliefs are justified and whether they are helping or hindering the situation. Self-limiting beliefs can be questioned and replaced with ones which help rather than impede performance. The client who asserts 'I'm hopeless at job interviews' restates this as 'Some interviews have gone well for me and others not' and similarly 'I always fall to pieces under pressure' becomes 'When I am well prepared, I can withstand interview pressure.'

It may be tempting to see our coaching and mentoring conversations as talking about change, while the real change happens out there back in the client's world. Hawkins and Smith's model of Systemic Transformational Coaching (2013: 33) provides a helpful challenge here. They describe the importance of the 'shift in the room' when a change in the client's assumptions, thinking, feeling or behaving occurs in the session. New behaviour that the client identifies as desirable can be rehearsed in the session in order to help embed it back in the workplace. The emphasis is on what is happening in the room in order to change things out there. Gestalt approaches too describe the importance of heightened awareness of the here-and-now. We have found techniques which originated in Gestalt, such as role reversal and empty chair, to be particularly helpful for clients in bringing immediacy to the session, so that rather than talking about an issue, they experience it.

This section would not be complete without reference to The Skilled Helper model (Egan 2010). We find it both liberating and embracing complexity. Used wisely, it has enabled us to apply the ideas and approaches we have described above.

The wise coach or mentor

In this chapter we have defined coaching and mentoring at work. We have explained the nine principles underpinning effectiveness. We have shared approaches and models which have influenced us and which are commonly used. Now we turn to consider: What it is that makes a coach or mentor not just competent, but also effective, and wise?

Clutterbuck and Megginson (2005, 2010) have observed numerous coaches and mentors at work and they conclude that mature practitioners are those who, although informed by particular models and approaches, do not stick to them rigidly. Instead, they constantly ask themselves two key questions when working with a client: 'Are we both relaxed enough to allow the issue and the solution to emerge in whatever way they will? Do I need to apply any processes or techniques at all? If I do, what does the client context tell me about how to select from the wide choice available to me?' (Clutterbuck and Megginson 2010: VIII, 1: 7) They call this way of working: 'systemic eclectic'. These mature coaches or mentors are demonstrating the confidence to be able to 'let go' and freewheel with the client. This requires the wisdom to make difficult choices from moment to moment in the session. When we have experienced as clients the help of a 'wise' coach or mentor, what has made the difference? For one of us, it was like this:

> My mentor was just a natural. So natural that I didn't even notice his skills, but they were certainly there. He wore his experience lightly, keeping himself in the background. But he was himself, he showed me that he cared, he gave me enough time to talk and think. He could be very challenging too, but he seemed to consider carefully when to be like this, watching me closely for my reactions. I was continually surprised at how well he seemed to know me. He would know just when to push and just when to hold back. I felt like I was moving along with my issues and targets and he seemed to intuitively understand when to say something and when to just stay quiet.
>
> I wanted to learn from him. I chose him because he knew how my organization worked and he knew the politics there. He shared his own experiences with me so that I felt I was with a real person and not just some 'professional front'. He gave me time. That was a big thing. I needed to make some changes at work, but wasn't ready at first. He never tried to move me too quickly into making those changes. There were moments when something would click. I may have suddenly opened my eyes to something and we would share that eureka moment together, he would be as pleased as I was! There were other difficult moments when we seemed temporarily to

be not connecting and he would take his time, give me time, and then ask if I would like to look at what was happening, together. This we would do and each time, although difficult, it brought our relationship to a new level of trust. The times when I sensed he had really understood, he didn't need to say anything, there was just a certain twinkle in his eye, a smile, a quizzical expression and in that moment I knew he was 'with' me.

So, what is this wisdom? Competences are tangible, wisdom less so. Wisdom seems to be about discerning what is needed at any one time and using sound judgement. To make such wise choices, the coach or mentor needs to be able to tune into the client on several levels at once. Such sensitivity, combined with caring, gives a special quality to the relationship. People talk about 'connecting', being 'in tune with one another', moving together 'in harmony'. These expressions attempt to capture the essence of being with a coach or mentor who is wise as well as competent, who trusts their instincts and intuition as much as their knowledge and skills, who knows when to hold back and do nothing, and when to move forward and actively engage, who uses all their senses to communicate a real belief in the worth and capacity of the client to achieve what they want and value.

Summary

In this chapter we have:

- Described how coaching and mentoring ideas and practice are becoming embedded in the culture of many organizations.

- Defined coaching and mentoring as learning relationships which help people to take charge of their own development, to release their potential and to achieve results which they value.

- Explored the similarities and differences between coaching and mentoring.

- Explained the key principles which underpin effective coaching and mentoring.

- Shared some influences on our practice.

- Concluded with thoughts about effective and wise practice.

2 How can I be an effective coach or mentor?

- Introduction
- Knowing yourself
- Assessing the benefits of coaching and mentoring
- Clarifying your role
- Building a learning relationship
- Developing core skills
- Creating a working agreement
- Managing a productive relationship
- Maximizing client resourcefulness
- Using a framework and tools and techniques
- Reflecting on coach and mentor competencies
- A coaching and mentoring checklist
- Summary

Introduction

The purpose of this chapter is to help you to be an effective coach and mentor, and to use coaching and mentoring skills effectively at work. You may already be a coach or mentor, or wondering whether you want to become one. You may be interested in how coaching or mentoring skills could help you to become a better leader or manager. You may be considering whether coaching or mentoring could benefit your organization or profession. You may want to know more about the skills and processes of coaching and mentoring, and to develop your practice.

In this chapter, we describe how coaching and mentoring differ from other helping relationships. We consider the qualities of the effective coach or mentor and show how you communicate these and use your coaching and mentoring skills most effectively. We explore how you can establish, sustain and conclude the learning relationship. We discuss how frameworks and tools can help you and your clients to make the most of coaching and mentoring.

While the chapter addresses questions about coaching and mentoring chiefly from the coach or mentor perspective, it may also be of interest to actual or potential clients. We include practical exercises, checklists and activities, as well as case examples designed to illustrate key points.

 Where you see this sign, there is an activity for you to complete. The questions assume that you are already involved in coaching or mentoring. Even if you are not yet actively involved, you can reflect on what your answers might be.

Knowing yourself

One of the most important things that you bring to coaching and mentoring is yourself. The person you are, with your own style and strengths and qualities. Effective coaches and mentors are self-aware and reflect on how they work with others and their impact on people around them. So, a good starting point is to think about what you bring to the coaching and mentoring role.

 Take a moment to think about what characterizes you? What do you bring to coaching and mentoring? How do you influence others? How do other people describe you? What feedback do you have about your strengths and areas for development?

Ideas from leadership, personality and influencing style models and theories can be helpful in thinking about your strengths and areas for development. Some models have associated questionnaires which, when used wisely, can add to your self-knowledge.

As coaches and mentors we can reflect on how we choose and use influencing styles when working with clients. The examples below show how self-insight can help to improve coach and mentor effectiveness.

Alex knows that one of his strengths is thinking about possibilities and the future, and sometimes he does not notice the detail of what is happening around him. One of his coaching strengths is helping his clients to consider possibilities, ways forward and 'what if' scenarios. However, he realizes that he must be careful not to rush ahead too quickly and 'leave the client behind'. He works hard to pay attention and stay with each client's story, and to listen to how things are for them in the present.

Isabelle has a cool and analytic management style and brings an insightful calm clarity to mentoring sessions. However, her thoughtful reflective style can come across as a bit cold and off-putting for some mentees. She received feedback on a training programme that she needs to remember to smile occasionally and pay attention to non-verbal communication and making eye contact.

Finally in this section, remember that your clients learn

- *from* you, from your experiences, knowledge and insights;
- *with* you, during the learning conversation;
- *through* you, from the way you are, sometimes called your 'way of being'.

So, be aware that you may be seen as a role model in some way by those you coach or mentor. You may have a quality or characteristic which clients admire, aspire to or see as important in their development.

 Box 2.1 contains a list of qualities. Which do you think are most characteristic of you? Least characteristic? How do others see you? How can you use the qualities in coaching and mentoring?

Box 2.1   Some qualities of a coach or mentor

Are you someone who?
- is supportive of others
- is a good listener
- is not afraid to disagree and question
- is respected in your organization/profession
- can state what you want and need

- is receptive to new ideas and ways of thinking
- embodies your values and 'walks the talk'
- can think laterally and be creative
- is well known in your organization/profession
- is interpersonally skilled
- is able to take the long-term view
- is sensitive to other people's feelings
- is task-focused
- treats people fairly
- is resilient under pressure
- is considered in reaching conclusions
- can be trusted with confidences
- is easygoing
- is organized
- is curious
- is more a listener than a talker

Assessing the benefits of coaching and mentoring

There is an increasing body of evidence from business, the public sector and the voluntary sector of the benefits of coaching and mentoring. The benefits for the client of coaching and mentoring are particularly well documented, and there can also be benefits for the coach or mentor and for the organization (Garvey and Garret-Harris 2005; Steven et al. 2008). A survey of mentoring research papers from the USA and Europe reported that there were benefits not only for the client (40 per cent) and the business (33 per cent), but also for the mentor (27 per cent) (Megginson et al. 2006: 30).

Below are some responses that coaches and mentors might make when asked about the benefits for them:

- It gives me a sense of personal accomplishment.
- I have the satisfaction of helping others and seeing them develop.
- It's made me more self-reflective.
- It's challenging and keeps me learning.
- I have improved my interpersonal skills, particularly my listening skills.
- The skills are transferable – I can apply a coaching and mentoring approach in all sorts of work and non-work situations.
- I have greater visibility in my organization and recognition from others that this is valuable work.

- I've built better relationships with colleagues.
- I value the opportunity to share my know how and at the same time gain insights about people and organizations.
- I've become a bit more resilient.
- I've learned how to help people without feeling that I'm responsible for solving their problems.

Here are some examples of coaches and mentors talking about the benefits, and also the costs:

> **Jo, a doctor and experienced mentor, and someone who is keen to continue her own development:** I've helped several people to get clearer about their career direction, and to become more focused in their thinking. Now, I see them being successful and fulfilled. I hope I've put something back into the profession and encouraged people. I know how important that is, and it wasn't around for me when I started out. I've also learned a lot about myself, for example, just because I'm more senior doesn't mean that I know what's best for someone. Mentoring has made me more aware of how I deal with colleagues and patients. It does take time and it competes with other demands, but for me it is worth it.

> **Ryan, an HR director, who has developed a coaching skills programme for senior staff, and wants to develop a coaching culture:** Obviously, there are significant direct and indirect costs incurred in running a training programme. A benefit is that we have seen, over the years, a transfer of participants' coaching skills into everyday work situations and a coaching approach is becoming part of the way we work. We haven't yet tried to quantify the benefits, but qualitative evaluation shows that staff are using the skills and the mindset in both formal coaching and also in day-to-day work. For example, a colleague remarked to me that 'You can tell if someone has been on the coaching course – it shows in the way they approach problem-solving in meetings.'

> **Nita, a manager, who uses a coaching approach in the way she leads her department:** Coaching is an integral part of my job, not a separate function. I'm responsible for developing my staff, and we have a very positive coaching culture here. I see myself as a resource for staff, and the benefits are tangible in terms of improvements in performance and the development of individuals. What are the costs to me? Well, reminding myself that sometimes I need to bite my tongue and not rush in and fix things!

You can see from these examples that costs and benefits may be both tangible, for example, time or money, and intangible, for example, personal satisfaction.

In the following activity, take a moment to think about the benefits for you of being a coach or mentor, or using a coaching or mentoring approach.

 Complete the following sentences:

- I'm interested in coaching/mentoring because . . .
- What I have to offer in coaching/mentoring is . . .
- My experience of coaching or mentoring (whether formal or informal) is . . .
- What I want to achieve in coaching/mentoring is . . .
- The benefits for my profession/organization/clients are . . .
- The benefits for me are . . .
- The costs for me are . . .

What do your answers tell you about what you want to achieve through coaching or mentoring? Any surprises? Any questions raised?

Clarifying your role

In Chapter 1 we described some of the ways in which the terms coach and mentor are used. Being clear about how *you* see your role, and communicating this to others (for example, clients, staff, sponsors) will help you be an effective coach or mentor. This is sometimes easier for external coaches and mentors, whose boundaries may be more defined, than for internal ones.

One way to think about your role is to notice how coaching and mentoring are different from patronage and from therapy. Coaches and mentors may find themselves being asked to take on the role of patron or therapist or find themselves drifting into the role, and so clarity from the outset is important. In patronage, a senior person nurtures the career advancement of a more junior colleague, a protégé, literally 'one who is protected'. The patron may act as a sponsor for the individual and may use their own professional networks to aid the person's career or development. In therapy, a qualified professional helps to resolve difficulties which may be long-standing, personal and not necessarily work-related. In coaching and mentoring, the focus is the individual at work, and while this may encompass personal issues, coaches and mentors do not normally work in depth in the way that therapists might work. Table 2.1 summarizes some differences between the roles.

Patronage	Coaching and mentoring	Therapy
Career advancement	Problems and opportunities	Personal problems and difficulties
Career-related	Work- or career-related	Issues may be deeply personal/unrelated to work
Patron unlikely to be trained	Coach/mentor may have had training	Therapist is a qualified practitioner
Boundaries less important – may be intentional overlap	Coach/mentor agrees boundaries	Therapist operates clear boundaries
Patron often in same profession/field	Coach/mentor may be internal or external	Therapist is outside organization
Patron may open career doors	Coach/mentor facilitates learning and development	Therapist helps to resolve problems
Patron is senior	Coach/mentor may be senior/colleague/junior or independent	Therapist is impartial and independent
Patron does not expect feedback	Feedback is part of the learning relationship	Amount/use of feedback dependent on therapeutic approach

Table 2.1 Patronage, coaching and mentoring, and therapy

 In what ways does this list of coaching and mentoring characteristics fit with your coaching or mentoring role? Is your role clearly different, or not, from that of patron or therapist? Do your clients see it the same way?

In the examples below, a mentor and a coach talk about how they see their role.

Emil, a mentor: I've been a mentor for several years for fellow professionals, helping them think through career and work issues. Of course,
I have a good network and sometimes that's helpful, but my role isn't
to smooth their career paths. In fact, over the years one or two have
left the organization and that's been right for them, they've moved on
to new pastures. Occasionally someone brings something that I'm not
skilled to deal with, for example, a relationship issue or a health
problem, and then we talk about how they might get help elsewhere.

Angela, a coach, has a career background in counselling. She is an
excellent listener and she is respectful and pays close attention to
what her clients say. However, she has been wondering whether she
sometimes steers her coaching clients, in her words, 'to get to the
bottom of things' rather than 'to get on with things'. She says, 'Maybe
I'm more interested in insight than action.' She decides that in future
she will pay particular attention to this, and ask clients what they
want to focus on in each session, and what outcomes they want.

Another way to think about your coaching and mentoring role is to consider
how it is different from that of expert helper. Being an expert helper is central
to many jobs and careers, and perhaps to yours. As coach or mentor, although
you may have experience and expertise, your primary role is to help your
client to find for themselves resourceful ways forward in dealing with issues
facing them. You help the client to generate their own solutions, which are
more likely to be successful than solutions proposed by you.

The next exercise will help you to reflect on how much expert helping you
do in your job.

 How much expert helping do you do at work?

To what extent are the following usually true, or not? In what ways
are coaching or mentoring different from your work role?

- I know more about the subject than the person I'm helping.
- People seek out my knowledge and experience.
- I know what facts or information are relevant to solving things.
- I ask questions to gather relevant information.
- I can usually give people the right answer or some options.
- I gather facts and evidence.
- I sort irrelevant from relevant information.
- I generate options for people.
- I propose solutions for people.

It can be difficult to unlearn expert advice-giving habits. Having the right mindset can help. Remember that client issues are rarely 'puzzles', by which we mean that they are not like a crossword puzzle, with only one set of right answers (Revans 1983). Client issues often have many possible answers and the best way forward or the best answer for the client depends on the client. Remember too that clients are resourceful and your role is to develop that resourcefulness. Advice giving, however well intentioned, comes from the assumption that you know better than the client. There may be rare occasions where giving guidance may be appropriate. However, if your coaching conversations are peppered with 'why don't you?' and 'have you thought about?' and 'could you?' then notice that what you are doing, under the guise of asking questions, is giving thinly disguised advice. Shaun Lincoln (Sulaiman 2006) suggests an activity for those considering becoming mentors: 'Test yourself. Can you listen for more than ten minutes without giving advice? If you can't, you might want to hesitate.' We would add here that, after hesitating, you might continue reading this book, in order to further your self-development!

Table 2.2 illustrates the differences between expert and coach or mentor.

Expert	Coach or mentor
Expert knowledge is key	Facilitation skills are key
Knows answers	Elicits client's views
Provides direction	Provides a 'map'
Puzzle-solver	Facilitator/enabler
Gathers/analyses information	Enables information-gathering
Facts and logic	Facts, logic and feelings
Assumes problem can be solved	Assumes problem can be managed
Wants to fix the problem	Wants to help the client to fix or manage the issue
Advises, evaluates, tells, instructs	Asks, reflects, supports, challenges

Table 2.2   Some differences between coach or mentor and expert

Below, a coach and a mentor, who are both experts, describe how they work.

> **Jack is an interpersonal skills coach** for senior executives. He helps clients to improve their influencing and conflict resolution skills. He is familiar with research on these topics, and shares this 'expert' information with them when appropriate. However, Jack focuses initially on each client's experience of what is helping and hindering their effectiveness. He helps each client to identify what changes are important to them and their organization, and to look for appropriate situations where they can try out and refine new skills. He shares expert research with a light touch, rather than imposing it.

> **Ruth, a nurse manager,** uses a mentoring approach to develop the junior staff in her unit. She is highly experienced, and has realized over the years that 'If I just tell them the answer, or do it for them, then they don't really learn. I have to get alongside my trainees, to ask them questions which challenge and develop them, and of course I'm there as a safety net if they need it.'

If coaching and mentoring are different from patronage and therapy and expert helping, then what are they? In practice, you may find yourself filling a range of helping roles, depending on the client and the context. Underpinning all effective practice is the ability to communicate support. Support provides a confidential, non-judgemental listening ear. Support does not mean agreeing, rather it means communicating your interest and desire to understand how your client sees things. Communicating support will help the client to identify and use their own resourcefulness. Support can be the springboard to enable a client to challenge themselves. This self-challenge can be more powerful than challenges from others, because it is less likely to provoke defensiveness in the client and so be rejected by them. So, enabling clients to self-challenge is also a role of a coach or mentor. Another role is that of sounding board, where you provide a place for the client to talk through half-formed ideas and options and, importantly, offer a place for the client to hear themselves 'thinking out loud'. A sounding board can be a powerful catalyst to action. The role of networker can be a valuable one too, where you help the client to identify and develop their networks and build relationships. Sometimes a coaching role is required, helping the client to develop skills and abilities and confidence. Being a role model is also a part of coaching and mentoring. This can be explicit, for example, where a client seeks a mentor, who is senior and whom they respect and admire. Sometimes it is more subtle: we find that in successful learning relationships there is often something that the client admires about their coach or mentor, some quality or characteristic. Another role is that of critical friend, where you might offer your client constructive feedback. This is most likely to benefit the client when there is a high degree of trust in your relationship and the client feels supported. Sometimes as coach or mentor, you act as strategist, helping your client to look at the big picture and think more broadly and longer term about their context. Linked to this is the role of catalyst, helping the client to develop new perspectives and harnessing their creativity. You may find that in any one session with a client you take on several roles, depending on the client's needs, and that the roles overlap and run together.

  Box 2.2 summarizes these roles of a coach or mentor. Take a moment to think about which roles feature in your coaching and mentoring work. Are there any that you would add to this list?

Box 2.2   Some roles of a coach and mentor

- **Supporter:** a confidential respectful listener who does not judge or evaluate.
- **Challenger:** helps the client to challenge themselves, and offers empathic challenge.
- **Sounding board:** helps the client to explore 'half-baked' ideas and thoughts.
- **Networker:** helps the client to identify key connections and develop relationships.
- **Coach:** helps the client to develop skills and abilities.
- **Role model:** has qualities or attributes to which the client aspires.
- **Critical friend:** gives constructive feedback.
- **Strategist:** helps the client to look at the broad picture and think in the long term.
- **Catalyst:** helps the client to develop new perspectives and harness their creativity.

Building a learning relationship

How clients perceive the coaching or mentoring relationship is important. When their view of the relationship is positive, then coaching or mentoring is more likely to be effective. What is the learning relationship? Remember that clients learn from you, with you and through you, and some of these more intangible qualities of the relationship are not easy to capture in words.

Carl Rogers, writing about helping relationships, described how, in striving to be trustworthy, he sought to fulfil the 'outer conditions of trustworthiness' (1961: 50), for example, being punctual, maintaining confidences, being consistent. Over time, he realized that it was equally important to be 'dependably real' or congruent, a quality often described nowadays as genuineness. *Genuineness* involves being aware of your own feelings and being able to use them to connect with your client, rather than retreating behind a façade or professional veneer. Genuineness does not mean blurting out everything you are thinking or feeling. It does mean being aware of yourself and your reactions and being willing to engage with your client in the learning partnership. The more you are fully present and genuine in the relationship, the more your client is freed up to be likewise.

In the following example we see that genuineness may be challenging for the client, but may lead to learning. Notice how the coach is not judgemental. He simply states the impact of the client's words on him as listener, and asks a question.

> My coach interrupted me and said, 'I know that this is really important to you, but you're giving me so much detail that I'm having difficulty in following you. Is all this detail helping you?' I was taken aback. Was it helping me? No, and it wasn't helping him either! I'd just assumed that it was useful and I realized I do that at work too. I flood people with information. Although his comment was a bit of a jolt, it was powerful learning for me when he didn't pretend to be interested. Maybe that's what people at work do, they just pretend to be interested.

Respect means accepting and affirming another person as they are. As coach or mentor, you may not agree with or like all aspects of a client's behaviour or views, but you try to suspend judgement and evaluation. Demonstrating respect might be difficult when the other person makes a decision that you would not choose, as the following example illustrates. However, at times like these, it can be most powerful.

> Eventually, I ended up telling my mentor that, despite everything the firm had done for me, I still thought that this wasn't the right career for me. I know people find that hard to hear. They see my success and think that I'm being ungrateful or self-indulgent, but he was different. He listened very quietly and attentively. I guess I was expecting disapproval, but there wasn't any. I know he sees things differently, but he respects my view, and that means a lot.

The third important quality identified by Rogers is *empathy*, which is different from sympathy. Though both words derive from the Greek word *pathos*, meaning 'feeling' or 'suffering', the prefix 'sym-' indicates 'sharing' or 'being in agreement', whereas the prefix 'em-' indicates being 'in'. When we communicate empathy, we try to appreciate how it is to be the other person, to walk in their shoes, to experience the situation as they experience it, from within. Rogers described how communicating empathy involved more than trying in a detached way to understand 'about' someone. Empathy is a powerful tool in coaching and mentoring because it communicates to the client that you have understood, or at least tried to understand, their unique experience, rather than imposing your view or making assumptions.

A colleague is talking. Below are two potential responses. One is empathic, one is sympathetic. How are they different? Which is the empathic response?

Colleague: Fred is being impossible. We're jointly accountable for this project, but he constantly passes the buck. He turns up late to meetings, hands all the tough decisions to me, and when the pressure is on, he goes off sick, whatever that means.

Response A: He sounds terrible! I don't know how you cope!

Response B: You're finding it really tough – it seems to you that he's not pulling his weight.

Response A is more sympathetic because it implies *agreement* with the colleague. It is likely to lead to a conversation with the colleague about Fred, but not necessarily about what the colleague can do to change the situation. The risk with a sympathetic response is that we end up agreeing or colluding with a person, but not helping them to move forward in managing their problem.

Response B is the more empathic response because it reflects the colleague's experience as seen by them. Notice that it implies neither agreement nor disagreement, but tries to communicate *understanding*. Response B is likely to be more productive in helping the colleague to address the problem, because it offers support but stays focused on the colleague.

In effective coaching and mentoring, you communicate empathy, respect and genuineness to your client. Sometimes this happens quite naturally. Sometimes it may be more difficult. This may be because the client is different from you, for example, in culture, upbringing, beliefs or values. However, in effective coaching and mentoring, the client is acknowledged and valued as they are, and the coach or mentor seeks to understand issues in the way that the client experiences them. Communicating this willingness to understand helps to build the learning relationship, which is at the heart of change.

An internal HR coach for senior managers describes how he sees this:

> I think it's enormously important to listen to clients' stories – how they tell the story of who they are. My best coaching has been when I felt that there was a real relationship and connection with the client. The client says 'you really know me, you know the mix of my past and the context and the present', and so it's a special relationship. One client with whom I had such a relationship was going through a very difficult time – a work conflict – and I was able to 'hold' him psychologically through that process and be steady for him and with him during the ups and downs.

In the next section, we will look at some core skills which help you to communicate respect, empathy and genuineness.

Developing core skills

Active listening

There are some core skills which enable you to build a learning dialogue with your client, and to use coaching and mentoring frameworks and techniques wisely and appropriately. In our experience of training coaches and mentors, the single most useful skill, which underpins all others, is that of active listening.

Active listening is different from diagnostic listening, as illustrated in Figure 2.1. When the coach or mentor listens diagnostically, they are trying to sift and sort information, to analyse what is relevant or irrelevant, trying to find a solution. This kind of listening can be useful when solving a puzzle, as in the kind of expert helping described earlier. For example, a dentist asks a patient if a pain is stabbing or diffuse, whether it is worse after drinking hot or cold liquids. The dentist is eliminating potential diagnoses and narrowing the search for the correct one. They are deciding which information is irrelevant and filtering it out; deciding which information needs elaboration; and gradually refining and focusing options based on their expertise and experience.

However, when the coach or mentor uses diagnostic listening, it can be less than useful, because it puts them in the driving seat and they end up leading the conversation. They ask closed questions (usually about facts) to get information to 'solve' things, and they slip into the role of expert helping. They are more likely to listen selectively, filtering responses and paying attention only to what seems relevant to their own ideas about what's going on. When the coach or mentor listens diagnostically, they end up generating options and solutions for their client.

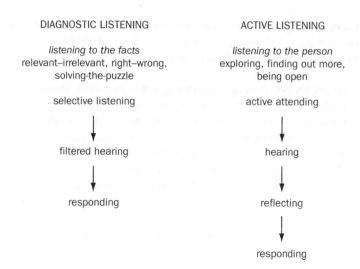

Figure 2.1   Diagnostic versus active listening
Source: Phillips and Pokora (2004).

In contrast, when they listen actively, they add value by helping the client to expand the client's understanding of the problem or opportunity so that *the client* can manage it better. When the coach or mentor listens actively, they are open to all information, including feelings as well as facts. They are free to follow rather than lead the client. In effect, they are holding up a mirror and saying, 'This is what I see/hear. Is that right? Is that how it is for you?' Active listening communicates that the coach or mentor is trying to understand the client's experience, and so it builds trust and a supportive learning relationship. Active listening, with a 'credulous attitude' (Kelly 1963: 174) tries to take in all information, verbal and non-verbal, factual and emotional, and to understand from the client's perspective. *For many people, it takes considerable effort to stop diagnostic listening and to start active listening.* The temptation to treat client issues as if they were puzzles, with one correct answer, and to try to 'solve' the puzzle, can be almost overwhelming. However, when the coach or mentor listens skilfully, the experience for the client can be intense. It can be powerful to feel that we have someone's full attention and that we are heard and understood as we are, without judgement or prescription or evaluation. Moreover, this experience of being heard and accepted can open up avenues for exploration in the coaching or mentoring conversation.

The following example shows how active listening can be used, and how it is different from diagnostic listening. Jane, a manager, is talking to a newly promoted team leader who comes to her with a problem.

A team leader describes the problems he faces in establishing an effective team: I feel as if I've been parachuted into a war zone. The department is divided, with factions sniping at each other, and so much unproductive conflict. We have a major deadline in four months, and it is vital that we start pulling together and stop wasting time and energy. Communication is breaking down – for example, at our weekly meeting, people become 'unavailable' at the last minute. I've inherited this situation – a hornets' nest – and I think part of the reason I was promoted was that senior management believed that I could sort it out. I suppose I should be encouraged by their faith in me, but . . .

Jane is trying to help. She is listening diagnostically and here are some of her responses:

- How many people are there in your department?
- Have you thought about involving the HR function?
- Could you try a team-building day?
- Can you renegotiate the deadline?
- How long has this been a problem?

These questions arise from diagnostic listening, and are easy to recognize. They include:

- suggestions framed as questions;
- questions to which the client already knows the answer;
- closed questions, which invite a one-word (often 'yes' or 'no') answer.

When you find yourself as coach or mentor asking a lot of questions to which the client already knows the answer, it may be because you have fallen into 'expert' helping and are trying to get the information to help you to solve the client's problem. Similarly with suggestions disguised as questions.

As an alternative, here are some active listening skills:

- ✔ paraphrasing the story;
- ✔ echoing key words or phrases, with a question mark;
- ✔ creating space by counting to three (silently!) before responding;
- ✔ summarizing the key parts of the overall message.

 If Jane uses active listening, what responses might she make? Can you think of some that you might try, using the skills of paraphrasing, echoing and summarizing? Some possible responses are given below.

Here are some examples of how Jane might show that she is actively listening:

- *Paraphrasing:* If I've understood you, it feels like a war zone, and you've been parachuted in to sort it out, and fast.
- *Echoing:* War zone?
- *Summarizing:* You're finding this a pretty tough situation to handle. You're new; external expectations are high; and the team seems to be in self-destruct mode.

These examples show how Jane could communicate to the team leader that she is actively attending and trying to understand his experience without filtering, judging or evaluating it. She is offering support to him, and as we will see in the next section, this will lead on to a conversation where he is able to challenge himself.

Encouraging self-challenge

While support is an important part of the coach or mentor role, clients want and need challenge. When clients are encouraged to challenge themselves, they can:

- develop insight;
- become aware of their blind spots;
- challenge self-limiting beliefs;
- notice previously overlooked strengths and resources;
- become more hopeful and positive;
- reframe their ideas and assumptions;
- focus on the future;
- implement action;
- become more strategic and proactive.

 Think of a time when you were helped with a difficult issue. What helped you to challenge yourself? Was there anything that made it more difficult?

Active listening serves a dual purpose. As well as supporting the client, it can enable them to self-challenge. Continuing with the previous example, let's look at how Jane's responses might help the team leader to do this:

- When Jane paraphrases: *If I've understood you right, it feels like a war zone, and you've been parachuted in to sort it out, and fast,* he realizes that he resents being 'parachuted in', even if he is supposed to be encouraged.

- When Jane echoes: *War zone?*, he notices that the metaphor of war is a strong one and he asks himself if things are really that bad.
- When Jane says: *You're finding this a pretty tough situation to handle. You're new; external expectations are high; and the team seems to be in self-destruct mode*, he wonders if all the team are in 'self-destruct mode'; maybe he is overlooking some potential allies.

Jane's interventions help her colleague to challenge how he sees things and to uncover some new perspectives. She is alongside him, working with him and their coaching conversation can move on from here. Similarly, when you use active listening skills, you build trust, by demonstrating that you are trying to understand how your client sees things. You also, as the example has shown, increase the likelihood that your client will challenge themselves.

Empathic challenge

Sometimes your client will need challenge to help them to move forward. Challenge is potentially strong medicine, and you earn the right to challenge by actively listening and challenging in an empathic way rather than a confronting way. As with too strong medicine, a too strong challenge may be rejected. So, it is helpful to develop your awareness of when challenging may be useful and your skill in challenging empathically. Getting the right balance of support and challenge for each client is important and we find that this needs careful attention. Below is a list of some areas for challenge, and indicators of when they may be appropriate. This is not intended to be a recipe book for challenge, or to imply that challenge is the appropriate response in each situation. Rather, it is intended to help you to notice the way in which the client tells their story and whether there are any new perspectives you can help them to uncover.

 Read through the list in Table 2.3. What is your experience of challenging in coaching and mentoring? Have you used any of these challenges, or any others? Have they helped your clients? Are there any that you use more frequently than others? Any that you rarely use? What do your answers tell you about your coaching and mentoring approach?

Challenge	May be useful when you experience the client as
Feelings: what is the client feeling?	focusing on what they are thinking or what is happening
Others' perspectives: how do/might other people see the situation?	seeing only their own viewpoint
Evidence: what are the facts to support or contradict the client's perspective?	generalizing or interpreting or lacking evidence
Resources: what are the client's internal and external resources, and which could they develop?	believing they lack resources or lacking self-belief
Ownership: in what way is the situation a problem or an opportunity for the client themselves?	talking about other people or the situation in general, rather that the impact on them
Patterns: has the client 'been there before'?	having a pattern, whether helpful or unhelpful, in their life or with the situation
Goals: is the client clear about what they want instead of what they've got?	focusing on what they don't want
Action: is the client willing and able to do something to move towards their goals?	finding it easier to talk rather than to act
The 'here and now': drawing attention to what's happening in the session and the impact on you	behaving in the session in a way which mirrors or contradicts how the client describes things outside it

Table 2.3 Areas for challenge in coaching and mentoring

Creating a working agreement

An effective coach and mentor has a clear understanding with their client about how they will work together, and this forms the foundation of a productive partnership and learning relationship. In formal coaching or mentoring, whether the coach or mentor is external or internal, an agreement or contract is important. Whether or not it is written, it should be discussed in the initial meeting. It gets the relationship off to a good start by involving the client and building the learning partnership. It also frees up both parties to focus their energy and attention on learning and development, rather than being distracted by unresolved questions or concerns. The coach or mentor models transparency by being open about what they can offer, and what they cannot, and how they want to work. This builds trust and creates the climate for learning. The working agreement is your opportunity to:

- agree with the client how you will work together;
- clarify any uncertainties;
- find out what they expect and want;
- explain what you can offer;
- answer their questions;
- deal with contractual issues.

Robert, a mentor for teachers: At the start of mentoring I ask the client quite a few 'what if' questions: What if we talk about something that cannot be kept confidential? What if you do not turn up for a session? What if we think mentoring is not proving useful? By asking these questions, I involve them in reaching an agreement, rather than imposing it.

Meg, a board-level coach: Over the years I have learned that it is helpful to be clear about the things, not many, which are non-negotiable. For example, sessions always take place away from the client's office, to free them up from job demands, and always during working hours, so that they see coaching as part of their day job. On the other hand, it is important to find out about, and be responsive to, how the client learns best, and be flexible about what will help them.

 Overleaf is a list of items that might be included in a working agreement for coaching or mentoring. Read through the list and note your response to each item. Would you include all these items in a working agreement? Would you add any? Which do you view as negotiable? Non-negotiable?

Practical

☐ Pre-coaching or mentoring introductory session
☐ Location – where will you meet?
☐ Frequency – how often will you meet? Minimum/maximum number of sessions
☐ Length of session – what would you prefer? Agree to?
☐ Payment – how much? Payment procedure?
☐ Cancellation – policy for missed session? What if the client is late?

Working relationship

☐ Preferred ways of working together
☐ Tools and techniques you might use
☐ Your values and the learning relationship
☐ Balance of support and challenge you will offer
☐ Feedback – 360-degree, other?
☐ How client learns best
☐ Framework or model you use
☐ Your expectations – work outside of sessions?

Professional

☐ Your qualifications
☐ Your experience/references
☐ Your responsibilities: legal, to the sponsor, to your profession or organization
☐ Any possible conflicts of interest?
☐ Note-taking – who takes? Who keeps? For how long?
☐ Supervision – your arrangements

Ethical

☐ An explicit working agreement
☐ Built-in ongoing review
☐ Confidentiality: extent and limits
☐ Clear role boundaries
☐ Ending session

Working agreements are particularly important where third parties are involved. They may take the form of a written contract, signed by all parties, and many mentoring and coaching schemes have formal contracts describing responsibilities and boundaries. A formal contract can specify what kind of information, if any, the sponsor will receive about the content and progress of mentoring or coaching. Sometimes third parties will want more information than the coach or mentor or client is prepared to give.

> **Stephanie offers an independent mentoring service** to staff identified as underperforming. She has verbally agreed with the organization sponsor that mentoring conversations will be confidential and separate from any organization processes or procedures. However, after mentoring a client for a while, she is asked by a concerned and well-intentioned sponsor to 'let us know how he is getting on'. In a conversation with the sponsor she reminds them of the verbal agreement, and formalizes this in writing. In future, she decides, she will use a written agreement from the outset.

Managing a productive relationship

Effective coaching or mentoring relationships have an outcome: they help your clients to achieve change. Regardless of whether a relationship extends over only one session or over many months or even years, it has a beginning, a middle and an end. At each stage – beginning, middle and end – you work to support and enable the client in making the changes they want and need in their life. You pay attention to the learning relationship and to client outcomes. There are different issues associated with each stage and below is an introduction to some of these issues.

Managing the beginning

Whether you are formally coaching or mentoring, or using the skills in your management or leadership role, clarifying expectations and focus will help you to establish a productive learning relationship. Some aspects of getting started with this are illustrated by the case example of Harry, a coach who is meeting a potential client for the first time.

> **Harry meets with a new client,** who is very keen to have some coaching, saying that Harry has been highly recommended by her colleagues. The client's busy schedule means that she wants coaching meetings in the early evening, as she would find it difficult to take time out of the day. Harry notices that the client is not very relaxed: she glances at her phone from time to time. Harry checks that he has understood the key points of her story and reflects to her that she seems concerned

> with time pressure, even during this first session together. This prompts her to talk more about how work pressures are affecting her.

Notice how Harry is **fully attending**. He pays attention to both the non-verbal and verbal messages from the client. He tries to maintain a relaxed and attentive posture, including appropriate eye contact, facial expression, tone of voice and leaning towards the client but not invading their personal space. He has cleared his mind of distractions, so that he can be receptive and open to the client. To communicate what he has heard, he reflects and paraphrases, clarifies and summarizes. All this is done tentatively, giving the client the space to correct any misunderstanding. They continue talking:

> In response to her request for evening sessions, Harry says that he understands that she will find it difficult to make time, but that he offers sessions only between 9 and 5. The client says she is very keen to work with Harry and says would be prepared to pay extra. He explains that he is unable to do this, and suggests tentatively that perhaps finding time in the day might help her to prioritize coaching. However, he also tells her that there are other coaches who offer more flexible hours than he does. On reflection, she agrees to work with him.

Notice how Harry is **clarifying boundaries**. He is clear about the working arrangements and what he can offer the client. He also says what he is unable to offer. This leads to a discussion about how they will work together.

> Harry explains the coaching process, and the framework he uses. He believes that it is important to agree goals and action plans at the end of each session, and check progress at the start of the next, and he asks whether this way of working will suit his client. He suggests that they meet fortnightly, within working hours, but she is concerned that her busy schedule will result in her missing some appointments, so they agree to meet every three weeks, within working hours, initially for three months.

Here Harry is **sorting out the working arrangements**. He is clear about how he works and is responsive to agreeing a workable schedule with his client. He discusses the framework and learning processes that he might use. Expectations and limitations are clarified, establishing trust and reducing uncertainties on both sides. They fix a date for their next meeting.

> Harry's client clears her diary so that they can meet within working hours, and they meet a few weeks later. By the end of the session Harry

has helped her to prioritize her aims for coaching. These are: to improve her presentation skills and her time management. They agree that these two issues are probably related. They discuss how coaching can help her to achieve these aims, and what she wants from her coach. She decides on some actions she will take before their next meeting.

In this session, Harry works on **focusing and prioritizing**. He helps the client to clarify and prioritize her aims, to focus her effort and attention and thereby increase the chance of successful outcomes. He enables the client to identify two key issues and also to commit to action before the next session.

In this example you can see that the coach fully attends to the client's expectations, clarifies boundaries and working arrangements and enables the client to prioritize. All these elements help to successfully establish their learning relationship. The list in Box 2.3 contains some questions for coaches and mentors, and summarizes the important aspects of managing the beginning.

 Which of these questions are most relevant in the kind of coaching and mentoring that you do? Are there any questions that you wish to add?

Box 2.3   Managing the beginning: some questions for coaches and mentors

- Am I able to give the client my full attention?
- Have we both been involved, as far as possible, in the decision to work together?
- Is this the right kind of help for the client at this time?
- Are we clear about the client's priorities for coaching or mentoring?
- Have we talked about the limits of confidentiality? Possible conflicts of interest?
- Have I described the framework I use? My professional background and experience?
- Have we talked about how the client learns best?
- Have we agreed time/place/note-keeping/financial arrangements?
- We have begun to establish a working relationship? How can I tell?
- Am I concerned about anything? Any unresolved issues that might benefit from supervision or support?
- Have I created the opportunity for the client to express any concerns or questions?

The ongoing relationship

Throughout the working relationship, you can help a client in a variety of ways, so that they are better able to do the following:

- *Reflect on the work they are doing*, both during and between sessions, and learn from experience. You create the reflective space that is so often missing in a busy working life.
- *Develop insight both about their situation and about themselves.* You enable the client to be realistic about but not constrained by their context. They can then identify what will help and hinder them in achieving goals.
- *Self-challenge, identify resources and develop their potential.* You help the client to challenge self-imposed limitations, and self-limiting beliefs and attitudes. They are supported in developing both internal and external resources which can help them achieve their goals.
- *Identify achievable change goals.* Goals vary in nature. Some may be visible, for example, achieving a performance goal; others may be harder to see, for example, sustaining a change in attitude. The value of a goal is the extent to which it helps the client to achieve the changes they want. You help the client to identify and choose change goals.
- *Plan and implement actions which help to achieve goals.* The coaching or mentoring session is an important catalyst, but the proof of the pudding, so to speak, is in the changes that the client makes back at work. You help the client to make realistic plans which they can implement.
- *Notice, celebrate and reinforce their successes.* You support the client by highlighting and acknowledging what they have achieved, and enabling them to do this for themselves, so that they are energized.

In the following example, the coach helps the client to reflect, to focus on strengths, to identify goals and to act.

> **John was a highly successful events organizer,** until a health problem meant that he could no longer drive, which was essential in his career. He described himself as 'washed-up' and 'fit for nothing'. He needed a coach to help him to identify and exploit the talents and resources that he still had, rather than focus on his limitations. The coach helped him to generate ideas about alternative career options. Together they planned how he might explore these options, and get started on moving forward rather than looking back. Experiencing some successes increased John's confidence and enthusiasm, and the coach supported him through setbacks. Although it took time, John was able to find a fulfilling alternative career.

Box 2.4 contains some useful questions for managing the ongoing relationship. Use the list to reflect on a coaching or mentoring role you have at present. What do your answers tell you about the ongoing relationship?

Box 2.4   Managing the ongoing relationship: some questions for coaches and mentors

- What has the client done as a result of our initial session/s? What has helped or hindered them?
- Has the client identified change goals? Made any action plans? Implemented these?
- Have I drawn the client's attention to what they have achieved, and any successes?
- Am I using the appropriate balance of support and challenge?
- Have we talked about how we are working together? What is helping or hindering?
- How would I describe our working relationship? How would the client describe it?
- Am I using all my resources to help the client, for example, knowledge, skills, experience, networks?

Managing the ending

In this stage, you help the client to bring the work and perhaps also the relationship to a conclusion. If the session is a one-off, the effective coach or mentor will ensure there is time at the end to address the relevant items from the list in Box 2.5.

Box 2.5   Managing the ending: some questions for coaches and mentors

- Are we clear about why we are ending, and when?
- Have we both been involved, as far as possible, in the decision to end?
- Is the client ready for the ending? If not, what can I do to help them?
- Have we acknowledged what the client has achieved?
- Have we reviewed how we have worked together?
- Have we discussed any work still to do? Considered how the client might take this forward?
- Have we discussed how the client will move on?
- Have we agreed what will be done with any notes?
- Has the client had the chance to make a good ending for themselves?

As a rough guide, in a two-hour session, 10–15 minutes might be set aside for this. Where a longer relationship is coming to an end, preparation for ending may take place over several sessions and form a significant part of the final session.

Remember too that every coaching or mentoring session has a beginning, a middle and an ending. Taking a few minutes at the end of each session to review the working partnership can produce powerful learning not only for the client but also for the coach or mentor.

Maximizing client resourcefulness

A key part of coaching and mentoring is developing your client's resourcefulness. Your belief in your clients is communicated in how you listen and respond to them: as Egan puts it, 'If you listen only for problems, you will end up talking mainly about problems' (2002: 83). So, it is important to listen not only for difficulties but also for resources, opportunities and potential. Here is an example of a coach who is listening for and developing her client's resourcefulness.

> *Julie:* I'm really unhappy with the way Steve (her colleague) upsets me; I just wish I was better at handling meetings with him.
>
> *Coach:* What would better look like?
>
> *Julie:* I don't know . . . well, I suppose I'd be confident in dealing with him and not let him get to me.
>
> *Coach:* Confident and not let him get to you?
>
> *Julie:* Well . . . not apologizing and then ending up resenting him.
>
> *Coach:* So if you weren't letting him get to you, and you weren't apologizing, what would you be doing?
>
> *Julie:* I don't know (pause). Well, I'd be standing my ground and keeping calm and I'd be saying to myself 'you can handle this'.

Notice how the coach's skilful questioning is drawing out ideas from Julie and developing her resourcefulness. The coach does not dwell on the difficulties but rather focuses on what could be. The coach assumes Julie is resourceful and helps her to access and develop her resources. The following quotation underlines how our assumptions as coaches and mentors can affect our approach and, potentially, coaching and mentoring outcomes.

> If we assume that our clients *do not* have the resources required to resolve the issues that they bring, then generally coaching will confirm

that assumption. If on the other hand we assume that our clients *do* have the resources required to resolve the problems that they bring, then again generally coaching will confirm that assumption. Sometimes, in the process, clients will discover resources that they (and we) knew nothing about.

(Iveson et al. 2012: 18)

Clients have all kinds of inner and outer resources, many of which may be underused and underdeveloped. Inner resources include their skills and abilities, their past experiences and learning from successes and failures. Outer resources may lie in people around them, their networks, their organization and the context.

So, when you work with your clients to draw out and develop their resources and their solutions, especially at times when they doubt themselves, you communicate your belief in them. The following quotation vividly describes the affirming experience of being listened to and believed in:

Imagine someone listening, not only to your words, but also to what's behind them – who even listens to the spaces between the words. Someone in tune with the nuances of your voice, your emotion, your energy – who is intent on receiving everything you communicate. Someone who listens to the very best in you, even when you can't hear it in yourself.

(Whitworth et al. 1998: xviii)

 Take a moment to think about how easy or difficult you find it to trust your clients' resourcefulness. Do you listen for the best in them? In what ways do you help your clients to discover and use their resources?

Using a framework and tools and techniques

Frameworks

A model or framework, when used sensitively, can contribute significantly to effective helping. There are many views on which framework or model is best for coaching and mentoring, but there is agreement that it is important for the coach or mentor to be clear about their approach. Some frameworks and approaches are outlined in Chapter 5, and one, the Egan Skilled Helper model, is described in detail in Chapter 6.

Box 2.6 Possible benefits of using a framework

- Communicates the values and assumptions of the coach or mentor.
- Demonstrates a professional approach by grounding practice in theory.
- Demonstrates transparency by clarifying underlying approach.
- Shares responsibility through discussion of the framework.
- Creates hope by using a tried and tested approach.
- Provides a reference point for deciding what work needs to be done.
- Encourages change by providing a map with direction.
- Focuses on key issues.
- Empowers the client if the framework is transferable to other contexts.
- Helps to guide purposeful coaching and mentoring conversations.

 Box 2.6 lists some benefits of using a framework. Which are important to you? Are there any that you might add?

Lucy, a mentor in a university mentoring scheme: People who come for mentoring are interested in the framework I use. I explain it to them and I think this reassures them that they are not being 'psyched out'. In fact, it's a framework which, after a time, they find they can use by themselves. I think that part of my mentoring role is to offer useful tools and techniques which people can try out in everyday work situations, and I say that right at the beginning.

Ed, an HR professional and coach: I'm a pretty good listener, but that isn't always enough. I use a framework as a map, to help me and the client to see where we are going and to check that we aren't going round in circles. It gives us both some structure which helps us to use time productively and ensure that we are moving forward.

 Here are some questions to help select the right framework for you.

- What frameworks do you know about?
- Which have you used?
- Have you had training in using a framework?

- What evidence exists to support the effectiveness of the framework?
- What has helped you personally in your development?
- What is congruent with your beliefs and values?
- What is relevant to your context?
- What do other coaches and mentors recommend?
- What would empower clients?

A cautionary note: a framework is only as good as the person using it. It is a useful guide, rather than a template. It should be used to help, rather than to unnecessarily constrain, the coach, mentor or client.

Tools and techniques

The effective coach or mentor knows how to use tools and techniques to help clients move forward in managing problems and developing their potential. You may like to use the tools and techniques that you have found beneficial. However, coaches and mentors should be wary of overusing their favourite approaches. There is a saying that if the only tool you have is a hammer, it is tempting to treat everything as if it were a nail. The most important consideration should be whether or not they will help the client in front of you.

Some tools and techniques are introduced in Chapter 8 with descriptions of how they can:

- provide a change of pace in the session;
- help the 'stuck' client to see their situation differently;
- appeal to the client's preferred learning style or way of working;
- enable the client to move out of their 'comfort zone';
- bring the 'out there' situation into the coaching session;
- access the client's hidden strengths and resources;
- offer the client a safe way of 'rehearsing' or trying out an approach;
- help the client to let go of the past and move forward.

Reflecting on coach and mentor competencies

The professional coaching and mentoring organizations are rightly concerned with establishing and maintenance of standards of practice. Many of them have developed competency frameworks which form the basis of their accreditation processes. Our key principles for effective practice reflect these competencies. Below are examples from two international professional bodies, the European Mentoring and Coaching Council (EMCC) and the International Coach Federation (ICF), which have been at the forefront of developing competence frameworks alongside codes of ethical practice.

The EMCC Competency Framework (2015) describes eight competency categories. These are:

1 Understanding Self
2 Commitment to Self-Development
3 Managing the Contract
4 Building the Relationship
5 Enabling Insight and Learning
6 Outcome and Action Orientation
7 Use of Models and Techniques
8 Evaluation

(EMCC 2015: online)

Attached to each category are descriptions of behaviours (called capabilities), which are indicators of competence in that category. The EMCC offers four levels of accreditation, and there are indicators for each level: the higher the level, the higher the capability. So, for example, at the Foundation level, the indicator of Commitment to Self-Development is 'Practises and evaluates their coaching/mentoring skills'. At the highest level, Master Practitioner, the indicator is 'Keeps up to date with and evaluates research and thinking on mentoring/coaching' (EMCC 2015: online).

The ICF identifies 11 core competencies, grouped in four clusters, and these are listed below:

A. Setting the Foundation
　　1. Meeting Ethical Guidelines and Professional Standards
　　2. Establishing the Coaching Agreement

B. Co-creating the Relationship
　　3. Establishing Trust and Intimacy with the Client
　　4. Coaching Presence

C. Communicating Effectively
　　5. Active Listening
　　6. Powerful Questioning
　　7. Direct Communication

D. **Facilitation Learning and Results**
   8. Creating Awareness
   9. Designing Actions
   10. Planning and Goal Setting
   11. Managing Progress and Accountability

(ICF 2016: online)

It offers three levels of accreditation; Associate Certified Coach, Professional Certified Coach and Master Certified Coach.

Whether or not you are interested in becoming accredited, competency frameworks are a useful backdrop against which to reflect on your practice. The safe and effective coach or mentor monitors their own competence and pays attention to developing their capabilities. The indicators offer descriptions of good practice which can help ongoing reflection and development. We say more about supervision, accreditation and self-development in Chapters 9 and 10.

A coaching and mentoring checklist

Finally, in this chapter, here is a checklist, which you might use as a starting point for reflecting on your coaching and mentoring. It is derived from the principles outlined in Chapter 1 and elaborated in this chapter. If your responses raise questions for you, you will find further discussion of each of these issues in this book, particularly in Chapters 4 and 9.

- Have we established a working learning relationship?
- Is the client clear about what they want from coaching or mentoring?
- Am I primarily facilitating rather than instructing?
- Is our work contained with appropriate boundaries?
- Is the client achieving change which they value?
- Am I using models or tools appropriately?
- Am I treating the client as a resourceful person?
- Am I communicating the core conditions and using skills wisely?
- Am I working ethically and paying attention to resolving any ethical dilemmas?

Summary

In this chapter we have:

- Invited you to reflect on your strengths and areas for development.

- Helped you to assess the costs and benefits of coaching or mentoring for you and your organization, and to consider your role.

- Described the core skills, and illustrated how they are used in a learning relationship.

- Considered how to establish and use a working agreement and manage the ongoing relationship.

- Explained the importance of maximizing client resourcefulness.

- Discussed the benefits of frameworks and tools and techniques, and considered how to use them wisely.

- Outlined two competency frameworks which might support your development.

- Provided a checklist based on the principles of effective coaching and mentoring.

3 How can I be an effective client?

- Introduction
- Getting the right coach or mentor
- Knowing yourself
- Having realistic expectations
- Negotiating a working agreement
- Thinking ahead and being strategic
- Being proactive
- Learning from support and challenge
- Using reflective space
- Developing your imagination
- Identifying your resources and working smart
- Setting goals and making action plans
- Developing skills, making changes and delivering results
- Summary

Introduction

The aim of this chapter is to help you to get the most out of coaching and mentoring by knowing what you can do to be fully active in and between sessions. It should give you some insight into yourself, and into what the coach or mentor might expect of you. It also aims to inform you about what you can expect from your coach or mentor, and how to get it.

The chapter starts by helping you to clarify how to get the right coach or mentor for your particular needs and wants. Throughout the chapter we refer to you as the 'client'. You may be an individual client, working with one coach or mentor, or you may be part of a team that is being coached. You will see how your personality preferences and learning style can affect the working relationship with a coach or mentor. Examples from coaching and mentoring are used to show differences as well as similarities. The importance of developing a clear working agreement is explained. Ways in which you can be proactive and make the most of the reflective space in sessions are outlined. There are examples of developing imagination, identifying resources, using skills, formulating goals and implementing action plans.

 Wherever you see this symbol there is an invitation for you to reflect upon how you can make the most of coaching and mentoring.

Getting the right coach or mentor

Box 3.1   What do I want from a coach or mentor?

Be aware that coaching and mentoring are described differently by different people and therefore, when choosing, do take care to read how the coach or mentor describes what they do, to see if it fits your purpose.

So what do you want, a coach or a mentor? You may even want both, for different needs in your life. Coaching at work is often about performance. It can be individual or team coaching. If you are being mentored or coached within the organization, it may be by your manager or leader, who may also be your appraiser or assessor. In this case, you will need to negotiate the agenda carefully, to ensure that it meets the expectations of both you and your coach or mentor. You may wish to benefit from the experience of a respected mentor who understands your profession or organization and who will share experience without expecting you to be a protégé. You may request 'off-line' mentoring or coaching either within the organization, or provided externally. This is particularly useful if it is an issue which is broader than a specific performance issue, or where there may be problems of confidentiality or conflicts of interest between you and your manager (see Table 3.1).

Executive coaching may be external to the organization. You may be paying an external coach or mentor yourself, or your organization may pay. In the latter case, it will be important to clarify and agree the expectations of all parties, the boundaries of confidentiality and the lines of communication.

When you have decided whether you want a coach or a mentor, internal to your organization or external, you will need to find the right person for you. For this, you need to know something about yourself. The literature on coaching

Internal	External
Advantages	*Advantages*
Easy to meet together	Can be totally objective
Knows the organization	Easy to maintain confidentiality
Can network for you	Clear boundary: you and work
Understands the politics	Likely to be uninterrupted
Has personal experience of obstacles	You may prepare more carefully
May know people you talk about	Conflict of interest less likely
May be able to access resources	Knows other networks
Disadvantages	*Disadvantages*
Sessions may be interrupted	May cost more
People will know	Travel takes time
Confidentiality may be harder	Need to explain about your work
Boundaries may be blurred and you may be more casual and informal	The coach or mentor may not be monitored the way an 'insider' is

Table 3.1   Internal vs external coaching and mentoring

and mentoring emphasizes that the chemistry between the client and the coach or mentor is significant. Knowing about your personality and the way you react to the support and challenge that will be given in coaching and mentoring will help you to make the most of the learning relationship.

Knowing yourself

What is it that you need and want in a coach or mentor? How do you learn best? What sort of person can help you most to gain insight, explore possibilities, set goals and deliver results?

Think of a time when you were helped in the past with a work issue or with a career opportunity. What was it in you, and in the person helping you, that really made the difference? Think of a time when someone tried to help but it didn't work. What was it about the way that person tried to help that didn't work? Was it something in them, or something in you, or both?

Here is the example of Tim who has looked around until he has found the right mentor.

Tim teaches in an inner-city secondary school. He was assigned an experienced senior colleague as his mentor. The mentor was generous with his time and in the way that he shared his considerable experience, but Tim found that the sessions were dominated by the mentor advising him what to do. What Tim really needed was some reflective space where he could talk over some of the concerns and opportunities arising in his new job. When he tried to raise issues, the mentor adopted a well-intentioned but nevertheless unhelpful 'if I were you' approach. Fortunately, Tim has now met another colleague, trained as a mentor, who is willing to act informally as a sounding board. He helps Tim to explore the issues on his mind, and reach his own conclusions. Tim continues to see the more experienced senior colleague from time to time, but uses those sessions to get advice on more practical aspects of lesson planning, marking and report writing.

 So, what sort of person are you: what do you know about your personality preferences; what makes you put your trust in other people to whom you turn for help; what makes you respect them; what makes you feel safe with them?

The list in Table 3.2 will help you to pick out your own personality preferences and clarify what sort of coach or mentor is best for you. Try ticking the characteristics that apply to you. *There are no right or wrong answers, just preferences.* You may want to tick one of each pair, or both in the pair, or neither may apply to you.

Characteristics	Characteristics
Reserved/Outgoing	Imaginative/Realistic
Objective/Subjective	Humorous/Serious
Vulnerable/Robust	Controlling/Adaptable
Challenging/Supportive	Empathic/Sympathetic
Involved/Detached	Directive/Non-Directive
Cool/Warm	Open/Closed
Active/Reflective	Fair/Just
Intuitive/Reasoned	Spontaneous/Considered
Practical/Conceptual	Transparent/Opaque
Problem-Solver/Listener	Leader/Follower

Table 3.2   Personality preferences when choosing a coach or mentor

When you have done this, think about the characteristics that you want in a coach or mentor and repeat the exercise. This time put a circle around the desired characteristic. You may find that you want someone like you, or that you would value someone who differs from you. If you have completed any psychometric questionnaires or inventories, they may give you additional information about your preferences.

Clients learn about themselves through dialogue with their coach or mentor. When this is effective, it will increase your insight into issues, problems and opportunities. It will increase your motivation to make the changes that are really wanted and the actions that will deliver results. The effective coach or mentor understands how to help you to motivate yourself and to believe in yourself. In order for you to make the most of this learning you need to be aware of how you like to learn.

Do you know anything about your preferred ways of learning? There is a learning styles questionnaire (Honey and Mumford 2006), which suggests that each of us has preferences for learning. For example, when we started to write this book we talked about how we would approach the task of writing. For one of us, it was a case of sitting in front of the computer and starting to write. For the other, it was a case of going to read other books on the subject before feeling able to start. Kolb and Fry (1975) suggest that there are four main approaches to learning: reflection, theorizing, pragmatism and action. People should be able to move between these styles and this is called the 'learning cycle'. The descriptions below will help you to identify how you learn best and what type of coaching and mentoring will suit your learning style.

 Put these in your order of preference:

- Applying ideas in practice
- Observing and reflecting
- Experiencing and doing
- Thinking and conceptualizing

So, what will you want from your coach or mentor: exploration, discussion, practical targets, skill development or action?

Figures 3.1 and 3.2 show how different learning styles are used at different stages of the learning cycle, and will help you to establish which are your most and least preferred styles. When thinking about how we learn, it is useful to remember that we do not learn from experience, but from reflection upon that experience.

When you are working with your coach or mentor, there is an opportunity to move through these different ways of working and learning as you go through the process. However, you may find that if your coach or mentor has a different learning style from you, it could affect your working

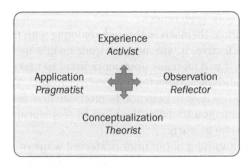

Figure 3.1 The learning cycle and learning styles
Source: Adapted from Honey and Mumford (1992).

PRAGMATIST	REFLECTOR
Keen to put ideas to the test	Careful and methodical
Loves practical activities	Doesn't jump to conclusions
May focus on task more than people	Doesn't like to be pushed into responses
Wants practical tips to use in real life	May appear unassertive
Needs time to practise and experiment	Needs time to think and consider options
ACTIVIST	THEORIST
Likes change	Likes logic and reason
Ready to experiment	Literal not lateral
Wants action	Asks challenging questions
Responds quickly	May not rate intuition
Likes fun	Prefers certainty and objectivity

Figure 3.2   Characteristics of the styles

relationship – the difference may be creative, or it may result in you feeling that you are not being understood or helped. There are two guidelines here. First, know your own preferences. Second, talk openly with your coach or mentor about *their* preferences and talk about what you need from one another. Then make sure that you can review on a regular basis how well you work together.

Having realistic expectations

Coaching and mentoring are not the answer for all issues and problems. The coach or mentor is a facilitator but not a fixer. You may seek help with an issue, a problem or an opportunity and you probably have the resources within yourself to manage that. But for whatever reason you may become stuck and unable to access those resources, and so seek some coaching or mentoring. The process will help you to become unstuck, it will release your own potential to achieve the desired results. It will work only if the relationship between helper and helped is balanced, with each person taking responsibility. This can be difficult to manage if coaching has been imposed on you. But even if it is imposed, you can still choose how to make the most of it. The coach or mentor is responsible for managing the process and for providing specific skills within a framework of ethical practice. The client is responsible for setting the agenda and for taking action as a result of the coaching or mentoring.

Much of the really important work in coaching and mentoring takes place between sessions when you are either reflecting upon the previous session, acting as a result of it, or preparing for the next session. In order to be an effective client, you will be proactive, not reactive. You will gradually become your own coach or mentor as you learn the skills and frameworks that have worked for you in the sessions.

> **Helen works in marketing.** She was sent for coaching by her line manager because of problems with team relationships during project work. She turned up expecting her coach to have all the answers. She was disappointed. The coach tried to get her to look at the problem from the perspective of the team as well as from her own point of view. But Helen was not ready to do this because she felt defensive at being 'told' that she needed some coaching. She attended two sessions but then went back to the manager and said that it had been a waste of time.

Helen's example is not uncommon. Readiness for coaching and mentoring is important. If it has been suggested by others, it does not always work. But in the next case example it did.

> **Tony is a medical manager.** He had never heard of coaching when his boss suggested that a coach might help him to deal with his difficulties in meeting deadlines at work. Although Tony did not understand what coaching was, he asked around and thought he would give it a try. He was recommended a coach who was outside his department but within the same organization. He arranged an introductory meeting where he negotiated how they might work together. By the time he arrived for his first proper session he had a clear idea of what to expect of himself and of his coach. They met on four occasions. This first session was mainly Tony talking and the coach listening as he revealed a lifelong problem with procrastination. They agreed some goals about charting his current tasks and prioritizing them. In the second session, the coach presented some approaches that others had used successfully and Tony was able to evaluate which of these might fit for him. He then tried some out before the next session. The third session was a debriefing of the action taken, with the coach helping Tony to formulate some specific, realistic goals and action plans. In the final session they evaluated the progress and talked about ending their working arrangement. Tony realized that he had a lifelong pattern of procrastination to change and that this would take time but he now had the confidence and skills to keep working at it.

In these two examples, both were referred for coaching but Tony was realistic, proactive and successful whereas Helen was passive and expected a magic wand instead of a coach!

Negotiating a working agreement

You have decided that you would like to start some coaching or mentoring. What next? You can find someone through personal recommendation or through coaching and mentoring networks and organizations. Before approaching someone, think through the type of working agreement you would like and have a look at a sample agreement in the previous chapter. Consider the aspects shown in Figure 3.3. In our experience it is important to address these questions and issues right from the start and to make sure you work with a coach or mentor who encourages open and honest discussion of all these aspects.

You will find useful information about these aspects in several of the other chapters. In Chapter 4, for example, we discuss what to expect in terms of good ethical and professional practice.

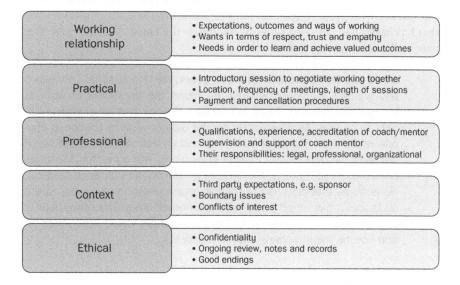

Working relationship	• Expectations, outcomes and ways of working • Wants in terms of respect, trust and empathy • Needs in order to learn and achieve valued outcomes
Practical	• Introductory session to negotiate working together • Location, frequency of meetings, length of sessions • Payment and cancellation procedures
Professional	• Qualifications, experience, accreditation of coach/mentor • Supervision and support of coach mentor • Their responsibilities: legal, professional, organizational
Context	• Third party expectations, e.g. sponsor • Boundary issues • Conflicts of interest
Ethical	• Confidentiality • Ongoing review, notes and records • Good endings

Figure 3.3 Aspects of a working agreement to be considered by the client

Thinking ahead and being strategic

'Being strategic' means thinking ahead about your own working or professional life. It may mean developing a vision of what you want to be in one year, two years, five years or ten years from now. Having a coach or mentor helps to keep your focus on the now and on the future. It is the responsibility of the coach or mentor to help the client to keep scanning the horizon, rather than getting bogged down in the activity of everyday working life.

Do you have a plan for your future?

Do you have a vision of where you want to be in five years' time?

Have you worked with someone to clarify your values and goals?

The most successful companies and organizations are constantly addressing these questions. The most successful people do it too, often accompanied by a coach or mentor.

To get the most out of coaching and mentoring, it will be part of your overall strategy for personal and professional development. In this way, you become the leader in your own life, rather than allowing your work to lead you. Clients who prepare for coaching or mentoring sessions by reviewing what has happened between sessions maximize the benefits of the reflective space with the coach or mentor.

> **David has had a mentor for three years.** He is a hospital consultant and wanted a mentor because he found the pressures of work at times overwhelming. There is constant change and never-ending targets to be met. As a senior doctor, he did not want to confide in anyone within the hospital and so he joined an action learning set which provides the opportunity to work one-on-one with a mentor. Meetings are every three months. He decides on the agenda for each session. He ensures that only half of the two-hour mentoring session is spent on issues which need to be resolved immediately. The other hour is spent in exploring longer-range issues, what his ideal future would be and how he might achieve that in practice.

Being proactive

As a client, it helps if you set the agenda for your coaching or mentoring sessions and allow your coach or mentor to facilitate that agenda. If you need help with a specific issue or problem, you may want your mentor or coach to be quite active in the process. Examples of this include helping you to role-play a particular scenario that has been problematic or practising a specific skill, such as assertiveness. Think carefully about what you want before you meet with your coach or mentor and then discuss how the session will address that. Make sure that the sort of working arrangement which you agree will allow for ongoing evaluation of the process and of the dynamic, in the working relationship. This can be helped by spending the final few minutes of each session with both of you saying what you feel has been achieved, what helped and what hindered. You can then agree targets for the next meeting, and for your time between sessions. Here are some examples of ways in which clients have been proactive.

Sarah, an administrator in a telecoms company, always arrives for her coaching session with a written list of things she wants help with, and she prioritizes them.

Bill, a sales manager in an oil company, thinks of a couple of situations at work where he wants help and then uses the learning from dealing with these in order to inform his judgement and skill in other areas. So, when he leaves the session and gets into his car he always talks into a dictaphone to summarize the session before driving off. He wants to capture the learning before he gets swamped with the next round of sales.

Pat, a social worker, keeps a reflective journal. She arrives in the session, opens the journal and picks from it some incident that has been especially significant.

Christian works in computers and likes to bring written reports and documents to reflect upon. He always writes a summary of the sessions in bullet-point form, bringing this with him next time, to review any action taken.

Martina is a lecturer and values just having space. She does not want to work from documents or reports, she has enough of those at college. But she always gives herself 30 minutes of quiet time to prepare for the mentoring session she has with a senior colleague.

 Think of a time when you were helped by someone. Consider what worked well for you.

Now think about your current situation. If you decide to go for coaching or mentoring what would you do to be proactive? Try to think of three ways that would work for you. Consider: your time; your usual ways of reflecting; how you learn; how you might prepare for a session; how you would act between sessions.

Learning from support and challenge

Any effective learning relationship will have an appropriate balance of support and challenge. If you read Chapter 2, you will know what the coach or mentor does in order to provide this potent mix in a way that empowers rather than overwhelms or overprotects. Everyone is different in the amount of support or challenge they want and need. Our needs vary at different points in our working life. Consider the example of Isaac.

> **Isaac has emigrated and is settling into a new job in engineering.**
> Mentoring was recommended to all newly recruited staff from overseas and Isaac was pleased to be offered this support. When he started to see his mentor, he was feeling very isolated, having left his family to come and work in a new country. Although he had been a high-flyer at home, he suddenly felt very much like the new kid on the block. He has a very understanding mentor who just gives him the space to talk about his feelings and who offers warm support. Isaac is relieved. He wants no more than this at first. Others are giving him the technical help he needs. He meets with his mentor on a monthly basis at first and after three months he says that he feels very supported and would now welcome some advice about whether to pursue a research opportunity to take his career to the next stage. His mentor becomes more active and helps Isaac to challenge himself about what he might achieve. This stage of mentoring is very powerful, but unnerving at times. Isaac says that he benefits greatly from this. He would have resisted too much challenge without support, and yet with too much support and not enough challenge, he would not stretch himself to the next stage of his career.

 Think about what you prefer in terms of support and challenge.

- Do you want to be challenged or do you want the sort of support that will enable you to challenge yourself?
- How would you ask for the sort of challenge that would work for you?
- What would you do if your coach or mentor got the balance wrong?

Using reflective space

One of the most significant benefits of coaching and mentoring is the opportunity in busy working lives to take stock, in the reflective space provided by the coach or mentor. At first, this may make you feel uncomfortable because while your coach or mentor provides the silence, you will search for thoughts, feelings and insights into the experiences that you have brought for discussion. You may try to avoid doing this because it is challenging and uncomfortable, even though it is very productive and helpful. A good coach or mentor will never expect you to talk about things that you do not wish to share. They will help you to decide what you really want to explore.

Some clients break the silence by changing the subject or using humour to distract their coach or mentor. However, if you can allow yourself to be psychologically 'held' by the attentive listening of your coach or mentor, then you will allow your inner voice to speak to you. Things which have been pushed down into your subconscious by the frenetic activity of everyday living can then slowly come up to the surface. You learn to listen to yourself. In terms of well-being, this is known to be very beneficial. It induces relaxation. You breathe more slowly and deeply, your pulse rate slows and you can then give voice to your wants, your needs, your problems, your issues, your opportunities and your dreams. Some people do this for 10 minutes every morning as a way of focusing on the day. If you are not used to doing this, then it may be worth trying to do it at some point in each day. You will then make more efficient use of the reflective space when you are with your coach or mentor. It is not just the time set aside that makes space 'reflective', it is the quality of the session.

 If you were to use a coach or mentor:

- How would you make most use of the time for reflection?
- What do you already do in your life that is similar to this?
- What difficulties might there be for you in working in this way?
- What qualities and interventions in your coach or mentor might help you (e.g. not having too much silence while you think about things, or asking your coach or mentor not to interrupt if you are thinking about something)?

Your coach or mentor will use skills of both non-verbal and verbal communication to support you in your thinking and exploration. They will reflect back to you what you say, they will question and prompt and clarify, challenge and summarize. They will help you to explore fully your 'story' of the issues, problems or opportunities that you wish to discuss and they will help you to prioritize the ones which need more immediate attention. You can then focus upon these in order to draw up wish-lists of possible ways forward. In order to benefit from this part of the process, you need to trust yourself and your coach or mentor. You also need to be open and straightforward so that your working relationship is one in which both of you take responsibility for the outcome. Undue dependency or indeed independence is not desirable. Interdependence and mutuality bring results.

> **Rosaleen, a PR consultant,** invariably arrives for her coaching session apologizing for being late yet again. She often sits down quite out of breath and explains that she has not had time to think about what she wants to talk about today. Topics of conversation have not been prioritized, and she tends to ramble. However, the skills of the coach in questioning, prompting and summarizing help her to become aware of the most important issue which needs change. She needs to be more strategic in marketing herself. The coach helps her to define specific goals and to make realistic plans for action. She could never have done this for herself because of her tendency to live for the moment and be constantly rushing from place to place. Having prearranged coaching sessions forces her to stop and reflect. It is this that brings change. Within six months of the first coaching session, she has implemented her marketing strategy and the work is coming in at a steady pace.

Developing your imagination

Clients often want to see a coach or mentor because they are feeling a bit stuck. They may lack the imagination to discover possibilities for moving forward. Their potential is being stifled. The most effective clients are willing to engage in approaches and exercises which develop the imagination, the 'what if' scenarios. Some people are born with a preference for imagination and intuition but others find this more difficult. All can benefit from mentors and coaches who help to 'think out of the box' or 'engage in blue-sky thinking'.

> **Chan is a financial manager.** He has been in his current job for several years and is well respected and established. He applies for an exciting new opportunity in another region. He is offered the job but if he moves, he will miss all that he has so carefully built up. He is given a week to decide whether he wants the job and he goes round in circles weighing up all the costs and benefits of going or staying. He cannot decide. Then he turns to a mentor for help. She knows his current job and she says (rather directly): 'You can take that job now or you can stay here and die slowly.' She is inviting him to use his imagination. The picture he paints in his head leaves him in no doubt that he

should accept the job. He does. It is the best move of his life. The job he leaves is gradually eroded after a series of painful reorganizations.

Greg has just qualified as a teacher and has one session with a mentor. He is about to take up his first teaching post but is not really sure that this is the career for him. He wants the mentor to help him to clarify his career ambitions. The other option he is considering is catering, because he has contacts in the restaurant business. After listening to his story and his doubts about teaching, his mentor asks him to close his eyes, try to breathe slowly and deeply, and to relax. He has to tell the mentor when he feels relaxed. This he does. The mentor then asks him to imagine himself in five years' time in a classroom in a school where he might have been teaching for that time. The mentor says, 'Tell me when you have a picture and describe to me what you see.' Greg says, 'I see an old man, bending over a desk, marking books.' The mentor helps Greg to fill in some details in the picture: what the old man is wearing; what he is thinking and feeling; what the pupils are doing. When the picture is complete, the mentor carefully asks Greg to bring himself back to this room and then to open his eyes again. He reminds Greg that he is back in the office and that he is Greg, a newly qualified teacher. The mentor notes how young and energetic he appears now and how different from the picture he painted of himself after five years of teaching. He asks Greg what he thought of the picture of himself that he had painted. He says, 'I'm horrified to think that could be me!' They then do the same exercise looking at the possible Greg five years down the line, working in a restaurant. A completely different picture emerges – of a vibrant, ambitious young man who is going places. Insight dawns. Greg decides to take up his teaching post, but to leave after the probationary year and pursue his career in catering. In only one mentoring session, with skilful use of his own imagination, a career decision is made.

You will notice how powerful imagination can be! It is important that such exercises are used safely and ethically. You can check whether your coach or mentor is working safely and ethically by looking at Chapter 4. Brainstorming techniques are used to generate as many possible ideas as you can in the shortest possible time. These techniques are useful in coaching and mentoring. To be of most use you might need to practise using them on yourself, for example, 'If I won the lottery.' They work best if the client is relaxed, is focusing on what might be rather than what is, is not hindered by 'but' or 'ought' but focuses on 'want'. If you are a 'yes, but' sort of person you will benefit greatly from learning how to change it to 'yes, if'.

Using your imagination

- Do you have a good imagination?
- Do you find it easy to imagine what might be, rather than just what is?
- Do you tend to say 'yes, but' rather than 'yes, if'?
- Which of these do you voice more: your 'wants' or your 'oughts'?

Identifying your resources and working smart

Coaching and mentoring are about releasing potential and delivering results. In order to do this, you need to identify your resources. Easier said than done! The process of coaching or mentoring will help you to become more aware of underused or unused resources. Some of these will be in yourself, and some will be in the people you live and work with. Some resources will be organizational or structural ones.

 Think about the personal resources you would bring to coaching or mentoring. For example: energy, passion, motivation, courage, stamina, persistence, resourcefulness, skills, knowledge, experience.

Now think of the resources that you could call upon in people around you. For example: their time, their know-how, their networks, their experience.

Finally, reflect upon the resources in your place of work: the context, the structures and the processes. Don't forget that time is a resource that is often underused or misused.

If you can identify and exploit resources, within yourself and in others, you will work smart and become more effective. Hopefully, you will open up many more possibilities by engaging the help, knowledge and skills of others at work and at home, and therefore you will not be alone in achieving your objectives.

When Marian first started seeing her coach, it was because she wanted to become more visible with senior managers in the supermarket chain where she had worked for 10 years. She had watched male contemporaries leapfrog over her in the promotion stakes. What was she doing wrong? She wanted her coach to tell her what was stopping her from getting promoted. Coaching has provided her with the opportunity to challenge herself about unused resources. She realized that she was not being proactive about getting promotion. She was not using the skills and resources on herself that she used so well when developing projects for the supermarket. She remembered times when she had made herself more visible in a previous job. At that time she had networked with senior leaders in the organization; she had found ways of showcasing her work at committee level; she had published in a national retailing publication and regularly went to her immediate superiors to inform them about ideas for innovative projects which she volunteered to lead. As a result of the coaching, Marian tries out some of these ideas again and brainstorms other strategies with her coach. The coach gives her some reading material on assertiveness and they practise together some presentation skills, which she then tries out for real at work. She identifies some trusted colleagues and asks for feedback on her new, more visible style. She then takes the feedback to a coaching session and, after reviewing with her coach, she modifies what she has been doing and has another go. At last, she is positively impacting upon her future instead of being overwhelmed by day-to-day matters at work.

Setting goals and making action plans

Goals and action plans are part of the intentional activity that is coaching and mentoring. Some performance coaches expect clients to articulate the goal for each session, before the session begins. The work is then focused upon achieving that specific goal. In mentoring, where the focus is broader, there may not be such a specific focus for each session. However, it is always useful to clarify for oneself, 'What do I expect to get out of this session?' and 'How am I going to make sure I get it?' You will find examples of goal-setting and action planning in Chapters 6 and 7. We advise that you also think about having a goal or goals, as well as action plans, to take away from the session. These can relate to changes you want: in thinking, in feeling or in acting.

A goal is best expressed as a specific outcome, not a vague statement of intent. You may go away from a coaching or mentoring session saying 'I want a better work–life balance' but that, as a specific goal, would be: 'In order to achieve a better balance I will leave work at a pre-planned time each day and I will spend one hour with my children each evening before they go to bed.'

A specific goal is SMART: **s**pecific, **m**easurable, **a**ppropriate, **r**elevant and in a timeframe. Goals help to make changes and changes help to deliver results. Your coach or mentor will help you to formulate realistic and meaningful goals that are in keeping with your values. They will also help you to develop the skills you need in order to act more effectively.

Developing skills, making changes and delivering results

This chapter started by considering what to expect of coaching and mentoring. It then focused on how you could put your own personality, preferences and resources into making it work. The outcome of the coaching or mentoring will hopefully be change: small change or life-changing change. You will probably learn new skills and new ways of thinking, feeling and acting. These will enable you to turn your wish-lists and dreams into reality. The skills will deliver results for you. In order to learn these skills you will need to be open to learning, you will need to practise and get feedback, and you will need to monitor your progress – and all this in partnership with your coach or mentor.

Summary

In this chapter we have:

- Helped you to understand how to be proactive in order to get the most out of coaching and mentoring.

- Provided self-assessment questions to increase awareness of what you, as a client, want and need.

- Stimulated thinking about how to get the best fit between client and coach or mentor in terms of personality preferences, expectations, limits, knowledge, experience, resources and work context.

- Given an example of what an effective working agreement might contain and indicated how to discuss this with a new coach or mentor.

- Used several case examples of issues which may arise for clients, giving the opportunity to reflect on what to do in similar situations.

4 What are some ethical issues?

- Introduction
- How ethics is relevant
- Ethical standards
- Ethical responsibilities
- Ethical beginnings
- Confidentiality
- Practicalities
- Review, referral and ending
- Diversity
- Managing your practice
- Ethical decisions
- A final word
- Summary

Introduction

This chapter explores ethical issues and dilemmas in coaching and mentoring. It addresses questions often asked by coaches and mentors. These include the following:

- What practical and professional issues might arise in coaching and mentoring?
- What dilemmas might I face?
- What would help me to resolve them?
- How can I be proactive in minimizing avoidable difficulties and dilemmas?

It illustrates, with case examples, the ways in which coaches and mentors might work with their clients in anticipating, managing and resolving such issues.

How ethics is relevant

Ethics can be defined as a set of moral values or principles. 'Moral' relates to what is judged to be a right or wrong course of action, or good or bad behaviour. If coaching or mentoring is only one aspect of your job, you may wonder whether ethical coaching or mentoring practice requires particular attention. For example, if you work in Human Resources and a few times a year you coach participants on a corporate leadership programme. Or you are a health professional or head teacher who occasionally coaches and mentors junior staff. Or you are a manager who mentors new hires. Could these activities raise issues that require you to think from a coaching and mentoring ethical perspective? Perhaps you imagine that is unlikely, or maybe you have the opposite view or experience, that in fact it is quite possible.

The situation regarding ethics is clearer for professional and full-time coaches and mentors. Coaching and mentoring professional bodies have developed ethical standards, frameworks and codes of practice, and an external coach is expected to be a member of a professional body and to subscribe to its ethical standards. Indeed, it has been suggested (Passmore and Mortimer 2011) that when selecting potential coaches, questions should be asked about their supervision arrangements, ethical codes and how they would resolve an ethical dilemma arising from coaching in the organization.

Our experience is that consideration of ethical principles forms an important keystone which supports safe and effective practice, not only if you are a full-time coach or mentor, but also when these activities form a part of your job. This is illustrated in the example below.

> **Louise, a partner in a consultancy,** is mentoring Raoul, a promising young manager in the firm, as part of a talent management initiative. After working together for several months, it has become clear that Raoul, while successful at work, is just about coping. He is struggling with a demanding workload and the domestic pressures of a young family. At a partners' meeting it emerges that Raoul is being considered for promotion to a challenging new role, and Louise is unexpectedly asked to comment: 'You know him quite well, what do you think?'

How do you think Louise should respond?

Louise wonders about the right thing to do. Here are her thoughts:

- What would be best for Raoul? Surely more stress would not help him at the moment? I really don't think he could cope.
- On the other hand, this is a great opportunity for him. It wouldn't be fair of me to make a comment which might adversely affect his chances.
- What exactly have I agreed with Raoul about confidentiality? Can I say anything at all about the pressure he is under? Maybe I should make a general remark without going into specifics?
- Perhaps I'm taking too much responsibility here – it's Raoul who has to decide whether he wants the job. But what if he felt he had to accept a promotion and then couldn't cope?

Below are some ethical principles, based on the British Association of Counselling and Psychotherapy (BACP) (2016) framework, which can be applied to coaching and mentoring:

- Beneficence: doing good for those we coach or mentor
- Non-maleficence: avoiding or minimizing harm to them
- Autonomy: respecting their right to self-determination
- Fidelity: being trustworthy and honouring commitments we make
- Justice: being fair and impartial
- Self-respect: developing self-knowledge and taking care of ourselves.

Each principle is worthy in its own right. The difficulty comes, however, when one principle seems to come into conflict with another. This can leave the coach or mentor wondering about their best course of action. Louise is aware of these principles and her questions reflect the potential conflict between the principles. For example, if she comments on Raoul's stress levels, is she protecting his well-being but breaking confidentiality? Is this more likely to do good than do harm? Would this action ensure Raoul's autonomy or diminish it? Would it be fair to her other mentees?

> **Louise is a wise mentor** who is aware that she has a tendency to take too much responsibility for others. She decides that she should not assume responsibility for Raoul, or for how he might respond to the job offer. Moreover, it would be inappropriate for her to break mentoring

confidentiality. She thinks that it is important to be seen by her colleagues as someone who is clear about mentoring boundaries. So, she says, 'I do know Raoul quite well, but he knows himself best, so why don't you sound him out about this promotion?' She also realizes that this situation has highlighted for her the concerns that she has about the stress that Raoul is experiencing. She wonders whether she is overreacting, or whether he might benefit from additional help in managing stress. She decides that she will talk to him about this when they next meet.

Do you agree with Louise's decision? Would you have acted differently in her place? If so, what ethical principles would guide your actions?

This example illustrates how ethical dilemmas can arise in the workplace and how an ethical perspective can help to inform wise decision-making.

There is much discussion about professional regulation and ethical standards within coaching and mentoring, and in the next section some developments in this area are outlined.

Ethical standards

With the increasing professionalization of coaching and mentoring, the relevant bodies have developed their individual codes of ethical and professional standards, which can be found on their websites (see Appendix). These codes set out for their members both guidelines for good practice and also enforceable standards. They cover topics such as confidentiality, contracting, professional integrity, conflicts of interest, boundary management, managing and ending relationships, equality and diversity, supervision, and developing and enhancing competence. They set expectations for professionalism and ongoing learning and development, as well as highlighting essential do's and don'ts.

In addition to ethical codes issued by individual bodies, collective statements of professional standards and ethical codes have been produced. In 2008, a UK coaching and mentoring roundtable issued the first Statement of Shared Professional Values (UK Coaching Bodies Roundtable 2008). This Statement aims to bring together the best ethical practice from these organizations and proposes shared professional principles. A Professional Charter for Coaching and Mentoring (European Economic and Social Committee

2011), signed by four coaching bodies, acknowledges the individual bodies' codes of ethics and outlines a set of minimum ethical standards expected of coaches and mentors.

In 2016, the Association for Coaching (AC) and the EMCC issued a Global Code of Ethics for Coaches and Mentors, which is aligned with the 2011 Professional Charter. Included in the Code's purpose is to 'Serve as a guide for those individuals who do not necessarily identify themselves as a professional coach or mentor, but nonetheless use coaching or mentoring skills in their work' (AC and EMCC 2016: online). Including such a purpose is a recent development for the professional bodies, in explicitly proposing that codes can be useful not only for professional coaches and mentors but also for those using the skills at work.

In addition to the codes of practice of coaching and mentoring bodies, those of other professional organizations can be informative. These include business, nursing and medical professional bodies and, in the UK, the British Psychological Society (BPS) and the BACP.

As can be seen from this brief overview, professional codes and standards are continually evolving. Being up to date with the latest codes serves as a useful reference point for all those involved in coaching and mentoring, including purchasers of coaching and mentoring services. However, it is useful to remember that ethical codes cannot themselves provide solutions for all situations, but rather codes offer principles to be considered (Passmore and Mortimer 2011). It is also worth noting Hawkins and Smith's advice that coaches and mentors develop their own ethical standards and formulate these as more than a list of restrictions or 'must not dos'. They suggest finding a balance between 'conforming' rules, which restrict or prohibit actions, and 'enabling' rules, 'which give me permission to do what I might not otherwise have the courage or authority to do' (Hawkins and Smith 2013: 289).

Ethical responsibilities

The effective coach or mentor is responsible for considering their ethical perspective, and deciding with their client how they will work together. It is the responsibility of the coach or mentor to create a climate where ways of working can be discussed. It is their responsibility to monitor their standards of practice and reflect on how they are working. It is also their responsibility to be aware of other sources of help which they or their client might call upon if needed.

Being clear about ethical principles is important for several reasons. First, clarity guides the coach or mentor to work safely without doing any harm to the client.

> **Marco is an experienced coach:** I have a responsibility to be clear about the commitments I make, and to honour them. For example, confidentiality is very important. If I promise confidentiality and then let slip something that a client has told me, they may feel confused and let down and possibly even betrayed. When I am clear about what issues I might not be able to keep confidential, then the client understands this from the start and can take informed responsibility for what they tell me. Clarity applies to other areas too. I cannot normally undertake telephone coaching, and I say this early on, so that a client will not ring me up 'on the off chance', and feel hurt or rejected if I cannot speak to them. I've learned to be clear about what I can realistically offer, and not to make promises which I can't keep.

Second, when the coach or mentor is clear about their principles and preferred ways of working, they express themselves clearly to the client, and in so doing they encourage the client to do likewise.

> **Marco:** Occasionally a coaching relationship hits a bumpy patch – it's not unusual and it can be a real learning opportunity for me and the client. I used to worry about this, but nowadays I'm upfront with clients and say at the beginning that if either of us is having difficulties with the way things are going, I'd like us to talk to each other about it. I think it's been really helpful to say this, because it's made it okay, and given both of us permission to raise issues and learn from them.

Third, clarity encourages the coach or mentor to be aware of and sensitive to issues of difference and diversity, and how these may impact on the relationship with the client or on the fair provision of services. An effective coach or mentor monitors their potential blind spots.

> **Marco:** Increasingly I work with clients of different nationalities and cultures and I've learned to check my assumptions with theirs. For example, in the UK and the USA, individual recognition is often seen as important and desirable. However, in some cultures, group and extended family affiliation and loyalty are more important. In the past I struggled to understand why a client wasn't more motivated to achieve personal goals, until I understood their frame of reference. That situation was challenging, for us both, and made me think hard about some of my cultural beliefs that I had assumed were universal 'givens'.

Finally, clarity about ethical principles serves as a reference point to inform the decisions a coach or mentor makes and actions they take.

Marco: There have been some situations which were difficult. I've had to weigh up the risks of taking no action versus the risks of maybe acting too quickly or inappropriately. For example, where I've seen a potential conflict between my responsibilities to my client and my agreement with their sponsoring organization, I've found it useful to work through the principles, sometimes in supervision, and it's helped me to steer a path and create some clarity for myself.

Important as the principles are, they are not always the natural starting point. A coaching or mentoring relationship is usually approached with a mixture of hope, anticipation, concerns and questions, not a list of moral or ethical principles. Principles may seem to be rather tricky issues, best left unspoken, and yet asking questions such as 'how will we work together?' and 'what's important to each of us?' and 'what if . . .?' is often an excellent starting point for clarifying principles.

Ethical beginnings

In the following sections, we consider some issues that may be addressed in creating a working agreement. While it is often useful to have the working agreement written down, and professional coaches and mentors would normally include this as part of a formal contract, a written document is no substitute for a conversation. In the following sections, the advantages of establishing a clear working agreement are illustrated with examples. These advantages include:

- establishing a joint basis for ongoing review;
- demonstrating the coach or mentor's willingness to share responsibility;
- clarifying what each party can expect from the other;
- creating the opportunity to discuss questions that might otherwise remain hidden;
- establishing a ground-rule of openness and collaboration in the relationship;
- pre-empting confusion and unnecessary ambiguity.

Below are some important topics that may usefully be discussed in the initial conversation.

The client's issue

A natural place to start a coaching or mentoring conversation is to ask the client what they want to talk about. The coach or mentor asks this for several reasons. First, it communicates the coach or mentor's respect for the client and their agenda, and puts the client 'centre stage'. In this way, it supports them. Second, it encourages the client to clarify for themselves the issues and to begin to explore them. In this way, it empathically challenges the client. Third, it checks that the issues are appropriate for coaching and mentoring and not more suited to some other form of helping. In this way, it checks boundaries. Warning bells might ring if a client wants, for example, to unpack long-standing relationship difficulties with their partner, albeit that these are affecting their work. Coaches and mentors are not relationship counsellors and to accept this kind of assignment may risk the coach or mentor and the client getting out of their depth.

The working relationship

In addition to asking what issues are on the client's mind, the initial conversation should always include a discussion of how the coach or mentor and client are going to work together. Talking about 'how' gives the coach or mentor a chance to clarify ethical and professional issues, to understand more about the client's concerns and perspective, and to jointly agree a way of working. The 'what' conversation is, for most people, the more natural one. The 'how' conversation may be less natural and even a little strange or uncomfortable at first. However, it is one way in which mentors and coaches usefully make the un-discussable more discussable. It differentiates coaching and mentoring from other helping relationships and makes them potentially powerful. It resolves uncertainties and focuses attention and effort.

Setting the scene

Clients want to know, and coaches and mentors need to be clear about, what coaching and mentoring will involve. The skilled coach or mentor will be able to explain simply and briefly how they work, what they expect and offer, and any models or frameworks they might use. Box 4.1 contains an extract from a mentor's description of mentoring during an introductory session with a mentee.

Unspoken concerns or questions which remain unspoken may create distraction and impede the coaching or mentoring process. The following example illustrates how one coach addressed such a concern and established one aspect of a working agreement.

> **Brian has agreed,** with some encouragement from his boss, to some coaching sessions with an external coach, but he has doubts about

---

Box 4.1   Extract from an introduction to mentoring

Let me tell you how I usually work, and then we can decide together what would suit us. These sessions are an opportunity to explore the career issues you've outlined, and to develop goals and plans in relation to these. Rather than give advice, I will try to help you to reflect on problems or opportunities, and to clarify your goals and what you can do to achieve them. Mentoring works best if you come to each session with your ideas of what you want to discuss, and we'll start each session by agreeing how we use the time. Towards the end of the session, I'll ask about any action or plans, because doing things between meetings is important. It's helpful if you make notes of these plans, and bring them to the following meeting. It's also helpful to review the way we've worked together and anything we want to change for the next time. How does that sound to you?

---

the process and whether working with the coach will have any real benefits. At their first meeting, Brian is surprised and relieved when the coach says, 'I imagine you may be wondering whether coaching is right for you. I suggest that we take stock after three sessions to see how we're doing, and decide at that point whether we want to continue. How does that sound to you?' Brian responds positively, and they then start to talk about what would constitute benefits of coaching, how they would assess 'how we're doing', and what 'progress' would look like from Brian's perspective.

Here the coach has taken the initiative, perhaps picking up some verbal or non-verbal cues from Brian. In discussing 'how', the coach has helped to bring a hidden question to the surface and make it discussable. He has also demonstrated openness and shared accountability for the coaching process.

Professional background

Establishing the working agreement may involve the coach or mentor describing their own work experience and their training as a coach or mentor. They should be prepared to offer a brief description of their background and relevant qualifications and respond to client questions about these.

Bryony is a doctor and mentor in a Mentoring Scheme for colleagues in the region. She introduces herself to potential mentees by briefly explaining her career background and also her training as a mentor; she has attended a four-day non-accredited training programme. She tells potential mentees that she has been a mentor for a year; she has had several referrals in that time and has enjoyed the mentoring work. She has supervision three times a year provided by the Scheme.

Confidentiality

Limitations

Both client and coach or mentor need to be clear about what confidentiality is being offered and being sought. They should be aware of obligations and constraints imposed upon them by the law and by their profession or organization. As noted earlier in this chapter, members of professional bodies are required to adhere to codes of ethics and standards. In addition, organizations may have policies and procedures which impact on coaching and mentoring. Coaching and mentoring schemes have guidelines and protocols. It is unwise and unrealistic to offer or accept an assurance of total confidentiality. Rather, the coach or mentor should consider carefully what limits of confidentiality they can offer and sustain. The client should consider what confidentiality they want and be prepared to explore this with their coach or mentor. Both parties should consider how they would work in a situation where the limits were tested. In what circumstances might confidentiality agreements need to be reviewed? In the following example, a dilemma is successfully resolved.

> **Mari works within the HR function** of a large law firm and offers confidential coaching for senior staff, with the understanding that there is no feedback to the organization. In the course of a coaching session, it emerges that her client is struggling with an alcohol problem and her work is suffering. The client asks Mari to keep this information 'strictly confidential'. Mari believes that her first duty of care is to the client, but she is also concerned about the client's staff and colleagues, and the firm's reputation. Mari and the client together clarify the corporate policy on alcohol misuse. They explore the possibility of involving the local HR manager to help the client to get treatment. Reassured, the client contacts the HR manager.

Organization feedback

Where coaching or mentoring are sponsored by an organization, or are part of a change process or development initiative, the organization may ask for feedback. What information will be given, to whom, and in what format, needs to be agreed at the outset. Here is an example of how one coach responded to such a request.

> **Simon is asked to provide coaching for several senior executives** in a large financial institution. This is intended to support a leadership development and culture-change programme which the chief executive has initiated. Simon will see each executive for eight sessions over the course of a year. The chief executive is interested in any themes emerging which might impact on the overall development programme. She understands the need to respect individual confidentiality. Simon agrees that at the end of the year he will feed back to the chief executive his perception of any general themes emerging from coaching sessions, but in a way that protected individual confidentiality.

This agreement seems clear and straightforward, however, as the assignment progresses, some dilemmas emerge for the coach.

Simon is more than halfway through the assignment and the coaching seems to be beneficial for most of the executives. However, one person attended for an initial session only and has missed four subsequent sessions. Simon has followed up with the person, by email, and received no reply. Another person has told Simon that they have decided to leave the organization and want to use the remaining coaching sessions to plan their exit strategy and future career.

Examples such as this illustrate typical dilemmas that can occur, despite a seemingly robust contract between coach, client and sponsor. Simon questions whether it is ethical for him to receive payment for coaching slots which are not being taken up. Should he inform the chief executive of the non-attendance or does his confidentiality agreement preclude that? He wonders too about his discomfort about being paid by the organization for coaching someone who is planning to leave it.

Think back to the ethical principles outlined earlier in the chapter. They are: doing good, avoiding harm, maximizing client autonomy, being trustworthy and honouring commitments, being fair and impartial, and self-respect.

If you were Simon, what action would you take, if any, in relation to each person? How would the ethical principles inform your actions?

Public or private?

Another aspect of confidentiality concerns how public or private the coaching or mentoring relationship is within the organization. It is important that the coach or mentor and client share the same understanding of who knows about the relationship. Expectations of public vs private will vary according to context. For example, MBA students at a university were assigned a coach/mentor as a part of their study arrangements, and this was common knowledge. In contrast, in a health care setting, a mentoring scheme offered mentoring for all staff. Anyone could request a mentor, and the relationship was kept confidential unless the mentee wished to disclose it.

Confidentiality applies to smaller as well as more substantial issues, as this example illustrates.

> **A mentor happened to meet a mentee in a workplace setting** a few days after a mentoring session. In a misguided attempt to show that he had been fully attentive in the previous session, the mentor asked the mentee about his progress with issues they had discussed. The mentee looked embarrassed, and the mentor learned the lesson that he could not assume that it was appropriate to discuss mentoring issues anywhere other than within mentoring sessions.

Note-taking

Confidentiality also applies to any notes made during or after the coaching or mentoring sessions. If notes are being made, it is important to clarify the purpose. Is it to fulfil a legal or professional requirement? Is it to assist the coach or mentor? If so, in what way and what sort of notes are most appropriate? A contractual record of date and length of session is different from a reflective practice diary or a note of issues to take to supervision. If notes are to help the client, what will help them best? Who should make the notes – the coach/mentor or client? Will there be different sorts of notes from a session? Who keeps them? If the coach or mentor is keeping the notes, they should be stored securely and separately from any personal details or contact information about the client. Both parties should agree what will happen to the notes at the end of the coaching or mentoring relationship. The Global Code of Ethics states: 'Members will store, and dispose of, any records regarding clients, including electronic files and communications, in a manner that promotes confidentiality, security and privacy, and complies with all applicable laws and agreements' (AC and EMCC 2016: online).

Supervision

The effective coach or mentor will explain their supervision arrangements when discussing the working agreement. In supervision, the identity of the client is not normally disclosed, and the focus is on the coach or mentor rather than the client. When clients understand this, they can be reassured that their coach or mentor, by having supervision, is paying attention to their professional development and maintaining their competence. We say more about supervision in Chapter 9.

In this section we have discussed aspects of confidentiality that may be addressed in the working agreement and Box 4.2 lists some useful questions about confidentiality for coach or mentor, and client.

Box 4.2   Confidentiality checklist for coaching and mentoring

- What are the legal, professional or organizational constraints, obligations or entitlements which affect confidentiality?
- What will be confidential? What will not be?
- What will we do if something cannot be kept confidential?
- Is the relationship confidential?
- What about any notes or records? Who takes them? What for? Where are they kept? Disposed of how?
- What feedback, if any, is there to the organization? By whom? For what purpose?
- Does the coach or mentor have supervision? How is client anonymity preserved?

Practicalities

Time

It is important to agree where and how often meetings will take place and the number of sessions. This might be a formal contract: 'We will meet for two hours every six weeks, initially for five meetings. At our fifth meeting we will review the work we have done, and decide whether more sessions would be useful.' It may be more informal: 'Come and see me if there's anything I can help with', although experience suggests that this can be an unsatisfactory arrangement on both sides. Here is an example of an informal arrangement which did not work well.

Sheena has offered to mentor two new teachers in her school. She has suggested that they can 'feel free to drop in for a chat'. One has been to see her a few times, rarely taking up more than ten minutes of her time and says he finds the sessions valuable. He uses Sheena as a sounding-board, to think through decisions. Sheena is pleased to offer her support, but notices that his visits are becoming more frequent and wonders whether he may rely on her too much.

The other teacher has never been to see Sheena. In fact, he is struggling in his new job and he is concerned about appearing to be unable to cope. He notices that Sheena has not called him to ask how work is going, and assumes she is busy. Sheena meanwhile is puzzled. She had tried to be encouraging to both individuals, but one has yet to contact her. She does not want to put pressure on him, so she is reluctant to contact him.

It is clear that there are some dilemmas in this situation for the mentor.

 Imagine you are Sheena. What dilemmas do you see? How do these relate to the ethical principles of doing good, avoiding harm, maximizing client autonomy, being trustworthy and honouring commitments, being fair and impartial, and self-respect?

Here are some dilemmas that you might have noticed:

- Should Sheena leave each teacher to make their own choices about if/how often they see her? What is fair to both of them? Should she contact the one who has not been to see her?
- Should she have a discussion with the teacher whom she sees frequently? Should she share her concerns that he may be becoming over-reliant on her? How can she do this in a way that is not too challenging?
- What does each teacher understand has been agreed by 'feel free to drop in for a chat'? How clear is this agreement?
- Is there any agreement about confidentiality?

 Imagine that you are each of the teachers. What would you want Sheena to do? Anything you'd prefer her not do?

Finally, if you were Sheena, what would you do? What actions are possible? Which are preferable?

In this example, there were some difficulties with an informal arrangement. In the next example, a more formal agreement also encounters a problem.

> **Adeola, a health professional,** has agreed to offer mentoring to a newly promoted colleague, Tim, and at their initial session they establish that they will meet for an hour every fortnight. Tim frequently arrives rushed and late, with the result that sessions start late and overrun the hour. Adeola has begun to feel irritated and resentful and is concerned that mentoring is taking up too much time in her already busy schedule. She finds herself being rather short with Tim and looking meaningfully at her watch. In a review session, she shares her concerns with Tim. He is finding the mentoring very useful and has been unaware of the knock-on effect of late finishes. Adeola explains that while she is happy to set aside an hour a fortnight, she cannot overrun the finish time. They agree that, in future, regardless of when Tim arrives, they will finish at the end of the hour. Tim is responsible for arriving on time or, if not, having a shorter session. Adeola is responsible for keeping the agreed time slot free. Adeola is relieved to clarify their arrangement.

Place

The meeting place is important. Meeting in the client's office can present difficulties; interruptions are possible and job demands can intrude. Some internal coaches and mentors use their own offices, but this can emphasize any hierarchy/power difference between coach or mentor and client. Here too, everyday work pressures can interrupt. If both parties are travelling some distance, a hotel or conference centre meeting room at a mid-way point may be an option. Many external coaches and mentors have their own premises where privacy and quiet are guaranteed. For internal coaches and mentors, a quiet meeting room can be a satisfactory alternative.

In addition to agreeing where and for how long meetings will take place, it is useful to clarify whether there will be contact between meetings, either by phone or e-mail. E-coaching and e-mentoring are becoming increasingly popular and may form part of the relationship. In agreeing time and place, it is important that both parties honour commitments and do not cancel meetings or phone calls other than in exceptional circumstances. It is useful to agree in advance how they will handle such a situation. Box 4.3 lists some helpful questions for both parties.

Box 4.3   Time and place checklist

- Where will we meet?
- For how long?
- How many sessions will we have?
- What happens if one of us cannot make the meeting?
- What happens if the client does not turn up? Or is late?
- Is contact between sessions part of the way we will work?
- If not, what if an urgent matter arises between sessions?

Role conflict

There can be potential or actual conflicts between the role of coach or mentor and other relationships they have with the client. Even if confidentiality boundaries have been agreed, the coach or mentor cannot 'unknow' something that has been shared in a coaching or mentoring conversation. For example:

- A mentor is asked to give a reference for a mentee.
- A client attends a selection panel for a job and finds that their coach is on the panel.
- Mentor and mentee find themselves attending the same work meeting. A previous mentoring conversation has focused on the mentee's difficulties with a colleague who is also at the meeting.
- Coach and client meet unexpectedly in a social setting.

 If you were the coach or mentor in the above situations, what would you do? If you were the mentee or client, what would you want the coach or mentor to do?

While it is impossible to anticipate every contingency, it is worth considering possible conflict or boundary issues and agreeing in advance how these might be handled. Below are two case examples, the first where this was done and the second where it was not.

Jaime is mentor to Alice. While he is not her line manager, he does have indirect management responsibility for some of her work. He is likely to be asked to comment on her work for her annual performance appraisal. They agree, together with Alice's boss, that Jaime will limit any comments he makes to Alice's work performance and results achieved.

Chris is a coach and his client Mike has talked quite a bit in coaching sessions about his family, in relation to career and personal development issues. Chris and Mike live in the same town. They meet unexpectedly in a café, both with their families. Both are uncomfortable, and Chris makes polite conversation and leaves as quickly as he can. He reflects afterwards that he had not anticipated such an eventuality, or discussed it with Mike. In future, Chris decides, he will discuss with each new client 'what if we meet outside of our sessions?'

Review, referral and ending

Regular review with the client is a cornerstone of safe and effective coaching and mentoring. It can also be a powerful source of learning which can enrich the relationship. Box 4.4 lists some questions which might encourage a constructive review, so that responsibility is shared and any difficulties can be raised in a problem-solving rather than a blaming fashion. Notice how some questions invite the mentee to reflect on their own behaviour, emphasizing that this is a joint process involving both parties thinking about how they are doing.

Box 4.4   Questions for review of a session

- What has been helpful about this session (e.g. use of time, structure of the session, focus, pace, venue)?
- Anything that has been unhelpful or got in the way in this session?
- Anything in particular that I have done that has helped or got in the way?
- Anything in particular that you have done that has helped or got in the way?
- Anything you would like me to do differently next time?
- Anything you would like to do differently next time?
- Anything else it would be useful to talk about?

In the following example a coach and client review, after three sessions, how they are working together.

Coach: It seems as though the sessions have enabled you to get focused. I notice you are always ready to challenge yourself and are open to thinking afresh, and that seems to help you clarify what is important to you. A few times I have interrupted you and then wondered if that was useful or not.

Client: It has been powerful having this time to focus on me, and really think about where I'm going in my career. You have not judged me or given advice, but you have helped me to question myself and some of my ideas. I didn't always want to be bothered to write things down at the end of sessions, but I can see that it has been important in keeping me focused. Perhaps I should take time to prepare before sessions as well. I like the way that you sometimes give me space and sometimes interrupt me. At first the space was a bit scary and I realize now that it is challenging – it makes me think. Your interventions are helpful in keeping me on track. I would like more of them if you think that I am starting to ramble!

These comments illustrate how the review process creates dialogue, as perceptions and perspectives are shared. Notice that the coach is concerned that they might be intervening too much and the client is asking for more!

Referral

A skilled coach or mentor discusses with the client the scope and nature of the work they will do together and the possibility that at some point referral elsewhere may be appropriate. Sometimes coaching or mentoring is not the right kind of help and something else may be more beneficial. So, it is important to be aware of other resources, which might include occupational health, counselling, careers advice, training and development programmes. In our experience, being clear about areas which are not your expertise enhances, not diminishes, your credibility as a coach or mentor. Being clear about boundaries protects both you and your clients. The following examples illustrate how referral can operate in practice.

Clare is coaching an able young chemist, Hugh, who has just been appointed to lead a large project, with high corporate visibility. Hugh comes to the coaching session asking for help with thinking through the business strategy relating to this project. Strategy is not Clare's forte, and she says so. However, she is able to help Hugh create a list of potentially useful resources. On the list are names of several people in the organization, and he selects two who are particularly experienced in strategy, and agrees to contact them before the next coaching session. The list also identifies other resources, including online educational material, which might help him.

Minesh is mentoring Lisa, a newly promoted specialist nurse. While she is understandably keen to do well in her new role, she seems to him very anxious rather than simply keen, and he wonders if she needs some other kind of help. He talks to Lisa and she reveals that she had ongoing support for several years from a counsellor and a GP in managing anxiety and depression. Having recently moved location, she is now without these resources. Together they agree that Minesh will continue as her mentor for the time being, being aware of the boundary of their conversations and she will find counselling and GP support. He gives her the names of some counsellors who work in the area.

Endings

There are many reasons why coaching and mentoring relationships come to an end. Sometimes it is a planned ending, bringing to a close a productive working relationship. At other times, it may be more abrupt. An unforeseen event means that the relationship has to be cut short, for example, a family emergency or sudden job transfer. Sometimes the relationship is not working and the client needs to move on. Sometimes changes in job roles produce a conflict of interest. Sometimes a referral to another helper has been arranged. The nature of the circumstances will obviously impact on the nature of the ending.

Most endings involve a mixture of loss and gain on both sides. The skilful coach or mentor involves the client in managing the ending. This is particularly important if the coach or mentor has the initiative in ending the relationship. Involving the client helps to minimize any feelings of rejection. Conversely, if it is the client who has decided to move on, it may be that the coach or mentor experiences some feelings of rejection. However, a well-managed ending can be a time to acknowledge the relationship, work well done and goals achieved, as in this example.

Richard has decided to stop working as a coach. He gives his clients as much notice as possible. One client is particularly surprised and rather upset. Richard works with the client to acknowledge these feelings and plan what they need to do together to achieve a 'good enough' ending. He shares with the client the loss that he too is experiencing, but also the satisfaction of the work they have done together and what the client has achieved. He helps the client to identify resources to support their development, including other potential coaches.

Think of the ending of a coaching or mentoring relationship that you were part of. Was it planned or sudden? What thoughts and feelings did you have at the time? What helped you to manage the ending? Did anything make it more difficult for you?

Ideally, the ending will have been discussed at the start of the coaching or mentoring relationship. When this happens, and ongoing review is built into the relationship, the path for a good ending is smoothed. Allowing space for ongoing review will also ensure that, if a planned ending changes, there is time for discussion of how to manage this. If the coach or mentor has worked in a way that encourages the client to be proactive, then the client will have ideas about their future and can discuss these. The coach or mentor will help the client to clarify plans and to explore what help they will need in implementing these.

The final session is an opportunity to affirm what has been achieved and celebrate the working relationship. Wherever possible, there will be time put aside for this review. It will include a conversation about what is next for the client, so that they are adequately supported. It will also include clarification of 'what if we meet in the street/office/at a social event?'

Diversity

Overview

Diversity refers to the range of differences that may impact on coaching and mentoring. These include gender, race, sex and sexual orientation, disability, social or economic status, culture, race and religion. The effective coach or mentor is sensitive to issues of difference and diversity. The Global Code of Ethics (AC and EMCC 2016) includes sensitivities such as: avoiding knowingly discriminating; monitoring unconscious bias and inadvertent discrimination, including language; being respectful and inclusive; supportively challenging discriminatory behaviour in others and increasing self-awareness in relation to equality and diversity.

Awareness of diversity and difference may impact not only on an individual coaching or mentoring relationship but also on fair provision of coaching or mentoring services, and on the use of coaching and mentoring as tools for promoting equal opportunity (Clutterbuck and Ragins 2002). Below, we consider each of these areas in turn and then highlight one aspect of diversity: cultural difference.

Promoting equal opportunity

Clutterbuck and Megginson (2005: 42) identify coaching and mentoring as positive opportunities for developing diverse talent:

> Developmental dyads between people of different race and gender, or between able and disabled people, help to identify hidden causes of discrimination. They also provide a safe environment where people can discuss and develop tactics for dealing with cultural barriers to advancement.

Diversity mentoring such as this is one way of promoting equal opportunity and it can be an instrument for both personal and social change, increasing motivation in mentees and raising awareness in mentors. Reverse mentoring, where a younger or more junior person mentors an older or more senior colleague, has been used similarly. It can raise awareness in both mentor and mentee of, for example, age, gender or ethnicity differences. It also gives both mentor and mentee some insights into the experience of being junior or more senior in the organization.

The equal opportunity role of coaching and mentoring is being developed in some organizations to include positively managing and leveraging diversity. Coaching and mentoring are designed not only to address inequality but also to create added value. Differences are seen as positive advantages rather than as obstacles to be overcome. For example, Rosinki (2003) argues that coaches and clients can use cultural differences positively, so that cultural diversity and different cultural perspectives produce organizational as well as individual benefits.

Provision of services

When the coach or mentor is acting fairly and justly, they will want all clients to be able to access the benefits of coaching and mentoring. They will consider whether the approaches and frameworks used are equally applicable to all clients, whatever their background, gender, culture or age. Such awareness can lead to expanding and diversifying the ways in which coaching and mentoring are offered, for example, using e-mails, e-messages, text, mobile phone and other social media. E-mentoring and coaching can have benefits for disadvantaged clients or mentees. These benefits include the fact that it is more accessible than face-to-face coaching or mentoring, and that it may reduce the impact of status or hierarchy differences between coach or mentor and the client or mentee.

The individual relationship

Diversity and difference can affect the coaching or mentoring relationship itself. The coaching or mentoring intervention may be inappropriate, stereotypes of difference or real difference may impede communication, values and assumptions may conflict. The coach or mentor tries to be attuned to such issues, while also being aware of the possibility of focusing inappropriately on diversity when some other aspect of the relationship is more relevant or important.

Below are some examples of individual relationships in difficulty.

> **Keith is a long-serving senior manager who mentors junior staff** on a one-year leadership development programme. He has difficulty working with Peter, who expresses views such as 'I'm only here for the short term' and 'I don't owe this organization anything.' Keith is upset. He believes that the organization has invested considerably in Peter's development. He describes him as 'typical Generation Y'.

> **Kelly is a senior academic who mentors final year students at her university.** As a single parent, Kelly has worked hard to overcome obstacles to reach her senior position. She is mentoring Jeanette who describes herself as 'here for the social life mainly'. Jeanette has few thoughts about her career, and is intending to follow her boyfriend 'wherever he gets a job'. Kelly is infuriated at Jeanette's lack of ambition.

 What differences may be impacting on these relationships? If you were either mentor, what might help you in moving the relationship forward?

Culture and diversity

Culture is one source of diversity. A person's cultural frame of reference includes the underlying beliefs, values and attitudes which impact on their behaviour and on behavioural norms. Organizations, professional and work groups, teams, educational and social groups may each have their own particular culture, which may affect expectations of coaching and mentoring. Culture can also refer to national or ethnic differences between countries and peoples.

One well-known framework which identifies seven dimensions of cultural difference is that of Trompenaars and Hampden-Turner (2012). Their dimensions highlight differences such as: separating work and personal versus blending and overlapping them; being judged on performance versus being judged on the basis of, for example, age, gender, education and connections; objectivity and detachment versus display of emotion; and rules and regulations versus individual circumstances. It is easy to imagine how cultural differences such as these might impact on a coaching or mentoring relationship. Below is an example of a relationship where cultural differences may be important.

> **A mentoring relationship is in difficulty.** A mentoring scheme offers support for overseas health professionals working in the UK. The mentor views their relationship with the mentee as a partnership of equals, a collaborative endeavour focused on the mentee's needs, to help the mentee take charge of their own development. He finds the mentee frustratingly passive and acquiescent, willing to 'go along with' him but often asking for his advice, and looking rather blank when he tries to explain that advice-giving is not his role. He describes the mentee as 'rather formal', and notices that she talks only about strictly work-related issues, never mentioning family or life outside work. The mentee sees things differently. She had anticipated that the mentor, a respected figure, would steer and guide her in career choices. She cannot understand why the mentor, an older, wiser, senior member of her profession, will not provide more guidance. She is also confused by the mentor asking her about her ambitions and aspirations.

 In the example above, how might cultural differences be affecting the mentoring relationship?

It may be that the problems described in the case example above are due to differences in national culture or ethnicity. However, when reflecting on diversity and difference, we have to guard against the risk of attributing difficulties to cultural difference or diversity when the cause may lie elsewhere. Effective coaches and mentors use what they know about themselves and about others from *both* individual and cultural perspectives. Egan notes the importance of paying attention to both and uses the term 'personal culture' to describe 'the way that each individual lives out the beliefs, values, and norms of the larger social culture' (2013: x).

Improving diversity awareness

In addition to reflecting on their own first-hand experience, there are many models and frameworks which can help the coach or mentor to assess their diversity awareness and cross-cultural sensitivity, and we briefly introduce some of these.

Clutterbuck has developed a Diversity Awareness Ladder (Clutterbuck 2012) with five stages of awareness: fear, wariness, tolerance, acceptance and appreciation. The coach or mentor can reflect on their own inner conversation (and therefore their stage), and consider how to have a productive outer conversation with their client. Bennett (2004) describes six stages of cross-cultural sensitivity: denial, defence, minimization, acceptance, adaptation and finally behavioural integration. He identifies characteristics of each stage, and a developmental path from denial through to integration. Van Dyne et al. (2010), writing about leadership, describe cultural intelligence as an individual's ability to function effectively across cultures. Cultural intelligence involves not only cultural knowledge and awareness but also individual motivation and the ability to be reflective and then to plan and act appropriately.

Finally, in this section, Hay (2007: 149) gives some prompts to coaches and mentors to raise awareness of their 'fantasies and fears' in relation to a whole range of 'difference' factors which include some of the following: sexual orientation, age, cultural background, ethnic origin, race, colour, religious background, physical disability, learning disability, social class, accent, educational experiences and employment history.

Managing your practice

Working reflectively and getting supervision

Safe and effective coaches and mentors take time to reflect on their practice. There are many different ways to do this, including supervision, and we say more about reflective practice and supervision in Chapter 9. Coaches and mentors should know at least one person who can provide them with support or supervision.

Managing yourself

One of the ethical principles mentioned earlier in this chapter is self-respect. This includes allowing enough time for your personal and professional development and also taking care of yourself. It involves monitoring your well-being and ensuring that you have adequate emotional, physical and personal

---

Box 4.5   A checklist for assessing well-being

- Am I too tired to concentrate during the session?
- Am I hoping the client will cancel the session?
- Are my own concerns intruding on the sessions?
- Am I finding it difficult to give my full attention during a session?
- Am I worrying continuously before/after a session?
- Have I cancelled a session for non-urgent reasons?
- Am I avoiding supervision or support?

---

resources to work effectively. Coaches and mentors may risk doing harm, and at minimum will not do their best work, when they are stressed, overtired or overburdened with personal or work problems. Anyone who does a significant amount of coaching or mentoring will at some time find themselves wanting or needing to take a break and replenish their personal resources. Sometimes the break may be enough and sometimes additional support or supervision may be required. Box 4.5 provides a checklist of questions to aid in assessing your well-being as a coach or mentor.

Ethical decisions

In ideal circumstances, the coach or mentor has time to consider without undue pressure the best ethical decision to make. They have time to involve the client and to consult with a supervisor or support resources. The client has time to reflect on what they want and need, and what they expect from their coach or mentor.

Bond (1993) describes a framework used in ethical decision-making. Adapting and reworking this framework, the coach or mentor might ask the following questions:

- How do moral principles inform this decision? What does most good, least harm, is faithful to any promises made, gives maximum autonomy, and is fair?
- How does the law impact on this situation? What must I do? What am I entitled to do? What am I prohibited from doing? Are there any rules of my professional body or organization which define or limit my actions?
- What resources do I have which might limit or enable me? How much time and energy do I have? How much capacity, mental or physical? Am I working within my competence, or at the edge? How

much support am I getting from supervision or other sources? Am I overlooking potential resources or overestimating any?

- What is my personal view of the situation? What do I want to do? What is my 'gut feeling'?

Figure 4.1 shows that each of these aspects interlock and contribute to making a sound ethical decision.

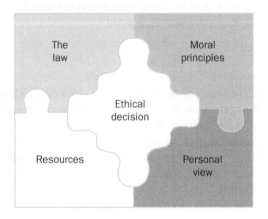

Figure 4.1   Ethical decision-making in coaching and mentoring

However, it is important to remember that ethical decisions are rarely absolutes. Carroll (2011) describes the final step in ethical maturity as learning to live with the decision made, even if with hindsight different or better decisions might have been possible. The process of resolving an ethical dilemma and living with any ambiguity, while it may be taxing, can be an opportunity for learning and development.

Sometimes the coach or mentor is faced with a decision which requires a rapid response. The following guidelines may help when making decisions under pressure.

- Don't panic. If you have just been told something difficult or troubling, that thing already exists, and the telling of it has not caused it to happen. If you have been told of something that might happen, it has not happened yet.
- Keep listening. It is all too easy, when anxious or concerned, to stop listening to the client and hear only our own inner voices: 'Oh heavens, what shall I do, what if . . .?' Try to keep listening.
- Take time. In almost all cases, you do not have to respond instantly. Check what you have heard.

- Listening is not necessarily agreeing or colluding. It is accepting the story of the other person and trying to understand it.
- Keep the focus on the client and give them space to arrive at their own answer.
- You have valuable perspectives to share but not to impose.
- Sometimes no action is better than the wrong action. If you decide to act, review your decision, even if only for a few minutes. If unsure, it may be best to reflect rather than act hastily.
- Create 'time out' if necessary. Having a break can give both you and the client the time to gather thoughts and consider resources.
- Get help. If you can, take the issue to supervision or support.

 Which of these actions might be easy for you? Which might you find harder to do? Are there any examples from your own experience where you have used these approaches? What was the result?

Will and his coach have been working together for several months, helping Will make the transition into a senior management role, which seems to be going well. The coach is surprised when Will starts a session by blurting out that family problems have been getting him down and this morning he felt like 'giving up'. Will is clearly upset, and says that everything seems hopeless. The coach is concerned, and in addition he knows that Will is facing a long drive that day followed by an important meeting.

 Imagine you are the coach. What are you thinking? What are you feeling? Which moral principles and ethical considerations are relevant here? What courses of action do you consider?

Imagine you are Will. What are you thinking? What are you feeling? What do you want from your coach? Anything you don't want them to do? What might help you?

The coach allows Will to talk about his feelings and about the family upset. Will has space to 'let off steam' and becomes visibly calmer as the session progresses. The coach wonders whether Will is temporarily upset or if there is something more than that, and so asks Will if he thinks he needs help from anyone else, for example, a doctor.

The coach does not get drawn too deeply into the family matters but helps Will to work through some strategies for coping with his feelings. The coach checks with Will how he will manage in the meeting he is attending later that day. They discuss whether Will is safe to drive, and also how Will could make contact with the coach before the next session if necessary.

A final word

It can be daunting to consider the ethical, moral and professional issues in coaching and mentoring and the potential moral and legal dilemmas which might arise. We are aware of this reaction, especially among some trainee coaches and mentors, who may feel concerned about 'what if . . .?' In reality, many of the ethical decisions we face are not overwhelming: they are commonplace and, for a trained and reflective coach or mentor, they are manageable. Only occasionally are we faced with very difficult and complex decisions. Nevertheless, ethical practice pervades all aspects of coaching and mentoring. The more thoughtfully we consider in advance our own boundaries, the more we help the client to consider and manage theirs. When we work in this way, we are more likely to prevent ethical dilemmas occurring, or handle them wisely if they do.

Summary

In this chapter we have:

- Described how ethics is relevant.

- Identified sources of ethical standards and highlighted coach or mentor responsibilities.

- Described ethical beginnings and endings in coaching and mentoring, and some ethical dimensions of a working agreement.

- Discussed managing review, referral and self-management.

- Highlighted some aspects of diversity.

- Considered ethical decision-making and decision-making under pressure.

PART 2
Approaches, Tools and Techniques

5 What are some approaches and models?

- Neuroscience, Mindfulness and Resilience
- Solution Focus and Appreciative Enquiry
- The OSKAR model
- Cognitive-Behavioural Coaching (CBC)
- The PRACTICE model
- Transformational Coaching: the CLEAR model
- Performance Coaching: the GROW and TGROW models
- Transactional Analysis (TA)
- Gestalt
- Systemic Coaching and Constellations
- Summary

In this chapter we introduce several approaches and models which can be used to enhance the learning relationship between coach, mentor and client, and which help clients to do the following:

- Take charge of their own development.
- Release their potential.
- Achieve results which they value.

Such models and approaches can usefully inform the practice of coaches and mentors, but the important considerations are:

- whether an approach or model is appropriate for this particular client, in this particular situation, at this particular time;
- whether an approach or model fits with your own key principles for effective practice.

Neuroscience, Mindfulness and Resilience

One of the most exciting recent developments in coaching and mentoring has been the growth in our understanding of neuroscience. This has extended knowledge of how different areas of the brain work, for example, the role of the pre-frontal cortex in planning, reasoning and problem-solving, and the role of the basal ganglia with regard to routine responses and habits. The coach or mentor may wonder why a client has such difficulty making changes, or why change does not happen very easily. It may be because the amygdala, the part of the brain which alerts the client to fear, and which processes many of our emotions, is responding to signals that are not in the awareness of the client.

For some clients there will be a natural tendency to stay with what is known, rather than to step into the uncertain territory of change and growth. For others, there may be a tendency to act impulsively, without considering the consequences of their actions. Such decisions will be partly influenced by the function of the brain, and some will be influenced by the action of brain chemicals. Dopamine affects motivation; adrenaline affects the 'fight or flight' response at times of fear and anxiety; serotonin levels affect our sense of well-being and happiness; and cortisol, often referred to as 'the stress hormone' is released in response to fear or stress. Not only does this knowledge inform the coach or mentor, it also helps those being coached or mentored to understand more about what affects will power and decision-making processes.

Our increased knowledge of the workings of the brain help us to re-evaluate the way that we use particular models with clients, for example, when choosing the questions that we ask and when considering the most appropriate intervention: *for this individual, with his or her unique way of viewing the world, in these specific circumstances.* Brann (2015) gives the example of a client who is currently suffering from stress, noting that: 'mental stress leads to habit behaviour rather than goal-directed behaviour'. She reminds us that this knowledge should inform the coach or mentor about when, and how, and what, goal-directed behaviour should be attempted by such clients.

Alongside developments in our understanding of the way in which the brain functions and influences motivation, is a greater understanding of the impact of mindfulness. It has been defined as 'Paying attention in a particular way: on purpose, in the present moment, and non-judgementally' (Kabat-Zinn, cited in Pemberton 2015: 80). Developing mindfulness can enable clients to become more accepting and resilient, with regard to both their strengths and their resistances. Resilience develops alongside a greater understanding and appreciation of self and others, and by paying attention to the workings of our inner and outer worlds:

Mindfulness is not the answer because it is popular and is being used by senior executives in FTSE companies, or even because research studies have shown that it changes the brain. It is right because you have a relationship of trust, and your client is open to exploring a different way of addressing their resilience gap. It is right when it is a genuine invitation, and wrong when it is an imposition driven by the enthusiasm of the coach ... The value of mindfulness is linked directly to its alignment with the client's style and openness to experimentation, and the coach's skill in positioning it within the purpose of the coaching relationship.

(Pemberton 2015: 92)

Pemberton reminds us that both the openness of the client, and the skill of the coach will affect the development of mindfulness. She also discusses how to develop resilience, the ability to tap into both internal and external resources when the going gets tough. There is a brief questionnaire to help clients, coaches and mentors to explore their levels of resilience and to reflect on how they have reacted at times of 'significant difficulty'. It includes aspects of self-belief, solution-finding, proactivity and emotional control (Pemberton 2015: 23). Here is an example of a mentor trying to tap into the resilience of her client despite his initial negativity about himself and his current difficult work situation:

The client had experienced several recent stressful life events. They affected his health and his work, his belief in himself and his ability to 'bounce back'. His level of resilience was very low but he had sought the help of a trusted mentor at work. The mentor knew that he was prone to negative thinking about himself and she listened carefully to his story. She also realized that he had been trying to remain positive and so she said 'So, given this very difficult time that you have had, and all the efforts you have been making to stay afloat, would there be a mantra, a few words, that would start to take you to where you really want to be?' As she said it, she wondered whether she was expecting too much of him, whether he had any resources left that would help him to visualize something better. She waited with bated breath and was amazed when he said, with energy, 'Go for it . . . and enjoy!' She noticed the wry smile that appeared on his face as he said 'and enjoy'. It was as if he could not believe that he had uttered such words, given his low mood at that moment.

He had found the resources within himself to move from hopeless to positive. This was resilience in action. But would it last? Would it really make a difference? Yes, it did. They checked out in detail how

'Go for it' might look and feel, and then they explored whether 'and enjoy' would be realistic, given his levels of stress at the moment. They also explored who or what might help or hinder his plan. He remained positive about 'having a go' and then he worked out an action plan. Within three weeks he had started, in small ways, to turn his life around. All those stressful life events were still there, but he had reconnected with his inner resources of courage, hope and resilience.

Solution Focus and Appreciative Enquiry

What is the Solution Focus approach? 'The SF approach to coaching places primary emphasis on assisting the client to define a desired future state and to construct a pathway in both thinking and action that assists the client in achieving that state' (Cavanagh and Grant 2010: 54). It is both positive and pragmatic. This approach is based on treating clients as experts in their own lives, with a focus on what they want to achieve now, rather than on what has brought them to this point. Coaching and mentoring focus on:

- finding what works and doing more of it;
- finding what does not work and doing something different;
- finding and using resources rather than focusing on deficits;
- finding and building on successes;
- exploring possible and preferred futures;
- exploring what is already contributing to those futures.

Some of the techniques which are used to help people are: focusing on what clients say they will do, not on what they will not do; using questions of scale, such as 'on a scale of 1 to 10, where are you now? What would it take to move you from where you are now to where you would like to be on this scale? How much is good enough?' Questions about how someone is coping with a difficult issue at work would not concentrate on the problem but would focus on client resources to solve it: 'I can see that . . . is very difficult at the moment . . . and I am noticing that you have still managed to . . . I am wondering how you have managed to do that.' In this example, helping the client to be aware of their strengths may enable them to move forward. There are the classic questions: 'Tell me, what is already going well for you?' and 'When . . . worked well, what was it that was different?'

An exercise in positive psychology, to help clients move towards a goal that seems unattainable, is explained this way:

> Visualise yourself on one side of a gap, with the goal on the other side. Now let's construct bridges over that gap. Let's consider your

top five strengths, and see how each one can be used to connect you
to what you truly want to be.

(Kauffman et al. 2010: 161)

The coach begins with the client's top strength, for example, persistence. The coach invites the client to develop an action plan, a road map for 'crossing the bridge', using that strength of perseverance. Then the client is asked to create another bridge with their next highest strength and the process is repeated with the other four strengths. Two other techniques are useful, the first is to help the client to get into the habit of affirming what is going well, the other is to encourage the client to remember that tiny steps make a big difference!

Solution-focused approaches are widely used by coaches and mentors to promote change and development in organizations because the approach encourages a focus on the preferred future, rather than on the deficits of the present.

Releasing the potential for change is an important aspect of positivist approaches which also include Appreciative Enquiry. In Appreciative Enquiry, the aim of the mentor or coach is to help the client through a four-stage cycle.

- *Discovery*: through dialogue involving systematic enquiry the client is helped to identify within a particular focus the elements that they find challenging, interesting and energizing and to which they can commit.
- *Dream*: the client is encouraged to project positive elements of the existing situation into a positive vision or dream of how the future ideally might look.
- *Design*: the client thinks through and designs a strategy to achieve the articulated vision or dream.
- *Destiny*: the client focuses on implementing the vision, and, importantly, sustaining and developing the energy, hope and enthusiasm and positive relationships underpinning the design.

(Pask and Joy 2007: 212)

In this approach, the mentor or coach focuses on change from the outset. Below is an example of some questions used in Appreciative Enquiry, for a client who is having problems with their team. Rather than asking what is wrong with the team, the mentor or coach invites the client to think about the strengths of individual members and a time when they worked to achieve something that the client valued.

- Describe a high point experience in your senior leadership team – a time when you were most engaged or excited!

- Without being modest, what is it that you most value about yourself and your contribution to the team?
- What do you most value about the team and its contribution to the organization?
- What do you think are the core factors that give life to the team?
- If you had three wishes to heighten the vitality and health of the team, what would they be?

(Cooperrider and Whitney 1999: 11–12)

Such questions are valuable in trying to develop new perspectives and uncover blind spots which prevent the client from moving forward. They energize and give hope. There are some similarities between the discovery, dream, design and destiny cycle of Appreciative Enquiry and the three stages of Egan's Skilled Helper model. Both approaches encourage the client to focus on their preferred future and both can be used by coaches and mentors for both individual and organizational development.

The OSKAR model

- Focus on solutions rather than problems.
- Start with the view that people are competent.
- Expect success and progress.
- Make the least change and expect the greatest result.
- Keep doing what works and stop doing what does not work.

In addition to the core qualities of listening and empathizing, a coach or mentor who is using an SF approach 'offers a new level of effectiveness to the coaching conversation. Rather than identifying what's wrong or looking for barriers to progress, the focus is simply on finding what works' (McKergow and Clarke, www.sfwork.com).

OSKAR stands for:
- **O**utcome. This is expressed in terms of the difference that the client and those around them *want* to see as a result of the coaching. The so-called 'miracle question' may be used, for example, 'If someone were to wave a magic wand and all your problems vanished overnight, what would be happening that is not happening now? What would not be happening that is happening now?'
- **S**cale. 'On a scale of 1 to10, where would you say that you are now in relation to this problem? And where would you like to be?'
- **K**now-How. The emphasis here is to find out what works, or what has worked 'rather than what won't work or what has gone wrong'.

Clients would be encouraged at this point to extend their knowledge by finding out information between sessions: 'Many coaching models stress the importance of the coach asking questions and drawing out knowledge from the coachee . . . the search for know-how may be extended to include other people and teams . . . the know-how is of course all about what works, or what has worked, rather than what won't work or what is wrong' (McKergow and Clarke, www. sfwork.com).

- **Affirm.** The coach or mentor affirms specific qualities and behaviours of the client. This has a positive impact on the working relationship and it also helps clients to realistically affirm themselves.
- **Action.** The action should build upon what has already been found to work for the client. Small steps are the most realistic way forward. 'Because these actions are built on what is already working, we can be very confident that they will be effective, and the coachee will usually be very motivated to try them out' (McKergow and Clarke, www.sfwork.com).
- **Review.** The focus at this point is on the positive 'What has worked well?', 'What is better?' The focus is kept on the positive results of action and the client may be asked: 'On a scale of 1 to 10, how much have things improved?' and 'What do you think helped or hindered?'

McKergow and Clarke highlight the benefits of using OSKAR:

- future focus of the approach;
- emphasis on progress rather than on setbacks;
- emphasis on 'what works' and 'doing more of it' rather than on 'what hasn't worked';
- encouragement for the client to share their wisdom about 'what works'.

Cognitive-Behavioural Coaching (CBC)

CBC approaches focus on achieving specific performance outcomes. These approaches have developed from Cognitive-Behavioural psychology, based on earlier work by Beck (1976) and Ellis et al. (1997). They use knowledge of the ways in which thinking, feeling and acting are interrelated and affect client outcome. They focus upon present experience and future possibilities with a 'solutions focus'. They use techniques of behavioural reinforcement to accentuate positives and reduce negatives. They have a common aim to help clients formulate and achieve specific, measurable, realistic goals within clear timeframes. Several research studies have affirmed the effectiveness of CBT in bringing about specific changes in thinking, feeling and doing. Cognitive-Behavioural Coaching is being extensively used by organizations, such as the National Health Service, which recommends CBC as part of a 'coaching for health strategy' for individual patients, as well as providing coaching and mentoring as part of leadership and management development. Neenan and Palmer (2001: 17) describe the CBC relationship as 'a collaborative relationship that helps individuals to focus on problem-solving in a structured and systematic way'.

Williams et al. (2010: 38) summarize five main goals of CBC:

1   Facilitate the client in achieving their realistic goals.
2   Facilitate self-awareness of underlying cognitive and emotional barriers to goal attainment.
3   Equip the individual with more effective thinking and behavioural skills.
4   Build internal resources, stability and self-acceptance in order to mobilize the individual to their choice of action.
5   Enable the client to become their own self-client.

They suggest that the approach may be of most benefit when other action models are not enough to help the client to change, or when there is 'a cognitive or emotional block' that is preventing change, including anxiety, avoidance or stress. Several coaching and mentoring models have developed from Cognitive-Behavioural and solution-focused theories of change and development.

The PRACTICE model

This model has been developed by Palmer (2007): 'The sequential steps of the PRACTICE model facilitate the coaching conversation and help orientate the client towards understanding the problem, developing realistic goals, selecting feasible solutions and their implementation, and finally reviewing progress' (Williams et al. 2010: 41). There are seven stages in the model:

1   **P**roblem identification
2   **R**ealistic, relevant goals
3   **A**lternative solutions generated
4   **C**onsideration of consequences
5   **T**arget most feasible solutions
6   **I**mplementation of **C**hosen solution(s)
7   **E**valuation

The coach or mentor initially invites the client to tell their story and not necessarily to immediately focus on any problems. This is so that the coach can learn about the client. Once the client has started talking about relevant current issues and concerns, the coach will feed back what she or he has heard earlier in the session with regard to relevant strengths, qualities or competencies already mentioned by the client. The coach will also help the client at this stage to focus on times when the current issue is actually less of a problem, and why that might be. At this stage, typical questions may be: 'What's the issue you would like to talk about today? What would you like to change? Are there any examples of when this is not an issue for you? How would you know if you woke up tomorrow morning and the issue had been solved? What would be different or better?'

After the telling of the story and the awareness of strengths and resources available to the client, the process moves straight to 'goals'. The client is asked: 'In the light of what you have said about this issue, what would you now like to achieve?' The client is helped to shape up one or more SMART goals (specific, measurable, achievable, realistic and in a timeframe). In relation to that specific goal or goals, alternative solutions are generated by exploring and noting down possible options that could be used to achieve the goal.

The consequences of these solutions are then considered with questions such as 'What might happen when . . . or if . . .?' 'How useful do you think that (course of action) would be?' Rating scales can be used to help this process: 'On a scale of 1 to 10, how useful would that be?' This would be used to open discussion rather than to close it down, to ensure that the client is not going to embark on action which could have a strong possibility of failure.

After a full consideration of the consequences of any action taken by the client, the coach focuses upon targeting the most feasible and practical solution so that coach and client can start to plan some action that would move the client forward. At this point, the coach would help the client to break down the chosen action plan into manageable steps.

The final part of the process is for the client to come back and for client and coach or mentor together to evaluate the success of the proposed 'solution' to the client's problem. Rating scales can be useful here: 'On a scale of 1 to 10, how successful do you think that was in trying to solve your problem or in helping you achieve what you wanted to achieve?'

Transformational Coaching: the CLEAR model

Hawkins and Smith (2013) developed Systemic Transformational Coaching after several years of coaching, training and supervision with executives and leaders in large organizations. While embracing the principles of action learning, they discovered that all too often the action outside of the sessions did not take place.

> Our experience made us skeptical that insight alone could deliver sustainable behaviour change. Developing new behaviours cannot be left to the coachee to address after the session. Under pressure, at work, we will not experiment with new, untried and potentially risky behaviours, we will instead get triggered by our old ones . . . Now, in transformational coaching, we aim to complete the full cycle of action learning (think, plan, do, review) in the coaching session. We ensure now that the action stage happens live in the room, at least once, followed by reflection and an agreement on how to implement the change back at work.
>
> (Hawkins and Smith 2013: 33)

They developed the CLEAR model, which has five stages:

1   CONTRACT. Listening to the client and system.
2   LISTEN. Jointly making sense.
3   EXPLORE. Generating new options.
4   ACTION. Creating a difference in the room.
5   REVIEW. Reflecting on the shift and how to embed it.

The key feature in this model, which distinguishes it from many others, is facilitating and working with 'the shift' in thinking, feeling or acting that needs to take place within the session because if the change does not happen in the coaching session, it is unlikely to happen back at work. Hawkins and Smith noted various ways in which shifts were evident during the session. These included: the way clients talked about their issues; the way they framed the 'problem, issue or challenge'; their use of metaphors and their feelings about the situation; their body and breathing; their emotional expression and engagement and the way they related to the coach or mentor.

Performance Coaching: the GROW and TGROW models

GROW is a popular coaching model developed by Whitmore (2002) for performance coaching. It has been used extensively in executive coaching and coaching at work. With the emphasis on performance and outcome, the GROW sequence starts by asking the client to identify a *Goal* or outcome which they want to achieve. Once this is identified, the coach helps the client to track back to their current *Reality*. Once the client has explored where they are now and where they want to be, they are then helped to explore all the *Options* for getting there. Finally, having decided upon options, the client explores the *Will* to act.

TGROW is a variation of the GROW Model, developed by Downey (2003) to address the issue of starting with 'the story' before setting a specific goal. The coach or mentor starts by helping the client to clarify and explore the *Topic* that they would like to talk about, before asking them what *Goal* they wish to work on.

Several writers on performance coaching and executive coaching base their ideas on the 'inner game'. Much of the thinking in performance coaching originated from sports coaching, including the difference between the 'outer game' of performance and the 'inner game' of attitude and psychology. Gallwey (2000) states that the outer game of improved performance will only be possible if there are changes in the inner game of thinking and feeling, so that emotional interference does not come between potential and achievement. He cites the following examples of the sort of interference which gets in the way and stops us focusing on the goal: fear, doubt, lack of confidence, the 'be perfect' driver, anger, boredom and frustration.

The coach helps the client to identify interference and then to work with it to minimize its impact. This leads to 'relaxed concentration', which in turn leads to performance that flows. The relationship between this approach and sports coaching is obvious. We all recognize 'flow' in excellent performance, whether it be playing tennis, playing the piano or public speaking. Downey gives useful examples of listening for emotions when the client tells their story. When the client starts talking about their dream, he listens not only to the external reasons why the client thinks this cannot be achieved, but also the internal reasons, 'the interference' which perhaps had never been articulated before. Although Whitmore, Gallwey and Downey keep their focus very much upon outcome in coaching, they also use skilled listening and questioning to be facilitative with the client, rather than directive. In fact, Downey calls his approach non-directive coaching: 'Coaching is the art of facilitating the performance, learning and development of another' (2003: 21).

There are several features in common between Whitmore's GROW model and The Skilled Helper model (Egan 2010). For further discussion of the Egan model, see Chapter 6. Both approaches highlight the important relationship between wanting and acting. Both focus on articulating specific goals for change. Both test commitment to the goal. However, the differences are in the sequencing of events. In Egan's approach, commitment is tested before options and action plans are drawn up. In both models it is important for the coach or mentor to be flexible and not to follow the model rigidly. Egan often reminds that: the model is for the client, not the client for the model!

Transactional Analysis (TA)

Transactional Analysis (TA) offers a way of increasing awareness and understanding by looking at 'transactions' within the self and between others. The theory states that in any communication we may operate from one of three ego states, Parent (P), Adult (A), or Child (C) (Figure 5.1). In the Parent ego state, a person may interact from either a Critical Parent ego state or a Nurturing Parent ego state. When interacting from the Child ego state, it may be from the Rebellious Child or the Adaptive Child state.

Berne (1976) shows how to understand, and work with, the way that the past impinges on the present. Sometimes clients get stuck and can only interact and respond in limited ways. Ideally, a person can flexibly move between different ego states as the occasion demands. These ideas form the basis of Transactional Analysis. TA ideas and techniques are widely used in coaching and mentoring. Coaches and mentors who use TA may notice certain 'scripts' which come from particular Parent, Adult or Child ego states. Examples of such scripts might be: 'I must always be perfect'; 'I cannot succeed'; 'One day I will be found out.' People learn scripts early on in life but they are not always 'in awareness' at the conscious level and they can develop into unhelpful 'games' in later life. The effective coach or mentor can enable the client to identify, challenge, and change both scripts and games.

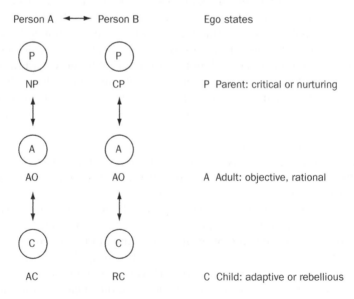

Figure 5.1   Transactions and ego states

TA can be used to help the client understand why certain relationships are not working. Either the client is stuck, or the person with whom they are having difficulty is stuck. Self-limiting patterns or 'scripts' for relating to another person can be perpetuated. TA can highlight these and then clients can rehearse different responses which make both parties feel better about each other. It gives the client new perspectives and resources. TA can also be used in coaching and mentoring supervision, as a way of reflecting upon and reviewing the 'contracting' aspects of working together. Hay (2007) gives some useful illustrations of how this can be done as part of the ongoing review process in supervision. In some situations with certain people, we may have a tendency to revert to certain patterns of behaviour and ways of thinking. These tendencies can be triggered by the way the other person is acting. To change our behaviour, we need insight into these patterns, but we also must want to change them.

People are able to move between any of the ego states, in any transaction. If person A is operating from Parent state, it may well induce in person B the Child state. In Parent state, the person can be either critical or nurturing. Either way, this could produce in person B a 'Child' response, either overly adaptive and conforming, or rebellious. Sometimes such transactions can be useful and creative. Often, they are counterproductive. A person needs to be able to access all three ego states, and to respond appropriately to the ego states from others, in order to be resilient in their transactions.

Sometimes a comment or a situation can trigger a certain reaction. A bullying manager may trigger the 'rebellious child' in a colleague. A difficult employee may trigger the 'critical parent' in a manager. The task of the mentor or coach is to help the client to be aware of what is happening and to identify, and then rehearse, appropriate responses. These skills are useful: listening to the story of the transactions; identifying themes or patterns; reflecting these back to the client; explaining Parent, Adult, Child (PAC) ego states; giving examples of these that relate to the transaction described; asking the client to practise from different ego states. Below is the result of how a team leader has been helped to reframe specific responses in a work situation:

> *Team member*: These meetings are a complete waste of time. Nobody has any good ideas, I don't want to waste my time attending them when I have important work to complete. (RC, Rebellious Child ego state)

> *Team leader response*: You don't have any choice in the matter. (CP, Critical Parent ego state)

> *Reframed response*: Would you like to tell us what would make the meetings work better for you? (Adult ego state)

Gestalt

Gestalt is a process that focuses on developing awareness and turning that into action. Coaches and mentors work with a 'Cycle of Experience'. Gestalt practitioners conceptualize this as a cycle which moves through: sensation; awareness; energy/mobilization; action; contact; resolution/closure; withdrawal of attention. When the coach or mentor is fully aware of what is going on in the here and now, they work in an appropriately immediate way. This can make a real difference to clients, who learn that it is safe to be authentic with the coach or mentor, and so they are more likely to be authentic in their other relationships. The Gestalt approach would not be appreciated by all clients, but it may be useful with those who have the ability and willingness to be supportively challenged, as well as the capacity to reflect on both their internal and external worlds. Coaches and mentors who have a background in psychology, psychotherapy, or counselling will be mindful of the importance of communicating empathy, warm respect and genuine interest to their client as the client grows in self-awareness, self-understanding and self-challenge. 'Contact' is a key concept. The challenge for the Gestalt coach is the capacity to stay in contact with the client while, at the same time, allowing the process to emerge. For this to be effective the coach or mentor has to relinquish the need for certainty and control. Bluckert outlines some core assumptions:

- Clients are always doing the best they can.
- Change occurs when the client is fully in contact with 'what is'.
- Heightened awareness helps people into new ways of seeing, choosing and acting.
- Each context and situation has its own dynamic which needs to be understood; so-called 'unfinished business' holds clients back from realizing their potential.
- Exploring the 'here and now' provides the best opportunities for learning and growth by such questions as 'What are you aware of now?' (Bluckert 2010: 83, 89).

Clients are helped to develop an honest awareness of what is happening in themselves in the moment-to-moment encounter with the coach or mentor. They are encouraged to 'make contact' or 'meet' all parts of themselves: their work and workplace; their colleagues and friends.

Gestalt theory asserts that change occurs, paradoxically, not by moving to the future, but by remaining fully in contact with the present. However, making contact with 'what is' means getting in touch with parts of the self which have been disowned or denied, maybe because important basic needs have not been met or satisfied in earlier experiences. The difficulty of doing this cannot be overestimated and in Gestalt theory, there are four major obstacles to making contact with the self. Two of these are introjection and retroflection. Introjects are the 'shoulds' and 'oughts' which may have been acquired from parental and other adult expectations. These interrupt contact with what the client 'wants'. Retroflection occurs when clients turn inwards with their real thoughts and feelings, perhaps in the workplace, where they do not feel safe to express themselves and where, for example, they may have allowed themselves to become invisible or overlooked.

A client may have lost contact with what they really think and feel. If the coach or mentor can stay fully present with them so that they feel safe enough to make contact with what they really want and need, this can be powerfully liberating for the client. Contact leads to the sort of 'connectedness' that develops from shared honesty and transparency and from the willingness to empathically challenge when contact is being interrupted. It is this quality of connectedness which enables the relationship to be transforming for the client.

The insight, learning and change that can be achieved through a Gestalt approach can be very powerful. Coaches and mentors who wish to use this approach need to ensure that they are providing the right balance of support and challenge for their clients.

Systemic Coaching and Constellations

Coaching and mentoring are activities which help clients to develop themselves within the specific systems of their current lives, whether at home or at work. This approach embraces not just the client, as Clutterbuck asserts:

> Coaching the client must inevitably involve coaching the system . . . Now we see a range of approaches that allow clients to explore their own systems and make informed choices about how they relate to and interact with those systems . . . I do not think that it is possible to be truly effective as a coach without supporting the client to become more aware of the systems in which they belong.
>
> (2012: viii)

Whittington (2012) has developed an approach to working with relationship 'systems'. He calls this 'working with constellations'. This active approach allows the client to 'experience' their own 'constellations' during a session with the coach or mentor:

> A constellation is a practical intervention that can illuminate the invisible and unspoken dynamics behind a relationship difficulty, a

stuck issue or a persisting challenge. Constellations provide a way of exploring and classifying almost any kind of relationship system – between people and teams across and within businesses but also any other kind of relationship from the intra-personal to the abstract.

(Whittington 2012: 34)

Many coaching and mentoring approaches rely on the client talking about their current issues and opportunities but this is a totally different way of working. It is an experiential way of working. 'A constellation encourages participants to "get out of their heads" and work from their "felt sense" – at an intuitive level of "knowing" that is very different from our normal understanding of knowing' (Whittington 2012: 39). Whittington explains that the largely non-verbal language exchange experienced during a constellation

frees leaders, coaches and consultants from their familiar stories and allows a deeper systemic picture to emerge. Standing in the truth of that picture – the first stage of a constellation, and referred to as mapping – is often enough to start to free up fresh energy and allow new possibilities to emerge.

This mapping helps participants to experience the 'interconnectedness' in systems and between people. Participants gain an experiential understanding of the way in which change in one part of a system affects the rest, and they learn how to work with these changes.

Whitmore asks: 'Why would dynamics discovered in family systems have any relevance in business, organizations and executive coaching?' (2002: 6). He describes a system as a series of relationships and asserts that 'systems are sustained by a consistent set of naturally occurring organizing principles. These principles are seen time and time again and are experienced as balancing forces that move all human systems towards wholeness' (2012: 93).

Coaches and mentors invariably work with clients who have problems as well as opportunities within both work and family systems. Increasingly clients are high-performing individuals with multiple responsibilities and working in complex environments in varied locations, whether their job is chief executive, manager, supervisor or operative. An experiential knowledge of how to work with our own systems and constellations will enhance the working knowledge of the coach or mentor. All approaches which involve exercises which are experiential, require particular skills and supervision from the coach or mentor. They demand the ability to do the following:

- Use wise judgement to negotiate carefully and ethically with the client.

- Sensitively monitor client's reactions, resistance and responses, noting signs of discomfort or distress.
- Pace activities carefully allowing plenty of time to debrief the session.

Summary

In this chapter we have:

- Introduced several coaching and mentoring approaches and models.

- Given examples of these being used with clients.

- Helped the reader to reflect on whether an approach or model would be appropriate 'for this particular client, in this particular situation, at this particular time'.

- Invited the coach or mentor to evaluate specific approaches or models in relation to their own key principles for effective practice.

6 What is The Skilled Helper model?

- Introduction
- Why use The Skilled Helper?
- Using The Skilled Helper in a learning relationship
- Using the model wisely
- Using the stages of the model to achieve change
- Stage 1: What's going on?
- Stage 2: What do I need or want?
- Stage 3: How do I get what I need or want?
- Staying client-centred
- Summary

Introduction

In this chapter we present one model: The Skilled Helper. We introduce the model, describe its advantages and discuss how to use it appropriately. An overview of the model is given, followed by a detailed explanation of how to use each of its three stages. A case example illustrates the stages in practice.

The Skilled Helper is used worldwide. It has been continuously developed by Gerard Egan since the first edition of his book *The Skilled Helper* was published in 1975. Over the past decades we have trained many coaches and mentors who consistently tell us that it is robust and enabling. They find that the model and its associated skills are easily transferable to professional, leadership, management and work roles. In this chapter we share their experiences, as well as our own, in identifying hints and tips for using each of the three stages with clients.

Why use The Skilled Helper?

Coaching and mentoring provide the opportunity to change and develop, through working in a learning relationship with a coach or mentor. The client is stuck with an issue or opportunity and in the process of coaching or mentoring they become more hopeful about possibilities, and they develop the courage to act, to make changes and to achieve results. The Skilled Helper is a well-grounded, practical model for coaching and mentoring. Like many models, it is not 'one size fits all' and must be tailored to the individual requirements of each client.

We value the fact that The Skilled Helper has been updated and refined over many years, with constant feedback from users. It is informed by humanistic, cognitive and behavioural approaches to the understanding of the person, applying these to knowledge from social psychology about people in contexts and systems. The result is a pragmatic approach, which turns theory into practical application. Some advantages of using The Skilled Helper are as follows:

- Clients readily understand it and can easily use it.
- Coaches and mentors find it robust and enabling.
- It has been developed and refined – tenth edition published in 2013.
- It is an integrative model which can incorporate elements from a range of approaches.
- It puts emphasis on change, leading to valued outcomes.
- It is applicable across cultures.
- It is applicable in a variety of helping situations.
- It is positive and systematic.
- It is a framework that can be shared with the client.
- It is a framework that can be used by the client between sessions.
- It maps the process of coaching or mentoring sessions.
- Egan acknowledges the 'shadow side' of helping and the things that may adversely affect it but are not identified or discussed.
- Coaches, mentors and clients find the skills transferable to life and work.

Using The Skilled Helper in a learning relationship

Egan states that there are three goals of helping (Egan 2010). The first is to help clients manage their problems more effectively and develop underused or unused resources and opportunities more fully. Sometimes The Skilled

Helper is referred to, for the sake of brevity, as a problem management model. However, the goal of developing resources and opportunities is equally important and should not be marginalized. The second goal is to help clients become better at helping themselves. The third goal is to help clients develop an action-oriented prevention mentality. The Skilled Helper model helps clients to achieve these goals. There are three stages of the model as shown in Figure 6.1.

This practical model may appear to be structured because it is presented in stages, however, it is intended to be used flexibly according to the needs of the client. Egan has often stated that the model is for the client, not the client for the model. He emphasizes the importance of 'keeping the client in the driver's seat' (2013: x). The Skilled Helper is used within a coaching or mentoring relationship characterized by respect, genuineness and empathy. This respect ensures that the model, used well, always starts with where the client is. It focuses upon how the client is at the present moment and how the client would like to be. In that sense, coaching and mentoring are intentional activities. Underlying the helping process are communication skills which enhance the effectiveness of the coach or mentor. Consciously developed listening, responding and challenging skills are important throughout the

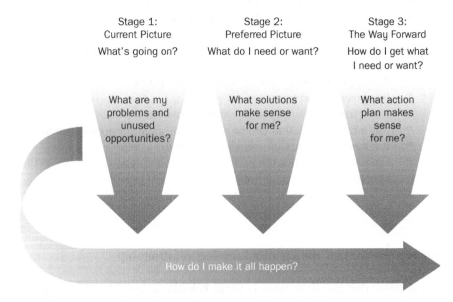

Figure 6.1 The Skilled Helper model

Source: Egan (2010: 70). From Egan, *The Skilled Helper, International Edition*, 9E. © 2010 South-Western, a part of Cengage Learning, Inc. Reproduced by permission. www.cengage.com/permissions

process. The effective coach or mentor tries to maintain the right balance of support and challenge throughout.

Using the model wisely

As with any framework, there are pitfalls associated with The Skilled Helper if used inappropriately. These include:

- using the framework mechanistically;
- being model-centred rather than client-centred;
- seeing goal-setting as solely rational and not attending to feelings;
- assuming that the framework is applicable in all situations;
- ignoring difficulties in the helping relationship;
- creating a power imbalance;
- focusing on what happens within sessions at the expense of what the client does between sessions.

One way of thinking about such pitfalls is described by Egan as the shadow side of helping. Egan says that the most effective helpers are wise, rather than smart. Wisdom, he says, involves understanding and managing the limitations of the models we use, the limitations in ourselves and in our clients and the contexts in which we operate. The shadow side of helping can be described as things which are not identified or explored, even though they affect the helping relationship and its outcomes.

Adverse shadow side issues for coaches and mentors may include:

- not having a coherent approach;
- or alternatively being too strongly wedded to only one approach;
- being caught up in the enthusiasm of the latest approach and applying it indiscriminately;
- having a favourite technique that is used regardless of its appropriateness.

Egan identifies shadow side issues associated not only with the helping relationship, but also with listening and responding, and with the stages of the model. More information on these topics can be found in the various editions of *The Skilled Helper*.

Using the stages of the model to achieve change

The interactive stages and tasks of The Skilled Helper model are shown in Figure 6.2. Each of the three stages has three tasks. The three stages are

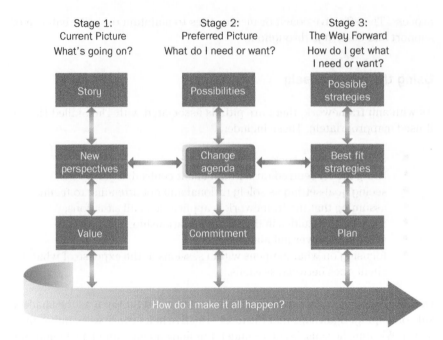

| Stage 1:
Current Picture
What's going on? | Stage 2:
Preferred Picture
What do I need or want? | Stage 3:
The Way Forward
How do I get what
I need or want? |

Figure 6.2   The helping model showing interactive stages and steps

Source: Egan (2010: 81). From Egan. *The Skilled Helper, International Edition*, 9E. © 2010 South-Western, a part of Cengage Learning, Inc. Reproduced by permission. www.cengage.com/permissions

designed to move the client forward so that there is change and action. In order for the client to be able to change, the coach or mentor must communicate genuine interest, respect and empathy. Coaching or mentoring will then develop into an effective working alliance. Reviewing the working alliance openly and honestly through frequent evaluation can be a direct source of learning and change.

The first stage

The first stage helps the client to clarify the key issue where change is needed or wanted. Three tasks help the client to work towards this clarification: first, telling their story; second, developing new perspectives; and third, focusing upon an aspect that will make a difference and add value to their life. In telling their story, the client is helped to elaborate their issue, concern or opportunity and to make sure that all facets have been explored. Then, the skills of the coach or mentor help the client to reframe or further expand the story, to include any new perspectives. Finally, the client is helped to focus and prioritize something to work on. When this, which Egan calls the value point, has been identified, the client can move on to the next stage which addresses the future and goals.

The second stage

The second stage helps the client to identify what they need and want in relation to the aspect of their story that they have chosen to work on. Three tasks help the client: first, imagining ideal possibilities for the value point; then formulating a goal, which Egan calls the change agenda, and finally checking commitment to the goal. In the first task, the client is encouraged to be creative in imagining the possibilities for a better future. The psychological importance of this stage is significant because by identifying 'wants' rather than 'oughts', the client is more likely to develop the hope and motivation to create a better future. The second task involves the client in finding a goal from all of their wants and possibilities. Goal-setting is at the heart of this model, and Egan calls the goal the change agenda. In the third task, the client is helped to test their commitment to the goal and to check whether the benefits outweigh any costs. The client's hope for change is developed into the courage to change. This leads into the next stage of the model, which deals with how the client will achieve their goal.

The third stage

The third stage helps the client discover how to get what they need and want, and to develop strategies for action. As with each of the previous stages, there are three tasks. In the first task, the client imagines possible action strategies to achieve the goal. In the second task, the client decides which of these strategies fits best with their resources. In the third task, the client is helped to formulate an action plan and decide the next steps.

Underlying all stages is the challenge for the client of constant incremental change. Egan reminds us that talking about change is not the same as doing it. The coach or mentor can ensure that change permeates the helping process. Change involves thinking, feeling and doing: the client may reflect, may become aware of feelings, and may act. What happens between sessions as well as within sessions is important for client growth and development and for achieving their goals.

We will now describe in detail The Skilled Helper process, highlighting the role of the coach or mentor in each stage. We will use a case example of, Steve, a client, to track the tasks of each stage.

Stage 1: What's going on?

Overview of Stage 1

The client usually goes to see a coach or mentor because they feel stuck with a problem, issue or opportunity. So, the coach or mentor gives the person space to talk about what is going on. In this first stage of the process, rapport is developed through the support that is offered while the client tells their story. Attending, listening, paraphrasing, reflecting thoughts and feelings, summarizing, probing and clarifying are skills that are needed throughout this process. In addition, empathic challenge is essential in order to identify areas that may have been overlooked or avoided. These areas could be inaccuracies or deficiencies in the client's perception of the situation, or they could be their underused resources and opportunities. New perspectives are developed from exploration of these areas. Finally, in the first stage, the coach or mentor uses the skills of focusing and prioritizing to help the client choose which aspect of the story to work on. They are helped to choose the aspect that would make a difference and add value to their life. Once this, the value point, is identified, the client can move forward. The key questions in this stage are shown in Figure 6.3. Each task will now be described in detail.

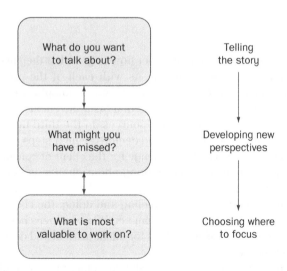

Figure 6.3   Key questions in Stage 1
Source: Adapted from Egan (2010).

Telling the story

The first task of the coaching and mentoring process is used whenever a client comes to talk about an issue, problem or opportunity which they want to work on. So, it may be at the initial visit, or at the beginning of a subsequent session, or at any point in longer-term work where an issue needs to be explored. The coach or mentor is first and foremost trying to build rapport to help the client tell their story. At this time the client needs space. Whether their storytelling is faltering, or words flow in a torrent, the space will help them to reflect and to hear themselves 'thinking out loud'. Skills of support and challenge are used to help the client open up all aspects of the issue that are relevant. Active listening skills are essential here, rather than diagnostic listening. Attentive active listening includes observation of non-verbal communication as well as listening to the words used. The coach or mentor:

- *Notes non-verbal communication:* eye contact, facial expression, posture, smiling or frowning, voice tone.
- *Notes any discrepancy* between non-verbal signs and words spoken.
- *Listens carefully* to thoughts, feelings and actions.
- *Uses silence*, when appropriate, to give the client time to think and to encourage them to elaborate.
- *Reflects* succinctly and tentatively what has been said by the client so that the client can hear it clearly.
- *Summarizes and paraphrases* to let the client know that they have been understood.
- *Uses open questions and probes* to clarify, challenge or check understanding.
- *Echoes key words* as questions, e.g. 'concerned?', 'pleased?'

Figure 6.4 lists some of the things that a coach or mentor might say in order to help the client tell their story.

Active listening skills and prompts help the client to relax and open up. They also communicate interest, concern and empathy. These qualities in helpers are known to influence rapport between helper and helped (Rogers 1961). Once the client has perceived these qualities in the coach or mentor, then trust develops. Trust makes challenge possible and more likely to be effective. Throughout the relationship the coach or mentor is trying to establish the right balance of support and challenge. Too much support may provide comfort, but no change. Too much challenge may provoke, but may produce resistance rather than change. Challenge has the power to make a

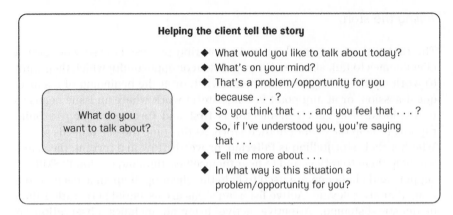

Figure 6.4 Prompts for telling the story

difference, but if too strong, or too early, it may be rejected. When the coach or mentor challenges with empathy and with the intention of facilitating self-challenge in the client, then it is more likely to be effective.

Developing new perspectives

This is the second task of Stage 1. The coach or mentor continues to use active listening skills and prompts to help the client to elaborate their story. In order to move forward it is important to check that no significant perspectives have been overlooked. The coach or mentor:

- enables client self-challenge;
- explores blind spots and new ways of looking at the issue;
- encourages the client to consider their strengths and resources;
- highlights any discrepancies in the story or the client's verbal/ non-verbal language;
- invites the client to look at the situation in different ways, e.g. others' perspectives;
- checks that nothing has been overlooked.

This second task in Stage 1 gives something of a reality check on the story. Possible resources that the client may have overlooked can be identified. Blind spots are explored and the client is encouraged to notice any self-defeating patterns of thinking, feeling or acting. The coach or mentor also helps the client to identify their strengths and strategies that have worked well in the past and which could be applied in the current situation. Each or all

Helping the client develop new perspectives

What might you have missed?

◆ Is there anything you may have missed?
◆ If X were here now, what might they be saying?
◆ When you have faced situations like this before, what, or who, has helped you? Could you use any of those resources now?
◆ Do you recognize any patterns of thoughts, feelings or actions that have occurred before in your life? Do you want to repeat them? Or change them?
◆ What personal and professional strengths do you have that you could bring to this situation?

Figure 6.5 Prompts for developing new perspectives

of these new perspectives may affect or reframe how the client views the situation. Figure 6.5 lists some prompts that the coach or mentor might use in helping the client to explore new perspectives.

One technique that may be useful at this stage is outlined by two coaches writing from a neuro-linguistic programming (NLP) background. Eaton and Johnson (2001) say that creative people can change perspectives or frames to look at things from different angles. They describe how, for example, the limiting frame of seeing everything as a problem can be changed to the productive frame of seeing everything as an opportunity. The coach or mentor can use productive frames to help the client. So, if the client seems to be bogged down with detail, the coach or mentor can ask the client a question about the big picture. This is one way of helping the client to develop new perspectives. A further way would be to get the client to imagine the situation from the point of view of another person. A role reversal exercise can be helpful here and there is an explanation of this technique in Chapter 8.

Egan (2006: 192) gives a useful list of things that clients are able to say when they have been helped to develop new perspectives:

- Here's a new angle . . .
- Here's something I've not thought of . . .
- Here's something I've overlooked . . .
- To be completely honest . . .
- Here's one way I've been fooling myself . . .

- Here's an important piece of the puzzle . . .
- Here's the real story . . .
- Here's the complete story . . .
- Oh, now I see that . . .

Choosing where to focus

In this task, the client chooses which part of their issue they will focus on. Earlier on, in the first task, the client was helped to describe their problem or opportunity: it was about 'putting all the pieces of the jigsaw out on the table'. In the second task, they elaborated and explored their story, and checked that none of the important pieces was missing. They may also have reflected on the size and scale of the issue; perhaps it was larger or smaller than they first thought. Now, the third task is to decide where to get started; which are the really important pieces? Egan describes this as the search for value and it leads to working on something that will make a difference to the client. This third task enables the client to focus and prioritize, and to find the aspect of the issue or opportunity that they want to work on.

Value is the part of the issue or opportunity which, if worked on, would have the most positive impact. In order to arrive at this point, the coach or mentor helps the client to do the following:

- *summarize* all the parts of the story;
- *focus* on the most important aspects;
- *prioritize* which part or parts to take forward.

Egan (2006: 193; 2010: 262) gives some principles for helping the client to decide which issues to choose to work on. We have adapted these as follows:

1   Check whether coaching or mentoring is the right kind of help.
2   If there is a crisis, help the client to manage the crisis.
3   Begin with the aspect that seems to be causing the most concern.
4   Begin with issues the client sees as important.
5   Begin with some manageable part of a larger situation.
6   Begin with a part that, if handled, will lead to some kind of general improvement.
7   Focus on a part of the issue for which the benefits outweigh the costs.

Figure 6.6 lists some prompts that the coach or mentor might use in this task.

Helping the client choose where to focus

What is most valuable
to work on?

◆ So, if I can try to summarize the key aspects
   of this situation . . .
◆ What seems most important to you out of all
   the things we've talked about?
◆ Which part of this have you got energy for
   tackling first?
◆ Is there something we could work on that
   would make a real difference to you?
◆ What feels like a manageable bit to work on?
◆ If you wanted to change one aspect of
   things, where would you start?
◆ Out of all of this, is there something we can
   take forward to work on?

Figure 6.6   Prompts for choosing where to focus

At the end of Stage 1 the client has identified something that they can
work on. They can now move forward to Stage 2, to think about what that
aspect would be like if it were much better: if it were ideal.

Summary of Stage 1

At the end of Stage 1, the client has explored their story, developed new
perspectives and chosen something to focus on and take forward.
     The coach or mentor has:

- Attended to the client's non-verbal and verbal communication.
- Listened actively.
- Responded empathically using reflecting, paraphrasing and
  summarizing.
- Echoed key words.
- Used silence to provide reflective space.
- Used open questions to clarify, challenge and check understanding.
- Provided a balance of support and challenge.
- Encouraged self-challenge in the client.
- Stimulated the client to reframe perspectives.
- Enabled the client to focus and prioritize.
- Helped the client to identify which aspect is most valuable to
  work on.

Hints and tips for Stage 1

These are some hints and tips from coaches and mentors to help you in Stage 1:

- Attentive listening, with few closed questions and plenty of reflecting, paraphrasing and summarizing, will be most helpful in order to build rapport and enable the client to tell their story. Resist the temptation to start diagnostic listening and to ask questions which help *you* solve the problem.
- If you find yourself asking lots of questions to which the client already knows the answer, stop! Don't assume that you need to know all the details of everything that led up to the situation presented by the client.
- If this stage has become a question-and-answer interview, rather than telling the story, pause and start to paraphrase and echo key words or phrases. A useful tip is to stay with recent and current events and keep focused on what is, rather than what was.
- When this stage is going well, you will feel as if you are following the content of the story, rather than leading it.
- In the second task of this stage, there may be many new perspectives to be discovered or very few or even none. Sometimes new perspectives emerge as the story is told, and the coach or mentor can then move straight to asking the client which aspect is of most value to work on.
- In helping the client to identify the value issue, the following question has often proved useful: 'Out of everything that we have talked about so far, is there one thing we could take forward to work on that would really make a difference?'

Example of Stage 1 in action

Steve is the client. His issue is 'work seems to be dominating my life'. He is helped to explore this issue and the ways in which it is a problem for him. He talks about the increasing pressure on him at work, his concern that work standards are slipping, having to work longer hours, spending less time with family and friends, and a general feeling that he is being driven by events, rather than being in the driving seat. As he talks, he begins to wonder whether putting work first is a pattern in his life, which has reaped rewards but also had some costs. He is asked, 'What would your colleagues say about you if they were here now?' and he is surprised when he replies that they'd say, 'Good old Steve, you can always count on him to get things done.' He realizes that while this is a compliment, such a perception may be contributing to his problem. He is asked about his strengths and resources, and recognizes that since he is the manager of his department, he has some power to reorganize work. Perhaps he is not currently using this power. He also realizes that as work has taken over his life, he is spending less time with family and friends and has got out of the habit of taking exercise, which used to 'recharge my batteries'. He is asked, 'Out of all of the things we've talked about, is there one thing that we could take forward to work on that would really make a difference?' and he identifies 'what I need now is to get a healthier balance back into my life'. This is his value issue.

Stage 2: What do I need or want?

Overview of Stage 2

Figure 6.7 shows the tasks and key questions in Stage 2.

The second stage moves the client from the state of being stuck which they probably experienced when they arrived for coaching or mentoring to the hope which arises from describing their wants and needs. In order to begin work in the second stage, the coach or mentor asks the client to restate their

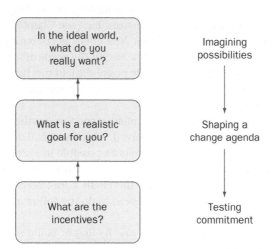

Figure 6.7   Key questions in Stage 2
Source: Adapted from Egan (2010).

chosen value issue. This becomes the focus for imagining an ideal scenario. If the coaching and mentoring has been effective in the first stage, the client has removed any blinkers, and so in this second stage they can explore all sorts of exciting possibilities in the ideal scenario. The client is invited to imagine possibilities, then to select from these possibilities some aspect/s which they can shape into a specific goal. This leads to the choice of a *wanted goal*. A wanted goal is powerful in psychological terms. The driver for change is intrinsic, not extrinsic. The goal that is chosen is really wanted, and so is more likely to be acted upon. Finally, in this stage, the client checks their commitment to the goal. Commitment moves the client from hope to courage, and from courage to action. This final task will help the client, in the next stage, to follow the goal thorough to action and results.

Imagining possibilities

The first task of Stage 2 helps the client to access their creativity and to imagine their ideal scenario for the value issue. Two things are important in this task. First, the focus is the ideal future, not the current situation. Second, the focus is '*What* ideally do you want or need?' not '*How* can you get it?' The 'how' question is not asked until later on in the model.

The coach or mentor asks the client to imagine the ideal and to describe what it is like. Notice that they ask the client to describe what it IS like rather than what it would be like, i.e. to picture the future as if they were already there. The coach or mentor can invite the client to use methods that stimulate their creativity, for example, drawing, sculpting or writing. Such methods may also include visualization or brainstorming (see Chapter 8). The purpose of this task is to open out possibilities. The client is encouraged to think the unthinkable, in a positive sense, because within the seeds of apparently unrealistic ideas may be the germ of a realistic possibility. In this first task of Stage 2, the client is helped to access their valued 'wants' and to minimize the constraining effect of 'oughts'.

To make this happen, the coach or mentor encourages the client to imagine that the value issue is successfully resolved, with their ideal outcome achieved. They are asked to produce as many ideas as possible in a short space of time, describing what this ideal is like. Keeping it short and sweet encourages uncensored responses, which can tell the client a lot about what they really want. The coach or mentor helps the client to do the following:

- Let go of their current reality and feeling of being stuck.
- Imagine the ideal future.
- Stay future-oriented.
- Focus on what, not how.

- Generate a large quantity of ideas.
- Create hope in the possibilities.
- Have fun and avoid self-censure.
- Give themselves permission to dream with their eyes open.

Figure 6.8 lists some brainstorming prompts the coach or mentor can use.

Some coaches or mentors find brainstorming difficult, and some clients do too. It may help if, when listening to the story in the first stage, the coach or mentor has picked up cues about whether the client has a preference for visual or kinaesthetic or auditory mental imagery. They can then choose the appropriate brainstorming prompts.

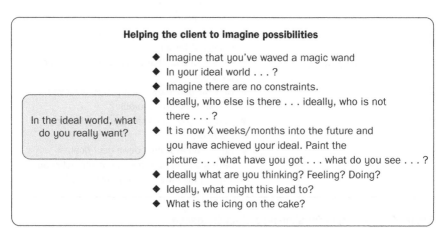

Helping the client to imagine possibilities

In the ideal world, what do you really want?

- Imagine that you've waved a magic wand
- In your ideal world . . . ?
- Imagine there are no constraints.
- Ideally, who else is there . . . ideally, who is not there . . . ?
- It is now X weeks/months into the future and you have achieved your ideal. Paint the picture . . . what have you got . . . what do you see . . . ?
- Ideally what are you thinking? Feeling? Doing?
- Ideally, what might this lead to?
- What is the icing on the cake?

Figure 6.8   Prompts for imagining possibilities

Shaping a change agenda

Having helped the client to brainstorm as many 'wants' as possible, the coach or mentor then helps them to identify which of these are most important and which might be incorporated into a specific goal. The process moves the client from *wanting* to *choosing*. The coach or mentor helps the client to do the following:

- Critique their list of wants.
- Choose those that are most important to them.
- Consider what is realistic.
- Move from aims to outcomes.

- Identify a goal.
- Shape the goal so that it is specific and has a timeframe.
- Check the goal against their values.

Figure 6.9 lists some prompts that can be used to help the client refine their description of the ideal, so that they can create a specific goal.

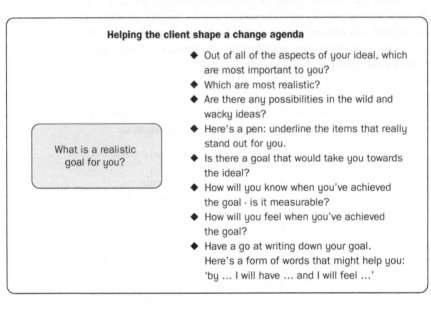

Helping the client shape a change agenda

What is a realistic goal for you?

- Out of all of the aspects of your ideal, which are most important to you?
- Which are most realistic?
- Are there any possibilities in the wild and wacky ideas?
- Here's a pen: underline the items that really stand out for you.
- Is there a goal that would take you towards the ideal?
- How will you know when you've achieved the goal - is it measurable?
- How will you feel when you've achieved the goal?
- Have a go at writing down your goal. Here's a form of words that might help you: 'by ... I will have ... and I will feel ...'

Figure 6.9   Prompts for shaping a change agenda

There are several mnemonics that may be used to help check the specificity of a goal, and we say more about goal setting in Chapter 8. One of these mnemonics is SMART. Eaton and Johnson (2001) define SMART as: **S**pecific, **M**easured, **A**chievable, **R**elevant and **T**imed, and they list focused questions to help a client develop a SMART goal, for example, 'How will you measure the achievement of the goal?' (2001: 31).

Testing commitment

The final task in this stage is to check how the client will feel when they achieve the goal. The coach or mentor asks: 'How committed are you to this goal?' If the client is not really committed, then the chances are that the goal will not be achieved. The client is helped to identify both costs and benefits. Forewarned is forearmed. There will always be costs, but the client can learn how to manage these and prevent them from subverting the wanted goal. They may also become aware of reasons why this goal has not been pursued before or not been achieved before. On the plus side, becoming more aware of the payoffs and rewards can strengthen the client's resolve. This increases the motivation to succeed and inspires the sort of courage which hopefully will propel the client to act and get results. One method of weighing the factors affecting commitment is cost-benefit analysis and we say more about this in Chapter 8. Whatever method is used in testing commitment, the coach or mentor helps the client to do the following:

- Identify incentives.
- Identify costs.
- Decide if it is worth the effort.
- Check whether incentives and payoffs outweigh costs.
- Consider who or what might help or hinder.
- Consider what has stopped them until now.
- Move from hope to courage and action.

Figure 6.10 lists some prompts that the coach or mentor can use to help the client to test their commitment to the goal.

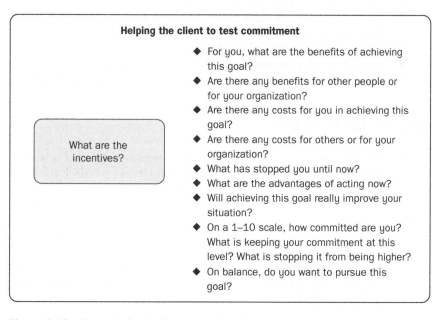

Figure 6.10 Prompts for testing commitment

The client may wish to redefine the goal at this stage if they realize that costs outweigh benefits. Or they may think that the goal is not sufficiently challenging and wish to set themselves a more stretching aim. Once the client has committed to a specific goal, coaching or mentoring can move to the third and final stage. Up to now, the focus has been on 'what': 'What is the present situation?' (Stage 1), 'What ideally do you need and want in the future?' (Stage 2). Now that a goal has been set, the client can move on to Stage 3, 'How'. They are helped to plan 'How will you achieve the goal?' At the end of Stage 2, some coaches or mentors think that the most important work is now done and that the client can do the action bit for themselves. Not so. There is still important work to do in the final stage.

Summary of Stage 2

At the end of Stage 2, the client has imagined possibilities in relation to their value issue, chosen a specific goal, and tested their commitment to achieving the goal.

The coach or mentor has done the following:

- Encouraged the client to picture themselves in the future.
- Used prompts to help the client to imagine their ideal.
- Given permission to suspend reality.
- Enabled the client to formulate a specific goal which describes what the client will have achieved.
- Identified important client values.
- Helped the client to test their commitment to the goal.
- Checked how the client will feel when they have achieved their goal.

Hints and tips for Stage 2

- Whether this stage is the beginning of a session, or part of a session, ask the client to state the value issue in their own words. It may take a few iterations before they get it right. Being clear about the value issue, and even writing it down, will help the client to get started in imagining the ideal.
- Be aware that the pace may be different from the previous stage. In this stage the coach or mentor models energy, imagination, creativity, hope and optimism. It can be more upbeat and energetic. For some coaches and mentors, and clients, this is liberating. For others, it can be more of an effort.

- If brainstorming is used, it can be useful to write down the ideas as they are spoken by the client. Check whether they wish to write or whether they would like you to write for them. Either way, the output of the brainstorm is theirs and should be given to them at the end of the session. Ideas should be written down verbatim, without judgement or discussion. In order to produce as many ideas as possible in the shortest time, the coach or mentor encourages a fast pace.

- The best ideas often emerge right at the end of the brainstorm. Encourage the client to keep going with the brainstorm – a useful prompt is 'Give me three more things that are there in your ideal.'

- Some clients are grounded and realistic, and find it difficult to imagine the ideal. Encourage them: 'if your wishes came true' or 'if you were being really selfish'. Quote Einstein, who said that imagination is more important than knowledge. Imagining possibilities liberates the mind. It is often from a seemingly implausible idea that a new possibility emerges and hope dawns.

- If you have written down the ideas generated in imagining the ideal, give the client the pen for the critique task. Let them decide whether they prefer to tick off the brainstormed ideas one by one, or whether they want to scan the list and pick out those that seem most significant.

- When helping the client to set a specific goal, listen carefully to them. It is not necessary to laboriously go through each element of, for example, the SMART criteria, but rather to highlight any areas of ambiguity.

- Some simple checks can help with this. Does the goal include the word 'I'? Does it have a completion date? Does it describe what the client will have achieved? Statements of wishes ('I will try to . . .' or 'I hope that . . .') are not goal statements!

- Writing down their goal and reading it aloud may help the client to refine the goal and check that it is right for them.

- When looking at costs and benefits, remember that intangible aspects, for example, feelings and values, may be just as important for some clients as more tangible costs and benefits.

- When clients have reflected on advantages and disadvantages of achieving their goal, they may choose to redefine or amend it. Sometimes a new perspective may occur to them and the most useful thing will be to go back to a previous stage and tell the story of that perspective. It is important to be alert for such possibilities and not to push on with a goal which is not right for the client.

In the case example, we saw how, at the end of Stage 1, Steve was helped to clarify the value issue that he wanted to work on. In this stage, Stage 2, Steve is helped to imagine his ideal in relation to the value issue, to shape two specific goals, and then to check his commitment to those goals.

Steve's work in Stage 2

Steve's value issue is *'I need to work on getting a healthier balance back into my life.'* He is encouraged, by the skilful use of the prompts, to think about what it would be like if he had actually achieved that. He is asked to imagine himself at a future time when he has the ideal healthier balance and to describe, as if he were there, what that is like. He is asked about what he is doing, ideally and what he has stopped doing. He is asked to describe his ideal day, what he is thinking and feeling, and ideally what others – colleagues, friends and family – are saying about him. There are a great many items on his brainstorm list, here are just a few:

- *Feel more energetic.*
- *Let go of work at the end of the day.*
- *Others say 'Steve is conscientious but not a pushover.'*
- *Arrive home with batteries recharged not depleted.*
- *Reconnect with friends and social life.*
- *Reorganize work and it gets done more efficiently.*

Steve is helped to review his list and underline the items that are most important to him. From these items, he generates two goals: *'By the beginning of next month I will be doing 30 minutes exercise each evening after work. and I will feel healthier and more energized. Within the next two weeks I will have agreed with my director the reallocation of some of my work. I will feel pleased that I have regained control of my life, although I may miss some of the work I have delegated.'* These are specific goals, Steve thinks that they are realistic and he will know when they have been achieved. He can meet the director within two weeks and thinks that 30 minutes exercise each day is manageable, sometimes by walking home from work or sometimes by going to the gym. Steve is asked about the incentives for achieving these goals; what are the benefits for him and others, and what might be the costs. He weighs up the pros and cons and decides that on balance these goals are right for him and will be a significant step towards a healthier life balance.

Stage 3: How do I get what I need or want?

Overview of Stage 3

This is the final stage of the coaching or mentoring process in relation to a specific issue or opportunity. A realistic goal has been set by the client, and the coach or mentor has checked whether it is really valued and wanted. Now is the time to plan how it will be achieved. The coach or mentor helps the client to move from 'what' to 'how'.

The three tasks in the final stage help the client to open up a range of possible strategies, to evaluate which of these makes most sense for them and then finally to develop a plan of action. In this stage, hope and courage are translated into practical action. The coach or mentor remains client-centred and does not become directive. The value of the work of previous stages will be undermined if this stage is rushed. Active listening and empathy go alongside action planning for results.

When the action plan is agreed, the coach or mentor discusses contingencies in case the plan does not succeed. This is the responsibility of the coach or mentor. Because action takes place within a learning relationship, failure can be viewed as a learning opportunity, not a disaster. The client can come back to report on action and results. At that point, the cyclical nature of this model becomes evident, as the client returns to tell their story. The key questions in Stage 3 are shown in Figure 6.11.

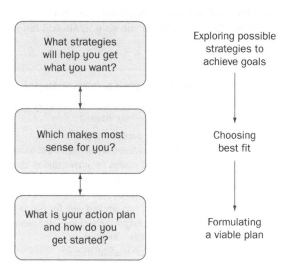

Figure 6.11 Key questions in Stage 3
Source: Adapted from Egan (2010).

Exploring possible strategies to achieve the goal

The first task in this stage is to generate possible strategies for achieving the goal. Egan reminds us that there are more than just one or two ways to achieve our goals, there are many ways. The aim is to help the client get in touch with as many different strategies as can be thought of, whether or not they seem feasible at this point. In this task, 'off the wall' ideas are encouraged. Helping the client to think 'outside of the box' may generate strategies that might otherwise not have surfaced. The client can include strategies used by others even if they have not yet been used by the client. This helps to broaden the canvas. The coach or mentor uses prompts appropriately and does not tell the client what to do. Rather, they help the client to do the following:

- Restate the goal.
- Brainstorm possible ways to achieve that goal.
- Be creative.
- Have fun.
- Keep going and generate lots of ideas.
- Suspend any evaluation or judgement.
- Piggyback on ideas.

Some prompts which can help the client to explore new or overlooked strategies are listed in Figure 6.12. Notice that these prompts are not directive. The client supplies their own answers. The effective coach or mentor steers clear of becoming directive and making suggestions. Beware of prompts such as 'Why don't you . . .?' or 'This worked for me so you should try it.'

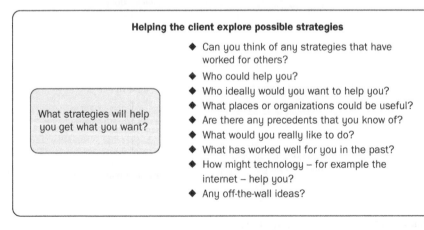

Helping the client explore possible strategies

What strategies will help you get what you want?

- Can you think of any strategies that have worked for others?
- Who could help you?
- Who ideally would you want to help you?
- What places or organizations could be useful?
- Are there any precedents that you know of?
- What would you really like to do?
- What has worked well for you in the past?
- How might technology – for example the internet – help you?
- Any off-the-wall ideas?

Figure 6.12   Prompts for exploring possible strategies

When this task is successfully accomplished, the skilful coach or mentor has helped the client to generate ideas about strategies and to develop these ideas. The client's resources and energy have been tapped. The client begins to see routes to their goal and so they are more likely to believe in themselves and in their capacity to get what they want or need. They develop a can-do attitude which will sustain them during the action phase. Clients who are stuck with a can't-do attitude are more likely to lose motivation when they encounter the inevitable obstacles on the way. When this task is done well, the client has been helped to maximize the use of their resources, both internal and external, and to increase the probability that they will achieve their goal.

Choosing best fit

The next task is to help the client to decide which of the strategies is the best fit for them. The client reviews all the possible strategies that they have just identified. They are invited to pick out ones which are most attractive and which match their resources. Or, it may be that a new strategy emerges for the client as they review the list. Because the client is doing the choosing, this increases the likelihood that the strategies will work for them. It is important that the coach or mentor does not presume to know which strategies will be most powerful or effective. The coach or mentor works with the client to do the following:

- Identify the most attractive strategies.
- Select those that match the client's resources.
- Check for any unintended or unhelpful consequences.
- Consider whether the chosen strategies will achieve the goal.
- Check that strategies fit with the client's values.
- Look for helpful and hindering factors.
- Plan how to enhance positives and reduce negatives.

Egan lists some questions that can be asked at this stage (2010: 372) and we have adapted these in Figure 6.13.

Techniques such as force field analysis and SWOT analysis can enable the client to become aware of what may hinder and what may help in achieving the goal. In force field analysis the client identifies these factors in self, others and their work and social contexts. Having identified these, the client can look at ways of minimizing or diverting the unhelpful factors. There is a description of this technique in Chapter 8. In SWOT analysis, the client evaluates their strengths and weaknesses and the opportunities and threats which could affect the successful outcome of a chosen strategy.

Helping the client choose best fit strategies

Which strategies makes most sense for you?

◆ Which strategies are most appealing to you?
◆ Which fit best with your resources?
◆ Which will be most powerful in producing an outcome?
◆ Which seem best for your goal?
◆ Which fit with your preferred way of doing things?
◆ Which seem manageable and do-able for you?
◆ Which fit with your values?
◆ Which have the fewest unwanted consequences?

Figure 6.13   Prompts for choosing best fit strategies

Formulating a viable plan

In this final task of the model, the client is helped to draw up an action plan with a timeframe. Critical path analysis can be used to plot milestones and key actions. There is a description of this technique in Chapter 8. It is important that the realism of the intended actions is tested. Contingency plans need to be discussed so that, if obstacles get in the way, the client has a Plan B. Evaluation follows implementation and the client can use a follow-up session to review what succeeded, what failed, why, and what can be learned for the future. So, in this task, the coach or mentor works with the client to do the following:

- Identify the chosen strategy.
- Develop a workable plan of action.
- Identify key milestones on a timeline.
- Build an awareness of intrinsic and extrinsic rewards that will sustain momentum.
- Maximize the use of client resources.
- Develop a contingency plan.
- Consider whether a follow-up session is appropriate.

The coach or mentor will be aware of the way that inertia or entropy can prevent action from starting or prevent it being completed (Egan 2006). Inertia bedevils those who procrastinate. Entropy bedevils those whose plans get started but fall apart before completion. One of the responsibilities of the coach or mentor is to help the client to recognize whether either of these could come into play, and how to prevent this from happening.

The real test of whether the coaching or mentoring is successful is whether the client acts, makes changes and achieves the results that they

Helping the client to formulate a viable plan

What is your action plan and how do you get started?

◆ Working back from the goal, what are the key milestones?
◆ What are the main tasks that you need to complete? By when?
◆ What are you going to do first? Next?
◆ Who else needs to be involved? How?
◆ What/who could stop this plan from succeeding?
◆ What/who could help this plan to succeed?
◆ How committed are you to this plan?
◆ Will inertia or entropy affect you? What can you do about this?
◆ Is there anything we could do now to increase your commitment?
◆ How does this plan relate to the story that we originally discussed?
◆ What is your strongest incentive to implement this plan?
◆ What if plans go awry - what is your 'plan B'?

Figure 6.14 Prompts for formulating a viable plan

want and need. So, specific and detailed action plans are important. During this task, the client may discover some skill deficits that might impede success. Where this is the case, the coach or mentor will try to help the client to develop whatever is needed. Figure 6.14 lists some prompts that the coach or mentor might use in helping the client to formulate a viable plan.

It can be satisfying to complete the cycle of The Skilled Helper in this way and then there is a natural feedback into debriefing the results of the action in a future session. The effective coach or mentor will realize that work goes on not just in the sessions but, most importantly, between sessions as well. The work that the client and coach or mentor do together is preparation for the action that takes place in everyday life and work.

Summary of Stage 3

At the end of Stage 3, the client has imagined a range of strategies for achieving their goal; decided which of these fit best with their values and resources; chosen strategies and checked what might help or hinder them; developed an action plan and a contingency plan.

The coach or mentor has:

✓ Facilitated the exploration of possible strategies.
✓ Helped the client to evaluate strategies and choose best fit ones.
✓ Ensured that there is a specific action plan in a timeframe.
✓ Supported the development of a contingency plan.
✓ Checked with the client about how they feel about the plans.
✓ Provided the possibility of a session to evaluate action.

Hints and tips for Stage 3

- When helping the client to generate ideas for how to achieve the goal, aim to get some new ideas which are more than just a list of previously thought-through ones. The prompt 'What would you ideally like to do?' can be powerful in liberating the client's creativity.
- Take time over critiquing the list. There needs to be a full critique, leading to a choice of strategies for action.
- Force field analysis can identify important factors which will affect whether the action succeeds.
- Stay client-centred while in the active stage of action planning, and resist the temptation to start directing.
- A time line is a useful and visual way of helping the client check whether their plan is do-able in the time they have. Invite the client to draw the line – this is their action plan. Marking key milestones on the line will help them to ensure that important actions are included and so the plan is more likely to be successful.
- If the client asks directly for your experiences, then you might share them, with the proviso that 'This worked for me, but how do you think it would be for you?' When you give back to the client the responsibility for evaluating your experience, this ensures that the helping process remains client-centred.
- It may be useful at the end of this stage to ask the client 'On a 1–10 scale, how committed are you to your action plan? What helps you to be committed? Is there anything that we can do now to increase your commitment?'

Steve's work in Stage 3

In the example, Steve's goals are 'By the beginning of next month I will be doing 30 minutes exercise each evening after work. and I will feel healthier and more energized. Within the next two weeks I will have agreed with my director the reallocation of some of my work. I will feel pleased that I have *regained control of my life, although I may miss some of the work I have dele-gated.' His brainstorm of possible strategies to achieve these goals includes:*

- *Rejoin a gym.*
- *Have a gym extension added on to the house.*
- *Hire a personal trainer to come to my home.*
- <u>*Buy an exercise bike.*</u>
- <u>*Walk home from work instead of using the car.*</u>
- *Leave office at 5.00 p.m. each day.*
- *Start working from home on two days each week.*
- <u>*Meet with director in my office not his, so he can see work pressures.*</u>
- *Be well prepared with statistics of hours worked.*
- *Give him plans for who and what to delegate.*
- <u>*Rehearse this meeting with you and feel confident.*</u>
- *Plan beforehand what my 'walkaway position' with director will be.*

Steve then selects four strategies that particularly appeal to him, and underlines these. Two strategies address his goal that is to do with having 30 minutes exercise each day. The other two address the reallocation of work. He then looks at what will help and what will hinder his four chosen strategies, using force field analysis (Figure 6.15).

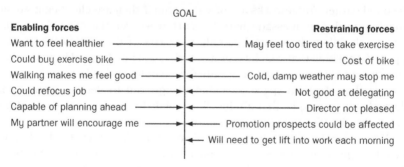

Force Field Analysis of Chosen Strategies

GOALS: 30 minutes of exercise each evening after work
Agree reallocation of work with director

GOAL

Enabling forces	Restraining forces
Want to feel healthier	May feel too tired to take exercise
Could buy exercise bike	Cost of bike
Walking makes me feel good	Cold, damp weather may stop me
Could refocus job	Not good at delegating
Capable of planning ahead	Director not pleased
My partner will encourage me	Promotion prospects could be affected
	Will need to get lift into work each morning

Figure 6.15   Force field analysis of chosen strategies

Steve considers how he can decrease the power of the unhelpful factors. He is then able to produce his action plan. Steve draws a time line, and describes his action plan as follows:

Steve's action plan: *'I will start walking home from work three nights each week for the first month and then review whether that is proving feasible. I will begin walking home from next Monday. In bad weather I will use the exercise bike instead. I will arrange the meeting with my director, in my office, for a date within the next two weeks. In the meantime I will have another session with you to rehearse the meeting. If I arrange that for next week, I will be able to come to the meeting having prepared what I think would be my position and what I think might be his.'*

The contingency plan is:

Steve's contingency plan: 'If I find after the first week that I have not kept to the exercise routine, I will talk to my partner and ask for support. Even if the walking home from work doesn't seem manageable, I will ride the exercise bike instead. If I have problems with arranging the meeting with my director, or if I start getting very stressed before we are due to meet again, I will contact you, as you suggested.'

In this case example, The Skilled Helper model has been used to help Steve progress from telling his story of work–personal life imbalance through to identifying specific action plans to make changes in his life.

Staying client-centred

As stated earlier, frameworks are of value only if they are client-centred, not model-centred. Our message here is, start wherever the client is. Let the framework follow the client. Use only the parts of the framework that are appropriate within that coaching or mentoring session. It could be that simply attending and listening are appropriate for a whole session because the client can use the reflective space to self-challenge and to decide upon action. Alternatively, it may be that all the client needs from the coach or mentor is some help with visioning the ideal future.

If the client has a clearly articulated goal, they do not want to be dragged back through Stage 1 and Stage 2 simply in order to use a model or framework. The wise coach or mentor will listen carefully and will check that the client's goal is clear and specific. If it is, then they can proceed to the next stage. However, if during the discussion about the goal, it becomes apparent that it is not so clear after all, then the client may be ready to tell more of the story about why this was chosen as a goal. It may be that the goal was not chosen by the client, but by a line manager or close friend, partner or colleague. If so, it may be in the category of 'ought' not 'want'. Until a goal is wanted, it is unlikely that the benefits will outweigh the costs and this is why action will not happen or will be half-hearted. Of course, sometimes in organizations we are told which goals, objectives or targets we will pursue, whether we like it or not. In that case, the coach or mentor has a more difficult job of helping the client to find the part that is meaningful to them within a larger objective which may not be.

Reviewing skills are needed throughout the process, as the coach or mentor works with the client in considering progress and appraising what is happening both within and between sessions. At any point in the process the client can return to the first stage to tell the story of how it has been between sessions. The skills of being able to go spontaneously with the flow of where the client is and apply the framework flexibly in the service of the client are perhaps the most advanced required of a coach or mentor. The Skilled Helper model is then used with integrity and wisdom, not mechanistically in the way a more inexperienced person may use it. It is used most effectively when it is known so well that it is in the background, with the client in the foreground. At this stage the coach or mentor has moved through the stage of conscious competence, to a level of proficiency that is characterized by unconscious competence.

In Chapter 7, a case study is presented. You are invited to put yourself in the position of a coach using The Skilled Helper to work with a client, Anna. You will use the skills and stages of The Skilled Helper model.

Summary

In this chapter we have:

- Introduced The Skilled Helper model and outlined its advantages.

- Highlighted the importance of using the model wisely, within a learning relationship, and with an awareness of potential pitfalls.

- Described how the three stages of the model can be used to help clients to release their potential and achieve results which they value.

- Explained each stage and its tasks, giving examples of coach and mentor questions, prompts and interventions and using a case example to track client progress through the stages.

- Identified useful hints and tips for each stage.

- Emphasized the importance of being client-centred rather than model-centred.

7   How is The Skilled Helper used in practice?

- Introduction
- Your coaching assignment
- The first session
- The second session
- Summary

Introduction

This chapter demonstrates the way in which The Skilled Helper model (Egan 2010) can be used in practice. A case study, with commentary, forms the major part of the chapter, and illustrates how the skills of effective coaching and mentoring are used intentionally within the model.

The Skilled Helper is described in detail in Chapter 6. There are three stages, each with three tasks. In the first stage, the client is helped to tell their story, to develop new perspectives and to choose an issue to work on that will make a difference. In the second stage, the client imagines a better future, develops a realistic goal and then checks its appropriateness by weighing the incentives against the costs. In the third stage, the client identifies possible strategies to achieve their goal, selects those that fit best for them and then creates an action plan.

In the case study, you are the coach and you use the model stage by stage. The case study is designed to help you to reflect on:

- How do I use the skills of effective practice with The Skilled Helper model?
- How do the key principles of coaching and mentoring, which are described in Chapter 1, operate in practice?

The case study explores the development of your learning relationship over the first two sessions. In each session you work with your client using all three stages of the model. The stages and tasks are highlighted **in bold** in the text as they are used in the session. At the end of each stage, there is a summary of how the model and principles have been applied. In the case study there are interactive prompts and questions. At various points you are asked to reflect on what is happening and consider how to respond.

 When you see this sign, there is a summary of how the model and principles of effective coaching and mentoring are being used in practice.

Your coaching assignment

You are the coach for Anna, who has recently been promoted to her first leadership role. She is highly intelligent and has no difficulty in grasping the technical aspects of complex assignments. Her previous boss described her as talented and impressive. The organization has recently conducted a 360-degree feedback exercise as part of a leadership development initiative. Feedback to Anna indicated that staff sometimes find her 'difficult'. Her boss has discussed the feedback with Anna and, as part of her personal development plan, she has agreed to have some coaching support. You are the coach and you have met Anna and her boss. In the meeting, you experienced her as polite but not overly enthusiastic. The outcome of the meeting was a plan to work with Anna, initially for four two-hour sessions, meeting monthly. You have also clarified the working agreement and discussed how you and Anna might use The Skilled Helper model to structure and support your work together.

The first session

This is your first session, and you are wondering how things will go.

 What are your hopes and aims for this first meeting? Any concerns?

Stage 1: What's going on? The story – new perspectives – value

The story: At the first session, you ask Anna to describe how things are at work. She starts talking animatedly about her new job, and as you listen and paraphrase, she tells you how happy she was until the 360-degree feedback exercise. Now, she says in a rather disgruntled manner, 'There is clearly a problem in the way people see me.'

How might you respond? You could:

- Ask a question: why do they see you that way?
- Make a statement: yes, the feedback indicates that there are problems.
- Reflect her words, in the form of a question: the way people see you?

You decide that the first two options run the risk of being too challenging at this early stage, so you choose the third.

Anna says, rather abruptly, 'Well, they certainly don't like me.' She begins to talk about how surprised she was by the feedback and how she is always 100 per cent successful in delivering on time and on budget, whatever it takes. Her job, she tells you, is extremely demanding and there isn't always time for 'handling everyone with kid gloves'.

You say?

- I know the job's tough, but don't you think you're being a bit defensive?
- So it's tough delivering on time all the time, and it's been a surprise to hear that you may have ruffled a few feathers?
- I imagine anyone would be stressed in your role.

The first option lacks empathy, and the third is more sympathetic than empathic, so you choose the second.

New perspectives: Anna looks a little taken aback by your response, as if she was expecting more of a challenge, but slowly she relaxes and begins to tell you how difficult it is being a newly appointed manager, being under scrutiny and being determined to do well. She talks about the constant pressure of deadlines, and how everything seems to rest on her shoulders. You notice that her demeanour has changed and the vivacious person has become quieter; the word that comes into your mind is 'smaller'.

You say?

- Rest on your shoulders . . . that sounds like a burden . . . is it?
- How does it feel to be under such pressure?
- And if your staff were here now, and heard you talking, what would they be saying?
- In the past, how have you handled being under pressure?

All of these responses could be helpful, and you use them in turn to help Anna to elaborate her story. She tells you how, under pressure, she becomes rather bossy, both with herself and with others. She talks about the way her management style changes from 'how I try to be – calm and even-tempered' into 'the gorgon'. As she says the words, she laughs at herself. You encourage Anna to tell you about the gorgon and she paints a verbal picture that has you both smiling, describing a gorgon prowling around a cave, terrifying all who dare approach!

You sense that Anna is now more willing to reflect on her behaviour, and challenge herself, so you risk a challenge: 'So, if you met the gorgon in a cave, what would you do?' Anna says immediately, 'Oh, I'd run like crazy and get away as fast as I could, and make sure I kept away!' She pauses for a moment, and then says, 'But, of course, staff can't actually run away.' She seems more reflective now, and she talks about how abrupt she can be with staff. In fact, she is finding the new role much tougher than she anticipated. She is even wondering whether this is the right job for her. She thinks that the technical aspects of work are much more satisfying than the people management aspects. This is why, she says, she would rather talk to you than her boss, because 'I wanted to talk completely off-line.'

 You are wondering what to say next in order to summarize Anna's problems. Try to complete this sentence: 'Anna, the current situation seems to be a problem for you in several ways . . .'

Compare your answer with the suggestions below, all of which describe ways in which the situation may be a problem for Anna. Does your answer include one or more of these points?

- The feedback has come as a surprise.
- You are hurt by the feedback.

- You are finding the new job harder than you expected.
- You are wondering whether you are on the right career path.
- You feel under constant pressure.
- You are aware that your management style can be less than perfect.
- Perhaps you don't feel appreciated for always delivering on time?

Having explored the situation with Anna, you ask her whether there is anything that you or she might have overlooked. She can't think of anything. You ask if she has any strengths or resources that might help in what is obviously a difficult situation for her. Anna replies that she is very determined and will do whatever it takes to improve things.

Value: You are not sure what is the most pressing or important aspect of the situation for Anna, and you are also aware that you have a limited number of sessions with her. You are wondering whether her question 'Is this the right job for me?' is within your remit, and whether it might be more than you can deal with in a limited time.

 What do you say next? Which of the options below do you prefer?

- So, out of all the things we've talked about, what seems the right bit for you to work on now?
- I wonder if you need to attend a stress management workshop?
- Perhaps you need to sort out your career issues first.

You select the first option because it offers Anna choice, whereas with the other two options you are making suggestions.

She says, 'Well, the career thing is a big issue, but maybe I need to see if I can get on top of this job first of all. That's what I want to work on, getting on top of this job and getting rid of the gorgon.'

At this point, you have reached the end of Stage 1, although not the end of the session.

SESSION 1: USING STAGE 1 AND APPLYING THE PRINCIPLES

You have worked through each of the three tasks of Stage 1 of The Skilled Helper. The model has enabled you to work intentionally.

Anna began by talking about the negative 360-degree feedback. You've helped her to explore the ways in which this a problem for her, and she has talked about her job and her career.

You've worked to establish a safe, trusting relationship with Anna, who was quite 'prickly' to begin with. At one point, you thought that she anticipated a critical challenge from you, but when she received support and empathic challenge, she began to relax.

You've challenged her and enabled her to challenge herself in exploring new perspectives.

She has been supported in identifying something manageable to take forward to work on.

You noticed that she is willing to laugh at herself, and you've been able to share humour together.

You've tried to ensure that Anna has autonomy in creating the coaching agenda. While you have steered the process, she has made the decisions about which issue to address.

You have helped Anna to focus on what she wants to work on now, while at the same time acknowledging that in the future she may explore broader career issues. You wonder whether it might be more appropriate for her to be mentored by a director if she decides to explore these issues.

The session continues.

Stage 2: What do I need or want? Possibilities – change agenda – commitment

Possibilities: Anna has identified something that would be valuable to work on: getting on top of her job and getting rid of the gorgon. You suggest that, rather than working on *how* she can achieve this, which may seem like an obvious place to begin, she could start by painting a picture in words of *what* would be happening in her ideal situation. You ask her to think forward in time, and picture herself 'on top of the job and rid of the gorgon'. What would it be like for her if things were going really well? You've noticed that Anna uses visual imagery in the way she talks, so you decide to include some prompts which might appeal to the visual sense.

What brainstorming prompts might you use? Try to add five to those below.

- So, imagine it's going really well . . . describe your day . . .
- Paint a picture of what you are doing?
- In your ideal, what are you thinking? Feeling?
- Ideally, what are people saying about you? About your team?

There are more prompts in Figure 6.8, p. 137.

Anna comes up with lots of ideas, however, many of them seem to be quite realistic. You encourage her to 'suspend reality for a moment and picture your absolute ideal, if there were no constraints'. Your prompt helps her to be more imaginative and Anna's brainstorm list covers a couple of pages. You struggle to keep up with writing each item down verbatim, but you manage. You wonder how on earth she'll be able to sort through all the items, and so you ask her how she wants to select the important points. You suggest going through the list item by item, but Anna is intuitive and prefers to scan the list. She underlines three items that seem most important to her:

- not losing my cool;
- we're all one team, not just me the boss;
- feeling calmer, happier.

Change agenda: You hope that by identifying the important elements of what she *wants*, Anna can now *choose* a goal. The items that she has selected are aspects of the ideal which are particularly important to her. She now needs to choose something that she can achieve, a goal which will take her towards those important aspects.

Can you think of a question that might help Anna to formulate a goal?

You ask a question: 'Anna, is there a goal emerging from the items that you underlined; something you can achieve, and want to achieve?' Anna says, yes, her goal is that within three months her group will be functioning as a team, and she will be part of the team and not, as she currently feels, apart from them. You ask her to phrase this as a SMART goal. Anna says, 'Within three months, the team will be working better with me, and I will feel more relaxed.'

 While this is a useful first attempt at getting a goal statement, there are some difficulties with it. Can you spot them?

With your help, Anna refines the goal statement. She makes two important changes. First, she focuses on achievements within her control, changing the goal from 'the team will' to 'I will'. Second, she tries to make the goal more specific and measurable. This is her revised goal statement:

> By the end of June, I will be acting calmly at work in all situations, and involving my team in responding to demands and deadlines, and I will feel happier.

 Is this a SMART goal? Are there any additional questions you might ask Anna at this stage?

Commitment: Before you start working on how Anna can achieve this goal, you want to check that it is the right goal for her. You ask her about the advantages and disadvantages of achieving the goal, the costs and benefits, both for herself and others. (There is a description of this technique in Chapter 8.) She thinks the advantages are pretty obvious: both she and the team would be happier and hopefully working more effectively. The disadvantages are less obvious; however, she notices that her goal is to *behave* calmly. She wonders if she will always *feel* calm. Maybe a disadvantage for her will be coping with how she is actually feeling at times. She also wonders whether the team's work will get done, or whether standards will suffer.

 How would you paraphrase what you've heard, and check if this is the right goal for Anna?

You ask Anna whether, considering both potential costs and benefits, this is the right goal for her. Anna decides that the goal is fine, and now she wants to work on how she can achieve it. You have reached the end of Stage 2.

SESSION 1: USING STAGE 2 AND APPLYING THE PRINCIPLES

Stage 2 enabled Anna to move forward by taking one part of her problem which she could work on, and picturing how that would be if things were much improved.

Anna found it easy to brainstorm. She was energized in this stage – it played to her strengths, and you mentally noted that brainstorming may be a useful technique to use again. While you were not sure how you would move from the ideal to the practical goal, the process seemed to flow.

You steered the process, and with plenty of reflecting and active listening, as well as using the framework, you helped her identify her goal. You found that being clear in your own mind about a format for a goal statement helped Anna to avoid the pitfall of setting a goal which was not really hers to achieve. The format 'by . . . I will have . . . and I will feel . . .' enabled her to set a goal that was within her control.

When you tested her commitment to the goal, she mentioned that work standards might suffer. You remembered that earlier on she had talked about getting the work done 'whatever it takes'. You wondered how important this was to her and whether you might have asked her. Maybe it would have been helpful to return to Stage 1 and explore this? However, the moment passed and you mentally logged it, and noted that perhaps it would crop up again.

Stage 3: How do I get what I need or want? Possible strategies – best fit strategies – plan

Possible strategies: There are 30 minutes until the end of the session. You wonder what would be a good outcome from this session for Anna. You don't want to leave matters in mid-air, but neither do you want to force the pace.

 What might you say to Anna now?

You say, 'Anna, I see we have 30 minutes left. You've identified a goal. Do you want to use the time to talk about how you might achieve your goal, or is there something else more useful that we could do?' Anna tells you that she thinks that a lot has been achieved already. She has focused on something which is manageable, after initially feeling rather overwhelmed by the 360-degree feedback. She says that in this last part of the session it would be useful to identify some actions for her to take between now and the next time you meet. You ask her to restate the goal, and then describe all the ways in which it could be achieved, even if they do not sound very probable. She restates her goal: 'By the end of June, I will be acting calmly at work in all situations, and involving my team in responding to demands and deadlines, and I will feel happier.'

 What prompts might you use to help Anna imagine all the different ways that she could achieve her goal? There are some in Figure 6.12 on p. 144.

In response to your prompts, here are some items from Anna's list, '101 ways to achieve my goal':

- identify role models . . . other colleagues who stay calm . . . talk to them;
- talk to my team more . . . involve them at the front end;
- take more notice of my own behaviour . . . notice what I do;
- take five, take time out to think before I start rushing around issuing orders;
- challenge deadlines . . . do I always have to respond instantly?;
- find some techniques on how to manage stress;
- join a relaxation class;
- take a holiday, have a break.

Best fit strategies: You ask Anna which of these she wants to do, which would fit with her values and resources, and which have the fewest unwanted consequences. Anna says, 'That certainly rules out taking a holiday, because I'd have a mountain of tasks to return to.' You agree that it's important that she chooses a strategy which does not add more stress at work and make the goal less likely to be achieved.

Anna decides that a good starting point would be to keep a record of her reactions in times of stress at work, and what happens to her when work pressures build. She says that this start point appeals to her. You ask, 'Because?' and she tells you that it appeals because it is something that she can do every day, it is under her control, and she will generate her own data.

Plan: Anna has identified a strategy, and you are wondering what would help her to put it into action.

What do you do next? What questions will help Anna firm up her actions? Help her to plan for contingencies? Help her to check that the actions will achieve her goal? There are some prompts in Figure 6.14 on p. 147.

Anna commits to the following actions, which she writes down:

- At the end of each day, I will note down any incidents where I have been under pressure. I will use three columns: what I was thinking at the time, what I was feeling and what I actually did.
- When I notice myself about to go into 'gorgon mode', I will 'take five', by getting a coffee or going for a walk around the block or finding some other distraction.
- When we meet again in a month, I will bring my notes and discuss with you what has happened.

You have reached the end of Stage 3 and of the first session.

C   **SESSION 1: USING STAGE 3 AND APPLYING THE PRINCIPLES**

In Stage 3, you enabled Anna to identify manageable actions she could take. Anna was supported in choosing actions which would not increase her stress levels too much – for example, by being too difficult to achieve or by having negative consequences. What she has chosen, however, does require her to reflect and notice her own behaviour, thoughts and feelings.

You were aware that, as the session progressed, you were feeling under time pressure. You remember that Anna's team members have said they often feel under pressure, and indeed so does Anna. You wonder whether you might have shared this observation with Anna and asked to what extent you and she were recreating in the session what happens at work.

However, you were pleased that, despite feeling concerned, you did offer choices to Anna about how to use the time.

You realize that you forgot to leave space at the end of the session to review with Anna how you have worked together. This would have been useful, especially since it was your first session. You make a mental note to ensure that you leave sufficient space for review at the end of the next session, which takes place, as planned, a month later.

The second session

Stage 1: What's going on?

You are wondering how to start the second session. You consider saying:

- Hello Anna, how are things?
- Hello Anna, let's start by looking at how you got on with your action plans.

Which option do you prefer? Why?

You decide that it's better not to make any assumptions about what's been happening, so you ask the more general question 'How are things?' Anna tells you that the past month has been an eye-opener for her. As planned, she has kept notes, and has been surprised by what she has found. First, she noticed how often she gets stressed at work. Second, she noticed her feelings: annoyance at requests, anxiety about her team's ability (and her own ability) to respond, and impatience with others. In these situations, she has tried to take time out and avoid getting irritated with those around her.

 What do you notice about Anna's reaction to this data compared with her reaction to the 360-degree feedback? Why do you think that is? Reflect this to Anna, balancing support and challenge.

You say, 'You know Anna, when you talked about the staff feedback it was as though you didn't really want to believe it, maybe it was a bit difficult to take in. Today it's different – you are challenging yourself, and sounding quite energized.' Anna agrees, yes, this is her data and something she can work with. She says, 'I want to get on and make some changes. I can see now what I need to stop doing. I'm just not sure what to do instead!' It seems as if Anna is firing on all cylinders, so you match her pace. You say, 'OK, let's try this. Choose three behaviours you'd be happy to lose, three gorgon behaviours, and three you want to substitute.' She says, 'I want to stop issuing orders, taking charge and demanding. I want to start listening, involving others more but not [she laughs] lose control.'

At this point, you share with Anna some research about the skills of effective influencers, which describes specific skills that they use. In fact, they do a lot of active listening and involving others, and yet they are certainly not people who have lost control. She is interested in this, and says that she's keen to give it a go, to try out some of these skills and new behaviours, and see what happens.

You have reached the end of Stage 1, although not the end of the session.

SESSION 2: USING STAGE 1 AND APPLYING THE PRINCIPLES

You trod cautiously at the beginning of the session. Anna is a client who has a lot of pressure at work and you did not want to recreate that pressure in the coaching session.

You invited Anna to tell her story of what had happened since your first session. It was clear that in carrying out her action plans, she had generated some new perspectives for herself since last time.

Since she was enthusiastic, it seemed appropriate for you to offer some challenges and suggest some additional new perspectives in the session. You talked about the research on communication skills, and asked focused questions. Your questions helped her to identify the value issue, which was 'developing new behaviours'.

As she described these behaviours, she talked about how she wanted things to be in the future, and so she began to move into Stage 2, talking about the ideal and possibilities.

The session continues.

Stage 2: What do I need or want?

 What do you do now? Which part of this stage will be most useful?

You say, 'Anna, remembering what we talked about last time, and putting that together with what you've said today, it sounds as though you have some ideas for a new goal, and now you want to get going with it?' Anna agrees. She wants to ask her team for suggestions, not assume that ideas have to come from her, talk less and not always jump in first. Her goal is: 'By the next time we meet, I will have spoken less and made fewer suggestions in our weekly meetings and elsewhere. Instead, I will ask for suggestions. I will feel pleased that I am doing this, and interested in whether I feel sufficiently in control!'

You are at the end of Stage 2, and midway through the session.

SESSION 2: USING STAGE 2 AND APPLYING THE PRINCIPLES

Given the work that you and Anna had done, your hunch was that you could quite quickly firm up a goal. Anna began to describe her ideal behaviour, and the goal, i.e. the change agenda, evolved from her description. It did not seem necessary to use brainstorming, as you had done in the first session.

You did not specifically ask Anna about the costs and benefits of achieving this goal, but you noticed that she was concerned about losing control, a potential cost of this goal. You have an idea about how to help her with this. However, you wonder whether you might have reflected this concern back to her, to give her the opportunity to talk more about it.

The session continues.

Stage 3: How do I get what I need or want?

An hour of your session remains. You suggest to Anna that one way of exploring possible actions would be to use the remainder of the time to practise some of the new behaviours. She could rehearse them, and notice how the words sound and how she feels as she says them, in particular, how 'in control' she feels. You explain the process and some options: perhaps you could take the part of a team member responding to her, or perhaps she could play both parts, physically moving between two chairs as she does so. (There is a description of this technique, role reversal, in Chapter 8.) Anna is enthusiastic to try this out and asks you to play the part of a team member. She tries out different scenarios and forms of words, and is quite heartened. 'When I hear myself, it doesn't sound like losing control at all, in fact it sounds better, more responsive, not just reactive.'

Anna writes down some specific actions she will try out between now and next time you meet. These are:

- I will do less telling and ask more questions.
- When feeling anxious I will let my team know, not by being aggressive but rather by saying something such as 'I'm concerned that . . .'
- Under pressure, I will continue to 'take five' and give myself time to calm down.
- I will read the article which you have recommended to me.

You check with Anna whether all these actions are do-able, and whether they fit with her goal.

As coach, in what ways have you influenced this part of the session? What are the potential advantages and disadvantages of the way you've worked?

In the time remaining, you suggest to Anna that you review together how you have worked over the two sessions, what has been achieved and what has been helpful or less helpful.

 What questions might you ask Anna? Compare them with the checklist of questions in Box 2.4 on p. 49. How do you think the sessions have gone?

↻ SESSION 2: USING STAGE 3 AND APPLYING THE PRINCIPLES

You have helped Anna to move from setting a goal to exploring different ways of achieving the goal, and finally to identifying specific actions that she will take.

You've used role reversal as a way of exploring possible actions that might work for Anna and finding the ones that suit her best. You followed your hunch that working in this more immediate way, i.e. trying out some new behaviour rather than simply talking about it, would be useful for Anna. She seems to have enjoyed this different learning method, and it has built the rapport between you.

Anna has written some specific action plans which she is confident are achievable.

You got rather carried away with how well the session was going, and realized afterwards that you forgot to help Anna to plan for contingencies and what she might do if things didn't go according to plan.

However, you did remember to make time to review with Anna how you have worked together in this session and the previous one.

A learning relationship has been established. You have established trust, worked with Anna, and enabled her to gain new perspectives and set achievable goals for herself.

Postscript

In the next two sessions, you continue this work. Anna builds her skills as she practises and refines the new behaviours. She plans an away-day with her team to reflect on how they are working together. She begins to try out skills with colleagues, so that she does less reacting and more clarifying of what is wanted and needed. As her confidence increases, she finds she can negotiate deadlines and reduce some of the pressure on her and her team.

Summary

In this chapter we have:

- Invited you to use The Skilled Helper model with a client, Anna, in a case study.

- Used interactive prompts and questions to help you consider how you would work with Anna over two sessions.

- Described the stages and tasks of the model and summarized how these occur in the case study.

- Reflected on how you can use the model and principles to support and guide the sessions.

8 What are some useful tools and techniques?

- Introduction
- Johari Window
- Karpman Triangle
- Career lifeline
- Role reversal
- Brainstorming
- Visualization
- Goal setting
- Cost-benefit analysis
- Wheel of work/life
- Force field analysis
- CAN model: conflict, assertiveness, negotiation
- Critical path analysis
- Summary

Introduction

This chapter describes some tried and tested techniques in coaching and mentoring. We have used all of these in our own work and found them to be valuable. We present them in the order in which you might use them if working with a framework which starts with helping a client to tell their story, then proceeds to ways of helping them to explore possibilities and set goals, and finally develops and manages action plans.

These tools and techniques can be powerful. The less experienced coach or mentor would be advised to familiarize themselves with the techniques in a safe and appropriate context before using them with clients. Each technique or approach is presented by addressing these questions:

- What is it?
- When should it be used?
- How does it work?
- What skills does the coach or mentor need?
- What are the advantages?
- What are the disadvantages?
- Are there any useful references?

Johari Window

What is it?

The Johari Window (Luft 1970) is a tool for increasing a person's self-awareness and understanding of how they interact with others. 'Johari' is an abbreviation of the first names of its inventors, Joseph Luft and Harry Ingham. The Window, which represents a person, has four panes or quadrants, as illustrated in Figure 8.1. Each quadrant represents an element of personal awareness:

- The public quadrant represents what is known by a person about themselves and which others also know about them.
- The blindspots quadrant represents things a person is not aware of about themselves, although these things are known to others.
- The private quadrant refers to things a person knows about themselves which they do not reveal to others.
- The unknown quadrant represents things about a person that are unknown both to themselves and to others.

A person can draw their own window, reflecting the relative sizes of each panel. Quadrants can change over time and in different situations. When a person seeks information, for example, by asking for feedback, the size of their public quadrant increases and so their blindspot quadrant decreases. When a person discloses information about themselves, the size of their public quadrant increases and their private quadrant decreases. Notice how change in the size of one quadrant affects the others.

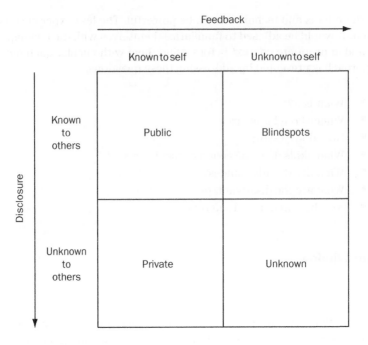

Figure 8.1   Johari Window

When should it be used?

The Johari Window can help clients to reflect upon how they see themselves in relation to others, and how they communicate with others. It can encourage the client to consider, for example:

- The blindspots quadrant: is there any mismatch between their view of themselves and how others see them? How could this be reduced?
- The private quadrant: how much do they share of what they are thinking and feeling? Could more (or less) disclosure improve trust and relationships?
- The hidden quadrant: do they have hidden talents or potential that is currently undeveloped?

How does it work?

The client is invited to draw their window and talk in as much detail as they wish about each quadrant and the relationship between quadrants. They can discuss any changes they would like to make in the relative sizes of the quadrants.

What skills does the coach or mentor need?

The coach or mentor needs to explain the Johari Window and prompt the client to consider the relative sizes of each quadrant, and their contents. For example, looking at the private quadrant, they might ask the client, either in relation to a particular context (e.g. a work team), or more generally:

- How much about your background and history do you tell others? About your personal and your professional life?
- How clear are you with others about what you are thinking? About what you are feeling? About your expectations of others? About what you want?
- What is the impact on your relationships of what you tell others, and what you do not tell them?
- Is there anything you would like to change? How would this improve your relationships and effectiveness?

What are the advantages?

The Johari Window can help a client to increase their self-awareness. They can review their assumptions about what information they can disclose or ask for, and whether they are getting useful feedback from others. They can gain insight into how others see them, and how their behaviour may affect the impression they make on others.

What are the disadvantages?

A client may feel that they 'ought' to disclose more about themselves or 'ought' to ask for feedback. There are risks in inappropriate disclosure and feedback, and clients should be encouraged to evaluate for themselves what might be safe and appropriate. The coach or mentor should avoid creating the impression that feedback and disclosure are always helpful, regardless of circumstances.

Are there any useful references?

Covey, S.R. (1989) *The Seven Habits of Highly Effective People*. London: Simon & Schuster.

Goleman, D. (1998) *Working with Emotional Intelligence*. London: Bloomsbury.

Luft, J. (1969) *Of Human Interaction*. Palo Alto, CA: National Press Books.

Luft, J. (1970) *Group Processes: An Introduction to Group Dynamics*. Palo Alto, CA: National Press Books.

Karpman Triangle

What is it?

The Karpman Triangle (Karpman 1968) is a way of looking at interactions between people. Sometimes people are stuck in unhelpful patterns of behaviour and they are unaware of these. When they recognize a pattern, they can make choices about changing it and behaving in ways which make them more productive and fulfilled. The Karpman Triangle describes one set of unhelpful patterns or 'scripts'. There are three roles: persecutor, rescuer and victim. These roles refer to states of mind. The persecutor role is 'it's all your fault'. The victim role is 'poor me'. The rescuer role is 'let me help you'. The roles are interdependent, so when one person breaks out of the script, or changes their role, the other two roles will change.

When should it be used?

The Karpman Triangle can help the client to become aware of patterns of interaction that they may unwittingly fall into, and which limit their behaviour and their potential. This awareness can enable the client to change their behaviour: to think, feel and act differently. It can also give the client useful insight into dysfunctional dynamics between others.

How does it work?

The client may notice that, in a particular context which is proving troublesome, they are habitually stuck in a role, and respond to others in a predictable way. They may find that they interpret experiences through the role, so it becomes a self-fulfilling prophecy. For example, a client may have a pattern of feeling helpless or powerless (victim) and looking for someone to help them (rescuer). They may see themselves as left out of important events and decisions or blamed by the persecutor when things go wrong. Challenging the victim mentality may help the client to reclaim their personal power, to become more assertive, and to take responsibility for their actions. Similarly, the rescuer may realize that others may not want or need rescuing. They can stop feeling guilty if they do not rescue others. The persecutor may see that they do not always have to take charge and take responsibility for others and their actions.

A person can find themselves in one of these roles as a reaction to the behaviour of another. The Karpman Triangle illustrates how the victim needs both an oppressor and a rescuer. The dynamic can go round and round with people caught in it, not realizing how they are being influenced to behave in particular ways, and Karpman called this the 'Drama Triangle', with predictable dramatic encounters. So, for example, the rescuer finds themselves blamed by the victim for not rescuing successfully: the rescuer has become the victim, and the victim has become the persecutor.

The client may be able to change the dynamic by noticing it, by re-framing their self-image and choosing to respond to others in a different way. For example:

> I must take care of everyone (rescuer)
>> becomes
> Sometimes people need help and sometimes they can take care of themselves

> I am hopeless and inadequate (victim)
>> becomes
> I have both power and also vulnerabilities

What skills does the coach or mentor need?

Skills of sensitivity as well as careful timing are needed. It can be challenging for a client to alter their view of themselves and their place in the world, especially if such role choices have affected much of their life. However, each client is different. Some clients change perceptions fairly readily. It may be that their role choices affect only a particular situation or group of people. A balance of support and challenge is needed and an awareness of the impact of trying out new behaviour. Suggesting further reading could be helpful to the client.

What are the advantages?

It can be liberating for the client to be freed from old, internalized scripts. Also, it can make the client aware of ways in which colleagues, friends and family may also be 'stuck'. This can help the client to try out different strategies with them. Powerful life changes can result.

What are the disadvantages?

Some clients may find it challenging to rewrite long-established scripts. When a client tries out new behaviour, colleagues and friends may be pleased, or may be upset. Support may be needed to help clients work through the realization that long-established scripts may have held them back. And finally, the coach or mentor (who, after all, may have their own scripts) should be mindful that scripts can play out in the coaching or mentoring session, with either party as persecutor, rescuer or victim.

Are there any useful references?

James, M. and Jongeward, D. (1971) *Born to Win*. Reading, MA: Addison-Wesley.
Karpman, S. (1968) Fairy tales and script drama analysis, *Transactional Analysis Bulletin*, 7(26): 39–43.
www.karpmandramatriangle.com

Career lifeline

What is it?

The career lifeline is a method of helping the client to look back at the development of their career in relation to other significant factors in their life. Having drawn a lifeline, they can then use this information to inform the discussion of future career plans.

When should it be used?

It can be used either as a start to a new coaching or mentoring relationship, perhaps in preparation for a first session, or as the occasion arises, for example, when a client is thinking of making a significant career move. It helps clients to do the following:

- raise awareness;
- identify 'choice points';
- spot external influences and internal drivers;
- note themes, patterns or trends;
- get a sense of 'the right time' for decisions and moves;
- see the factors which influence choices and decisions;

- identify threats;
- clarify values;
- link past to present;
- link present to future;
- identify resources and strategies.

How does it work?

The client is asked to make a pictorial representation of their career to date. They may choose to draw a graph in a timeframe, or a picture or other visual representation. If the lifeline is drawn as a timeline on a graph, the horizontal axis represents age in years and the vertical axis represents level of satisfaction (see Figure 8.2). One line may be drawn to represent career development and another superimposed to represent significant life events which may have affected the career lifeline.

In the example shown in Figure 8.2, the dotted line signifies the career journey through the years from age 15 to age 70. The solid line is the personal journey which sometimes intersects the career path, sometimes runs in

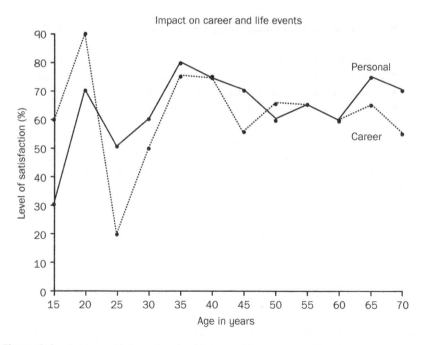

Figure 8.2   A career lifeline showing highs and lows across life stages

parallel and sometimes overlaps. In this example, the dips in levels of career and life satisfaction in the earlier years are far more marked. Some clients find the relationship between life events and career development very interesting. Others prefer to focus on a career lifeline, without a personal one. It is interesting to look at the obvious turning points and to explore what decisions were made at those times, what resources were available to the client, what influenced decisions, and what learning there may be now, from reflecting on these events.

After the lifeline has been drawn, the client is prompted to reflect on it. The coach or mentor may offer the client a list of questions, and the client can choose which they would find useful to explore:

- What do you notice about the line or about your drawing?
- Any patterns or themes about your career?
- How have you made educational and career decisions?
- Who/what has helped you in making decisions?
- Looking at high points, what inner strengths were evident?
- Looking at high points, what external conditions helped?
- Looking at low points, what would have helped?
- Looking at low points, what might you have done differently, if anything?
- What seem to be underlying values: the most important things to you?
- Identify three strengths that carry you through the hard times.
- What are the three most important features of a job for you now?
- What are your priorities for work–life balance?
- Where would you like to be in your career in X years' time?

Some people find graphs too limiting and prefer to be invited to draw a picture of the development of their career. The picture would still need to have some sense of development through time and possible linkages with significant life events.

What skills does the coach or mentor need?

This exercise needs plenty of time. It must be handled with sensitivity. The coach or mentor needs to leave enough time for adequate debriefing. The skills of active listening, open questioning, reflecting feeling, paraphrasing and summarizing are all essential. In addition, some supportive challenging may be helpful, leading to brainstorming possibilities for the future. At least one hour should be allowed for the exercise.

What are the advantages?

A career lifeline can be a way of accessing strengths, resources and values. It provides a creative way of looking at career development. It also provides a useful structure for a coaching or mentoring session.

What are the disadvantages?

It may trigger memories which need careful handling. Asking someone to reflect on their past may trigger memories of, for example, difficult life events. The coach should be ready to suggest further help and support if necessary.

Are there any useful references?

Bolles, R.N. (2002) *What Color Is Your Parachute? A Practical Guide for Job Hunters and Career Changers*. Berkeley, CA: Ten Speed Press.
Schein, E. (1990) *Career Anchors: Discovering Your Real Values*. San Francisco, CA: Jossey-Bass/Pfeiffer.

Role reversal

What is it?

Role reversal is an opportunity for the client to develop new perspectives on a problem by role-playing. It developed from the 'empty chair' technique used in Gestalt therapy.

When should it be used?

It is useful when the client is telling their story, in order to develop new perspectives and to challenge blindspots. It can also be useful when testing out new ways of negotiating or being assertive.

How does it work?

1 The coach or mentor asks the client to describe a typical scenario with person X, where there has been some difficulty or where the

      client wants to rehearse an interview or a meeting. They are asked to say exactly what X is like, what they might say, how they might feel and what they might do.

2   The coach or mentor then role-plays the scenario, with the client as themselves and with the coach or mentor playing the difficult person X. The scenario can be quite short, but enough time needs to be given for typical responses to be voiced.

3   There is then a debrief of what happened, asking the client to say whether X was portrayed accurately and, if so, what the client learned about both parties in the role-play.

4   It may be appropriate to then re-run that same scenario with the client trying out some different responses.

5   In addition, the client can be invited to be X while the coach or mentor takes the part of the client. This helps the client to empathize with X.

6   At the end of the exercise the debriefing should make clear what is role-play and what is reality.

What skills does the coach or mentor need?

The skills of role-playing. This requires clear instructions and the ability to flex between roles as the occasion demands. The skills of debriefing are needed to ensure that the client does not end up confused. Sensitivity is required because role-play can be a way of accessing previously unacknowledged ideas, feelings and actions.

What are the advantages?

It can bring a session alive. It is a quick way of finding out exactly what goes on in a difficult interaction. Skills of empathy, assertion and negotiation can be practised in a safe setting.

What are the disadvantages?

None, if it is done carefully, allowing enough time for debriefing. However, the coach or mentor should not assume that a client will want to use role-play. Some people do not like it at all. Some find it difficult to engage in a way that may seem artificial to them. Others engage readily but then find that the exercise touches a raw nerve. The wise and safe coach or mentor goes carefully and is ready to adapt at any stage in the process.

Are there any useful references?

Blatner, A. (1996) *Acting-In: Practical Applications of Psychodramatic Methods,* 3rd edn. New York: Springer.

Fritchie, R. and Leary, M. (1998) *Resolving Conflicts in Organisations.* London: Lemos & Crane.

www.mindtools.com has a section on role-playing.

Brainstorming

What is it?

Brainstorming is a technique that encourages creativity and lateral thinking by stimulating the creative right hemisphere of the brain. Hope, ideas, possibilities and optimism are encouraged, while critique and evaluation are discouraged. Brainstorming focuses on the future and possibilities, rather than the present situation and current facts.

When should it be used?

Brainstorming can help the client to describe their ideal future in relation to some aspect of the current situation. It can help them to respond creatively to questions such as 'How would you like things to be, ideally? What do you want instead of what you've got?' It can also be helpful in prompting the client to think creatively about different ways to achieve a goal: 'What are 101 ways to achieve X?'

How does it work?

The coach or mentor sets the scene and briefly explains the process, thus creating the conditions for successful brainstorming. They encourage the client to think forward in time, rather than staying in the present. The coach or mentor emphasizes that the client can:

- think about their ideal;
- take themselves to the future and imagine they are there;
- focus on what is happening in the ideal;
- generate as many ideas as possible, as quickly as possible;
- have fun: anything goes including seemingly implausible ideas.

The client is asked to imagine, in relation to the issue they have selected, what would be happening if things were much better, if they were ideal. They are asked to paint a verbal picture of their preferred future, as if they were already there. They are helped by prompts from the coach or mentor, who writes down verbatim all responses. The aim of the brainstorming session is to generate as many ideas as possible, regardless of apparent quality, and to encourage ideas even when the client is stuck, or has 'dried up'. Some possible prompts include:

- Ideally, where are you?
- Ideally, what are you doing/thinking/feeling?
- Ideally, what have you achieved?
- Ideally, what have you got rid of?
- Ideally, what have you gained?
- In your wildest dreams . . .?
- Ideally, what are others saying about you?

At the end of the brainstorming session, the client reviews the ideas and is helped to identify the most important ones and to formulate realistic goals. Brainstorming can also be used to identify possible strategies for achieving a goal. It follows a similar process, with the important difference that the client is asked to think about how they might ideally achieve their goal. The responses to the brainstorm are then used to identify realistic change strategies which will work well for the client.

What skills does the coach or mentor need?

Brainstorming is a fast-paced, upbeat process and the style of the coach should model hope and optimism. Staying focused, energetic and positive will encourage the client to produce as many responses as possible, and quantity rather than quality is what counts here. Their role is to encourage the client to stay future-oriented and think idealistically, since it is in seemingly implausible ideas that the seeds of possibility are sown. Some clients prefer to draw rather than use words, so coloured pens may be needed.

What are the advantages?

Brainstorming can be an effective way of encouraging clients to overcome problems and blocks, to reframe their ideas and think laterally, and to access the elements of the future that are really important to them. Brainstorming is powerful in helping people to identify what they really want, rather than what others say they should have, or what they think is achievable. It can tap into the values of the client and help them to establish goals and realistic action strategies which will work for them.

What are the disadvantages?

Brainstorming is a powerful process, with potential for harm as well as good. The client should not be left 'high and dry' in the face of a gap between their ideal and their reality, because this might leave them feeling hopeless or helpless. If this is likely, time must be allowed to help the client to identify realistic or feasible elements or actions from the brainstorming output. In this way, they can link the future with the present. In addition, clients can be surprised by their unexpected responses to brainstorming prompts, and it is important to explain clearly the brainstorming process in advance and check that they are ready to 'have a go'. They may need time after the brainstorm to discuss their reactions to what they have produced and any surprises. Also, some people find brainstorming difficult. The sensitive coach or mentor will 'stretch' the client without becoming too challenging or insisting on using a technique which is not helpful for that client.

Are there any useful references?

De Bono, E. (1992) *Serious Creativity*. New York: Harper Business.
Rawlinson, J.G. (1986) *Creative Thinking and Brainstorming*. Aldershot: Gower.
Rich, J.R. (2003) *Brainstorm: Tap into Your Creativity to Generate Awesome Ideas and Tremendous Results*. Franklin Lakes, NJ: Career Press.
Rickards, T. (1997) *Creativity and Problem Solving at Work*. Aldershot: Gower.

Visualization

What is it?

Visualization is a way of helping a client to imagine an ideal future. This could be an aspect of a current job that they want to improve, a new job, career, or any plan into the future.

When should it be used?

Whenever seems appropriate in trying to envisage a different or better future. It can be used as an alternative to brainstorming to develop wants and needs in a preferred scenario. It can be used whenever the client seems to be stuck and needs help in opening up possibilities. It can also be used to compare and contrast two or more different scenarios if each is visualized and debriefed in turn.

How does it work?

1   Explain the process to the client and ask if they would find it helpful.
2   Invite the client to make sure that they are comfortable and then to close their eyes and relax. They are then guided into relaxation, reminding them not to fall asleep! You can slowly remind them to relax their facial muscles, jaw, neck, shoulders, arms, hands and fingers. Then remind them to breathe slowly and deeply and gradually to relax their chest, abdomen, hips, legs, feet and toes.
3   Invite them to imagine their ideal. Let us take as an example a future job opportunity. The coach or mentor would ask the client to imagine their ideal job, perhaps that it is now X months ahead and they have been in the job for a while. Ask them to spend a few moments just getting into that picture, imagining what they are doing, who they are with, where this ideal job is and how they are feeling.
4   When they have built up a full picture, ask them to keep their eyes closed and, when they are ready, ask what they see. Prompt, if necessary, to get details.
5   When they have given you the picture, the full picture, you can then gently bring them out of the visualization by saying: 'Now you are going to leave that picture and slowly and gradually you can open your eyes and come back to this room, with me, on X date, in X location.'
6   When the client has opened their eyes, check they are OK.
7   Now debrief the visualization by helping the client to summarize what they found in their ideal picture that they want in their future job. They will also have probably clarified what they don't want!
8   Finally, the visualization exercise should lead to a critique of what will be realistic now to shape into some sort of goal.

What skills does the coach or mentor need?

This exercise can be a creative way of accessing ideas. The coach or mentor needs to appear relaxed and calm. It is best used by the experienced coach or mentor who has familiarized themselves with the technique in a safe and appropriate context before using it with clients. The process should be explained clearly and the client asked whether they would like to do this. While the client is visualizing, the coach or mentor needs to observe the client to check that they are relaxed. If there are any non-verbal signs of discomfort, the exercise should be reviewed immediately to see if the client wishes to stop. Appropriate prompts are used to guide the visualization (see the brainstorming section in this chapter for examples). Careful timing and debriefing are essential for safe practice.

What are the advantages?

Visualization frees up the imagination. It can feel very positive for the client. It helps them to access new and exciting possibilities. It can be a powerful way of comparing different scenarios.

What are the disadvantages?

Some clients may not like relaxation exercises or may find imaginative work difficult. It is important to check. It is possible that the gap between current reality and future dreams is so great as to make a client despondent. This would need to be addressed and time allowed for good debriefing. However, most clients are likely to find the exercise energizing and motivating. The coach or mentor needs to ensure that the client is well 'grounded' after the visualization experience and so it should take place well in advance of the ending of a session.

Are there any useful references?

McKay, M., Davis, M. and Fanning, P. (1981) *Thoughts and Feelings*. Richmond, CA: New Harbinger Publications.
Vickers, A. and Bavister, S. (2005) *Teach Yourself Coaching*. London: Hodder Arnold.
Whitworth, L., Kimsey-House, H. and Sandahl, P. (1998) *Co-active Coaching*. Mountain View, CA: Davies Black Publishing.

Goal setting

What is it?

A way of helping the client to focus on the future and on the outcomes that they want or need in relation to their problem, issue or opportunity. The client is encouraged to identify a specific goal (or goals), i.e. something that they can achieve. Setting and then achieving the goal make real the changes which the client has identified as important. There are various mnemonics that can help the client to set a specific achievable goal, including SMART and EXACT. An EXACT goal is: **EX**citing, **A**ssessable, **C**hallenging and **T**ime framed (Wilson 2014). Another useful idea is that of a well-formed goal (de Shazer 1991: 112), which is: small, relevant to the client, specific, achievable, hard work for the client, a beginning not an ending and doing something new rather than stopping doing something.

When should it be used?

It can be used at any point during the coach or mentoring session or relationship, providing the client is ready. Goal setting should not be imposed. Some clients move easily to goal setting. Others, perhaps those addressing difficult issues, may take longer to reach this point. Goal setting works well when the client has imagined the ideal future in relation to their issue, because it then follows naturally to ask the client about what aspects of their ideal may be achievable.

How does it work?

The coach or mentor explains the process, and checks that the client is willing to proceed. The client is invited to describe their goal using the following sentence:

'By . . ., I will have . . . and I will feel . . .'

After 'by', the client inserts a date. Specifying a date brings in a reality check. We find that short-term goals (days or weeks) are most useful for clients, even though they may have longer-term aims or ambitions.

After 'I will have' the client inserts a phrase with a verb describing what action will have been completed. 'I will have', rather than 'we will have' or 'they will have' ensures the client owns the goal and can influence whether or not it is achieved. 'I will have' is also a strong statement, a statement of achievement, rather than 'I hope to' or 'I will try to'; this challenges the client to identify a goal that they are really committed to.

'I will feel' checks that the goal is right for the client. There needs to be some positive emotion, even if only relief, attached to achieving the goal, otherwise it will not motivate the client.

The goal or mentor facilitates the process, however, it is important that the client is in the driving seat when shaping the goal itself.

What skills does the coach or mentor need?

As has been noted elsewhere, some clients find goal setting to be liberating while for others it can be challenging. The coach or mentor needs to be sensitive to the client and use the appropriate balance of support and challenge. They need to take care to move to goal setting only when the client is ready. They need to ensure that it is the client who determines the goal. It may take the client a few attempts to define and refine their goal, and the coach or mentor needs to allow space for this process and not rush it or take over.

What are the advantages?

Goal setting can help when clients are 'stuck' in their current dilemma. Because it is future-oriented, it can break a negative pattern of thinking and behaving, and mobilize hope and energy. It can help the enthusiastic client to capture their energy and convert hopes and wishes into specific outcomes. It can help when a client's ideas about the future are vague or half-formed, and bring their thoughts into sharper focus. Research (Page and de Haan 2014) suggests that positive coaching relationships with clear goals are more likely to have successful outcomes than those which are just relationship focused, and they stress the value of a collaborative coaching partnership which is goal-focused.

What are the disadvantages?

If the client feels that the goal setting process or the goal itself is being imposed on them, it will be of little benefit. A goal which seems to the client to be a target or an objective set by someone else will not have the motivating power of a goal which they own and define. The goal will feel like 'I ought' or 'I should' rather than 'I want' or 'I will.'

Similarly, when goal setting is introduced too soon into the coaching or mentoring process, before the client is ready, it will be unhelpful and seen as too strong a challenge or as an irrelevance.

Are there any useful references?

Davis, S., Clutterbuck, D., and Megginson, D. (eds) (2016) *Beyond Goals*. London: Routledge.
de Shazer, S. (1991) *Putting Difference to Work*. New York: Norton.
Wilson, C. (2014) *Performance Coaching*, 2nd edn. London: Kogan Page.

Cost-benefit analysis

What is it?

Cost-benefit analysis is a technique for comparing the expected costs with the expected benefits of a course of action, in order to decide whether to proceed. It can also be used to compare several possible options in order to choose the best one. A simplified version of cost-benefit analysis can help the client to evaluate their goal and decide whether to proceed, or whether the goal needs to be reconsidered.

When should it be used?

When the client needs to test their commitment to a goal or evaluate a proposed course of action.

How does it work?

The client clarifies their goal statement, and is then asked to list all the potential advantages of achieving their goal: for themselves, for other people and for their wider context, for example, the department, organization or family. They then list all the disadvantages for themselves and others and the wider context. The two lists can be thought of as balances on a set of weighing scales, and the client assesses whether the benefits outweigh the costs (see Figure 8.3).

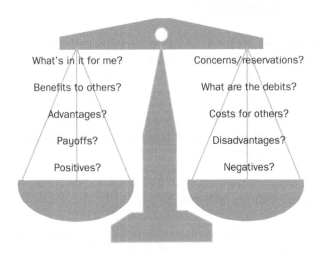

What's in it for me?   Concerns/reservations?

Benefits to others?   What are the debits?

Advantages?   Costs for others?

Payoffs?   Disadvantages?

Positives?   Negatives?

Figure 8.3   Cost-benefit analysis

What skills does the coach or mentor need?

The coach or mentor needs to use prompting questions to help the client identify all costs and benefits, some of which may have been overlooked.

What are the advantages?

The technique identifies the advantages of the chosen goal and thereby strengthens commitment to it. It also identifies disadvantages and can help the client to consider whether the gain is worth the pain, or whether any disadvantages could be minimized. It ensures that the client is really committed to a goal or course of action that is realistic for them.

What are the disadvantages?

The client may discover that the goal or action is unrealistic or not right for them. They may need to pause and reflect on how to proceed, or whether there is more exploration of issues needed. This may be seen as failure, and the client may become disheartened. If this is the case, the coach or mentor needs to be appropriately supportive.

Are there any useful references?

Egan, G. (2010) *The Skilled Helper*, 9th edn. Belmont, CA: Brooks/Cole.
www.mindtools.com describes this and other evaluation techniques.

Wheel of work/life

What is it?

The wheel of work and wheel of life pinpoint life and work activities and allow for exploration of areas of satisfaction and dissatisfaction. They also help to manage issues of work–life balance.

When should it be used?

Whenever the client is trying to prioritize and make decisions about work, career or work–life balance. It can also be used to help to understand why a client is feeling stressed, demotivated or demoralized at work or generally in life.

How does it work?

This tool is widely used by coaches and mentors. For the wheel of work, a blank template is provided, showing 10 possible hubs. Figure 8.4 gives an example of the 10 aspects identified by a client showing the least valued (1) as 'writing reports' and the most valued (10) as 'leading':

1   Clients are invited to make a list of 10 aspects of their work. They write these on a blank template of the wheel of work.
2   They are then given 10 stickers each with a number 1–10.
3   They are invited to place one of these on each spoke of the wheel according to how much they value that part of their work at present: 1 would indicate the lowest area of satisfaction and 10 would indicate the highest.
4   They are then asked to think about the proportion of time spent on each activity. For example, the client may put the '10' sticker on leading, indicating the highest value for that aspect of work, but the percentage of time given to leading is only 20 per cent of total work time.

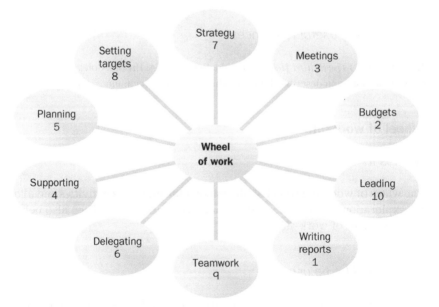

Figure 8.4   A wheel of work

The client can instantly see where the areas of satisfaction and dissatisfaction are. They may become clearer about what they value in work. They can also see the difference between what they want and need and what they have actually got. If this is the current situation with their job, they can then be invited to repeat the same exercise for their ideal job, and to compare and contrast the two wheels.

Another version of this is a wheel of life. This helps clients who have problems with work–life balance. The client can be invited to suggest their own categories for what they value in life. They may include areas such as partner, money, health, leisure, personal growth, spirituality, family, friends and career.

When areas on either of these wheels have been identified and prioritized, the client can move to goal setting around, for example, delegation, time management, career development, work–life balance, health, fitness and relationships. These exercises help clients to become clearer about what they value in work and life.

What skills does the coach or mentor need?

The skills of eliciting information from the client about the important categories in their life and work. The skills of open questioning and clarifying, as well as clearly presenting the techniques and instructing the client how to use them.

What are the advantages?

The wheels are a visual way of accessing important priorities and of noticing imbalances. They are something that can be done either in a coaching or mentoring session, or partly done between sessions.

What are the disadvantages?

The awareness of gaps between what the client wants and what they have got may require further support from the coach or mentor. This may not be a disadvantage, but is certainly something to consider.

Are there any useful references?

Francis, D. (1994) *Managing Your Own Career*. London: HarperCollins.
Robbins, A. (2004) *Awaken the Giant Within*. Riverside, NJ: Simon & Schuster.

Schein, E. (1990) *Career Anchors: Discovering Your Real Values.* San Francisco, CA: Jossey-Bass/Pfeiffer.

Vickers, A. and Bavister, S. (2005) *Teach Yourself Coaching.* London: Hodder Arnold.

Zeus, P. and Skiffington, S. (2000) *The Complete Guide to Coaching at Work.* North Ryde, NSW: McGraw-Hill.

Force field analysis

What is it?

Force field analysis is a technique derived from the ideas of the psychologist Kurt Lewin (1951). He said that all the forces and influences on a situation need to be taken into account in understanding that situation. If a person wants to change their behaviour, or change a situation, they need to look at the forces which might help move things in the desired direction, and the forces that are holding back change.

When should it be used?

Force field analysis can be useful at different stages in coaching or mentoring to do the following:

- Look at the forces which are holding a problem in place and those pushing for change. This analysis can help the client to identify blind-spots, new perspectives and a place to start in making changes.
- Test the realism of a goal and commitment to it. Force field analysis can help to identify the forces which support goal achievement and those that are restraining it.
- Test the feasibility of an action plan.

How does it work?

The following example illustrates how force field analysis can be applied to identify what will help or hinder goal achievement. In this example, the client's goal is physical fitness.

1   The client is asked to write down their goal statement with a vertical line drawn beneath it, as in Figure 8.5. Next, they draw horizontal arrows showing all the factors or forces which will support and assist the goal achievement, i.e. the *helping forces.*

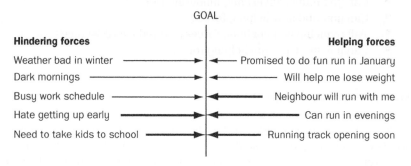

Force field analysis

By 31 December I will run three miles in 20 minutes
at least twice a week

GOAL

Hindering forces	Helping forces
Weather bad in winter	Promised to do fun run in January
Dark mornings	Will help me lose weight
Busy work schedule	Neighbour will run with me
Hate getting up early	Can run in evenings
Need to take kids to school	Running track opening soon

Figure 8.5   Force field analysis

2   The client is prompted to think about: forces under *their* control: things about themselves; forces dependent upon *others*: colleagues/ friends/family; forces *within the organization and wider context*: events, policies, norms.

3   The forces can be drawn in graphically, ideally in green, with bold arrows for large forces, and smaller, finer ones for less powerful forces.

4   The client then draws, ideally in red, all the *hindering forces* that will prevent them achieving the goal. As in Step 2, they consider forces under their control, forces dependent upon others and forces in the organization or wider context.

5   The final step is to consider which forces can be increased, diminished or diverted, to increase the likelihood of success.

This method could also be used to map the enabling and restraining forces impacting on a proposed action strategy. The action strategy would be drawn as the vertical line and the forces enabling or restraining successful implementation would be mapped.

What skills does the coach or mentor need?

The coach or mentor needs to prompt the client to identify the key helping or hindering forces. They then need to offer support and challenge to encourage the client to consider ways of shifting the balance of forces to increase the overall helping effect. The coach or mentor can use prompts, for example:

- Can you reduce/divert any hindering forces?
- Can you find new helping forces?
- Will reducing any enabling forces also reduce resistance?
- Can you increase any helping forces?

What are the advantages?

Force field analysis can make visible the positive and negative forces which have been previously overlooked. It can help the client reflect on their motivation, strengths and weaknesses, and also to reflect on the factors in their situation or context which will help or hinder them. Having identified these factors, the client selects manageable ones to work on and thus increases their probability of success.

What are the disadvantages?

No obvious ones, except that force field analysis is a visual representation, but not a science. A client may choose, even in the face of large restraining forces, to pursue a goal that is important to them.

Are there any useful references?

Lewin, K. (1951) *Field Theory in Social Science: Selected Theoretical Papers*. New York: Harper & Row.

Pedler, M., Burgoyne, J. and Boydell, T. (1994) *A Manager's Guide to Self Development*. Maidenhead: McGraw-Hill.

CAN model: conflict, assertiveness, negotiation

What is it?

There are many situations at work which require skilled negotiation in order to prevent or resolve conflict. CAN is a three-stage model which we have developed for understanding the processes of conflict management and for developing the skills of assertiveness and negotiation (Connor and Pokora 2007).

When should it be used?

Whenever the need arises. It can improve performance with individuals, groups or teams. It can help clients tackle difficult situations in meetings. It can be used as part of action planning.

What skills does the coach or mentor need?

The coach or mentor will need to model skills of empathy, assertiveness and negotiation. The ability to role-play will also be required. Alongside this, the coach or mentor needs to inspire the client with the confidence to 'have a go' at role-playing a conflict situation.

The coach or mentor can offer the model when a client experiences a conflict situation at work. It could be useful to go through all the stages of the model, rehearsing some of the skills and behaviours involved. This would require the coach or mentor to do some role-play in which they are the 'other party' in the negotiation. This would give the client invaluable practice and insight into ways in which the other party might experience them. It may be useful to reverse roles. The client is invited to get 'under the skin' of the other party by taking on their role, and the coach or mentor plays the role of the client. The debriefing of this exercise is important, in order to identify the learning points and to set goals for practising new ways of being assertive, and negotiating desired outcomes.

How is it used?

Box 8.1 demonstrates the process in full.

What are the advantages?

If the model is rehearsed within a coaching or mentoring session, it is an excellent opportunity for the coach or mentor to observe how the client might behave in a negotiation. Direct feedback can then be given and goals set for practice of assertiveness and bargaining skills.

What are the disadvantages?

Real life can never be completely replicated in a coaching or mentoring session. It is important to have a follow-up session with the client to check

Box 8.1   The CAN model

   Conflict → Assertiveness → Negotiation

CONFLICT

Conflict occurs when two or more parties want different things.

1   Understand the differences: ideas, values, power, processes, outcomes.
2   Listen carefully to the other party to find out where they are coming from.
3   Show that you empathize with their point of view or their expectations.

ASSERTIVENESS

Assertiveness means clearly, positively and realistically stating what you want.

1   Prepare your own case and consider how the other party will approach things.
2   Present yourself carefully: appearance, posture, facial expression.
3   Know what you want and be prepared to state it clearly and positively.

NEGOTIATION

Negotiation involves movement between different interests.

1   Be clear about what you want and need. List in order of priority what you could give to the other party without too much cost to yourself or to your organization and what you may not be able to give under any circumstances.
2   Negotiate. Acknowledge others' wants and needs alongside your own. Separate the person from the issue. Ask questions, find out what is behind the stated position. Be flexible to offers and creative alternatives.
3   Aim for win-win, but accept that compromise can also be a successful outcome. In many negotiations, the relationship as well as the outcome is important.

Note: Negotiation will work only if both parties are prepared to adjust to different interests.

how the negotiation went in real life and the learning from this. Forewarned is forearmed. Some of the recommended reading deals in more depth with reasons why all the best skills won't always work!

Are there any useful references?

Fisher, R. and Ury, W. (1987) *Getting to Yes*. London: Arrow.

Kennedy, G. (1992) *The Perfect Negotiation*. London: Century.

Stone, D., Patton, B. and Heen, S. (1999) *Difficult Conversations: How to Discuss What Matters Most*. London: Michael Joseph.

Critical path analysis

What is it?

Critical path analysis is a technique originally used when planning large, complex projects with interdependent activities and timescales. A simplified version can be used in coaching and mentoring to help the client to identify the action sequence necessary to achieve their goal.

When should it be used?

Critical path analysis is used in action planning when the client is considering the details of how they will implement their strategy and achieve their goal.

How does it work?

The client is asked to draw a horizontal line and mark their goal, with a date for completion at the extreme right. Working backwards from that date, they are then asked what needs to be done *before* that date in order to meet the goal deadline, and what needs to be done before that, and so on. Key actions, achievements and dates are plotted on the line, from right to left, eventually reaching the current date, i.e. the start point. The resulting line represents key actions and milestones along the path to achieving the goal. An example of using this technique might look like Figure 8.6 where a client is planning a team away-day on 23 October.

What skills does the coach or mentor need?

The coach or mentor may need patience and persistence in helping the client to stay focused on this task. Some may find it laborious, or over-detailed, and

1 Sept	10 Sept	15 Sept	8 Oct	15 Oct	23 Oct
Book venue	Meet facilitator	Circulate draft programme	Discuss with department	Circulate final programme	Team away-day

Figure 8.6 Critical path analysis

it may prove challenging for those, whether helping or being helped, who get bored easily or dislike detail.

What are the advantages?

A skilful coach or mentor helps the client to ensure the best possible chance of success when they act, and this technique can be a powerful aid. It identifies the sub-tasks which need to be completed, any that are interdependent and the timeframe associated with each. So, it enables the client to check the feasibility of goals and deadlines and helps them to clarify whether goals are achievable. The client may discover that their timescales need adjusting, or the goal refining, or that a critical step in the process needs more detailed consideration. Alternatively, this technique may confirm that the goal is achievable, and give the client a clear set of action steps. For longer-term goals, it is helpful in defining interim milestones.

What are the disadvantages?

The client may become disheartened if the goal proves unachievable in the timescale, and may need to be supported in redefining the goal or timeframe. It is important that they do not see this as a failure, but rather as a smart piece of advance planning.

Action planning does not always mean the end of a coaching or mentoring journey. In many cases the client will return to the next coaching or mentoring session to tell the story of what happened when they implemented their action plans. It is important that they feel adequately supported to return, even if plans have not gone entirely as anticipated, without feeling that they have 'failed'.

Are there any useful references?

www.mindtools.com describes critical path analysis and other planning techniques.

Summary

In this chapter we have:

- Introduced 12 tools and techniques that are used by coaches and mentors.

- Used a series of questions to evaluate each tool or technique.

- Explained the skills which would be needed by the coach or mentor and indicated where each tool or technique might be used within the coaching or mentoring process.

- Outlined the advantages and disadvantages of each tool or technique.

PART 3
Coach and Mentor Development

9 What is reflective practice, supervision and accreditation?

- Introduction
- Development
- Experience
- Reflective practice
- Supervision
- Accreditation
- Summary

Introduction

In Part 3 we focus on coach and mentor development, and in this chapter on the way in which experience, reflective practice, supervision and accreditation contribute to the development of the mentor or coach. In Chapter 10, there is an interactive case study raising issues for reflective practice. Chapter 11 addresses frequently asked questions. In Chapter 12, we share glimpses of nine coaches and mentors at work. They briefly talk about their coaching or mentoring role including any current issues or problems. They share high points, rewards, low points and difficult issues. They offer examples of what has worked well, and what has not worked so well. Finally, they share one piece of wisdom and a thought about the future of coaching and mentoring.

Development

Development is at the heart of coaching and mentoring work. In order to help clients, the coach or mentor continuously reflects upon their own practice. By doing so, they develop a more accurate perception of their levels of competence, they develop their capability and they monitor their capacity.

Hawkins and Smith (2006: 123, 206) identify three important elements for effectiveness:

- *competencies:* 'we see as the ability to utilize a skill or use a tool';
- *capability:* 'the ability to use the tool or skill at the right time, in the right way and in the right place';
- *capacity:* 'a human quality . . . rather than a skill and more to do with how you are rather than what you do' (2006: 123).

In order to develop these three elements you will need not only training, but also the experience of work with clients. It is important to reflect upon experience, not only afterwards, but also while it is happening. Reflection is valuable, particularly if you are not a full-time coach or mentor, but do use coaching or mentoring skills in your job. If this is the case, then formal supervision may not be appropriate. However, taking the time for reflection on the experience of using the skills – for example, in an action learning set or a co-mentoring or co-coaching arrangement – may well be useful. Development can take many forms. Here are two very different pathways. The mentor and coach have given permission for their names to be used.

> **Shelley was asked to coach staff** as part of her managerial role. She really enjoyed this aspect of her work but found difficulties with regard to confidentiality and experienced conflicts of interest in her role of both supporting the staff and yet ensuring that they achieved demanding performance targets. Some of her staff gave her feedback that the coaching was too hurried and too directive. She was upset by this and reflected on the situation. She decided that she needed to get some supervision for her work. She was amazed at how much this helped her to become more aware of herself and more confident in handling difficulties with staff. Her supervisor told her about some training opportunities and she has now started a certificate in coaching. She really enjoys meeting up with other coaches on a regular basis and is getting a much broader view of what coaching involves.

> **Gordon is a doctor,** who attended a mentor development programme. He enjoyed the programme, started mentoring, and a year later attended a follow-up day, where he met other mentors and heard about mentoring schemes. He influenced key stakeholders to fund mentor training for hospital consultants in the hospital where he worked. He helped out on these courses as a facilitator. At the same time he undertook research into doctors' attitudes to mentoring. He was able to use the research to influence his hospital to endorse a mentoring scheme. Further mentoring training programmes were run

and a group of trained mentors was established. These mentors, including Gordon, formed a support group, where they could practise skills and techniques and keep up to date.

 Read the list in Box 9.1, which elaborates on the six aspects of development shown in the Figure 9.1.

- In what ways are you currently developing?
- What would enhance your development?

Experience

We say to trainees on coaching and mentoring courses, 'The most important thing that you bring to your client is yourself.' The 'self' you bring includes: innate skills and abilities; values; personality; attitudes; experience of different types of people and relationships; knowledge of different organizations; and work contexts. We argue that this unique mix of knowledge and experience is what you bring to coaching and mentoring right from the start.

Figure 9.1   Six aspects of development

Box 9.1 Developing as a coach or mentor: a checklist

- *Experience:* what experience do you have of being a coach or mentor? Are there any ways in which you might extend this experience? Do you have experience of being a client? Do you get one-to-one support for yourself when you need it?
- *Reflective practice:* do you currently reflect on your practice both within and outside the sessions? Are you part of a coach or mentor support group? An action learning set?
- *Supervision:* do you have supervision? How regularly? Are you making the most of it?
- *Training:* what coaching or mentoring training have you attended? What future training would be useful to enhance your capabilities? Would you wish to pursue a course which had academic and/or professional accreditation?
- *Professional networking:* are you a member of a coaching or mentoring organization? Could you start up an interest group? Do you attend conferences and network to keep up to date with current trends?
- *Accreditation:* are you accredited or seeking accreditation by a national or international coaching and mentoring organization which promotes ethical codes of practice and/or which regulates standards in coaching and mentoring?

You may have been approached by colleagues at work, for informal help and guidance, or you may have a more formal coaching or mentoring role. Whatever the reason, it is useful to ask:

- Why do these people turn to me?
- What do I bring to them?
- In which of these situations do I feel most adequate or inadequate?
- What might help me to respond to them more effectively?
- Who could I trust to help me review my experiences?

Once you ask yourself these questions, and address the issues they raise, you have started to become a reflective practitioner.

> **Sue is a senior teacher** in a secondary school. In this role she was asked to mentor a junior colleague who was having difficulties managing particular pupils in his class. Sue spent a lot of time listening to stories of wilful and troublesome pupils but whenever she tried to help

the teacher to focus on his own responses to these pupils, he would change the subject. She began to feel quite powerless with him, she didn't want to work with him any more and yet she knew it was part of her role as staff mentor to do so.

 In Sue's situation, what would you have done?

Sue was fortunate that she was able to talk this situation over with a trusted colleague. She began to see that all the practical suggestions she had for improvement were falling on deaf ears and that she would need to take a step back and listen more empathically to his story before trying to move him towards action. This helped her to relax more in the session, and to listen to his anxieties and fears more fully before trying to work with action plans. She learned to be a mentor, rather than a teacher!

Reflective practice

Effective practice is reflective practice. Reflective practice involves an ongoing cycle of preparation, engagement/encounter with the client and then reflection on that coaching or mentoring work. The reflection may involve others, for example someone who offers informal feedback, a supervisor with whom you have a formal working agreement, or a peer supervision group (see Figure 9.2).

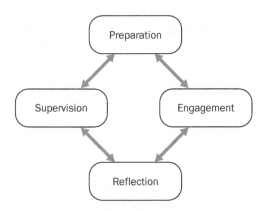

Figure 9.2   The four phases of reflective practice

Preparation: reflection before action

Preparation may involve any of a number of activities including:

- *extending* your knowledge of coaching and mentoring approaches and models;
- *learning* about appropriate tools and techniques;
- *doing* a continuing professional development (CPD) workshop;
- *finding* out about the organization or work context of your client;
- *ensuring* that you have considered how to work ethically with this client;
- *thinking* through what this client may want and/or need from you;
- *developing* an awareness of where your own limits and vulnerabilities may be;
- *becoming* aware of your strengths and how you will utilize them for the client;
- *checking* what a sponsor or manager expects from your work with this client.

Lara has realized how important it is to prepare before a coaching session. When she is meeting a client for the first time, she prepares how she will introduce herself and how she will negotiate a productive working agreement with the client. If the client has been 'sent' by the organization, she thinks through in advance of the first meeting with the client all the issues there could be concerning conflicts of expectation between the line manager, sponsor, client and herself as coach. She clarifies in her own mind what her stance is on confidentiality and rehearses how to discuss this with the client. She decides how to approach the issue of note-taking and records, and the practicalities of payment.

Ewan is mentor to a client in his own workplace: They have been meeting regularly for several months so that Ewan can share his experience of being a senior leader in the organization. He has got to the point of thinking that they are not making much progress and so he decides to attend a mentoring support group. In the group he rehearses some responses which he would like to use with his client. During the next session he uses creative questions to help the client shift the focus from problems to solutions. They both feel far more energized and positive at the end of the session.

Box 9.2   Some questions to address in preparation for work with a client

---

- What do I think the client wants and needs from me?
- What knowledge do I require for work with this client?
- What personal resources will I need?
- Will there be any boundary or confidentiality issues to address?
- What skills and tools will I need?
- What do I need to do before meeting my client?
- What would I like to achieve with and for this client?
- What will help and what will hinder, in me and in my client?

Engagement: reflection in action

At the heart of reflective practice is the encounter with the client, the capacity to be fully present with the client, and the ability to reflect on the session while it is happening (Figure 9.3). But what do you reflect upon within the session?

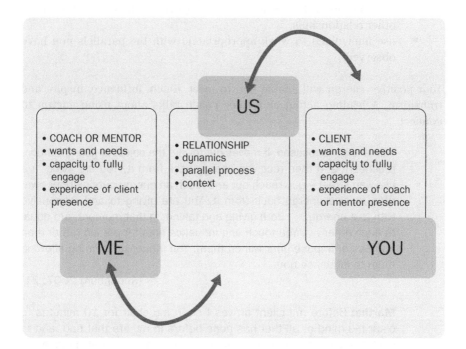

Figure 9.3   The dynamics of engagement

Let us start with *capacity* – in other words, 'how you are' with your client. We said earlier that the most important thing you bring to your client is yourself. The quality of your presence with your client will make a significant impact. The more fully present you can be in the encounter, the greater the level of engagement with your client. Presence involves awareness of self, awareness of the client, awareness of the space between and awareness of the developing relationship. To be fully present you need to do the following:

- be centred, grounded and alert throughout the session;
- focus all your attention on what your client is communicating both verbally and non-verbally;
- be aware of anything in yourself which is limiting you or distracting you from giving that full attention;
- notice what you are picking up and responding to, or conversely missing, from the client;
- spot patterns of thinking, feeling, and responding in both you and your client;
- notice what is happening in the dynamic of the relationship between you;
- reflect upon whether there are any parallels between the developing relationship in the session and the reports of the client about their other relationships;
- use immediacy to work appropriately with the parallels you have observed.

Your positive energy will enable you to meet, touch, influence, inspire and transform. A leading acting and voice coach talks about using energy to connect:

> Your energy is focused. It moves out toward the object of your attention, touches it and then receives energy back from it. You are living in a two-way street – you reach out and touch an energy outside your own, then receive energy back from it. You are giving to and responsive with that energy . . . Both giving and taking, in that moment, are equal to each other . . . You touch and influence another person rather than impress or impose your will on them. You influence them by allowing them to influence you.
>
> (Rodenburg 2007: 21)

> **Martha:** Before my client arrives I sit in my chair for 10 minutes to clear my mind of all that has gone before in my life that day, and to centre myself on the person whom I am about to meet. I close my eyes, take some deep breaths and listen to my body as I gradually

unwind. I notice that my muscles relax and gradually the noise in my head subsides. The noise, for example, of unfinished business or of tasks in my in-tray. As the noise clears, I sense some space and at this point I start to focus upon my client: what will he bring today?; what do I remember from last time?; what do I think he wants and needs from me today?; what can I give?; how can I ensure that however difficult the client, or his material, we will connect, we will truly encounter one another?

Let us turn now to a couple of lived experiences of coaches and mentors reflecting on their ability to engage fully with their clients.

> **Hal is an experienced mentor:** He knows his client well. They have been working together for some time now and they have a very productive working relationship. Hal usually emerges from the sessions energized by the capacity of his client to engage in their work together. The week before this session Hal had some bad news and wondered whether to cancel the session because he knew that his capacity to 'be with' his client would be affected. However, he decided to go ahead because he did not want to let his client down when the appointment had been agreed for some time. On the day, Hal was tired and found it difficult to concentrate. He noticed that this made him much more likely to be directive with his client, rather than really listening and allowing the client to arrive at his own conclusions. The atmosphere felt strained, as if the proverbial elephant was in the room without being acknowledged. As the session moved on, he wondered whether to apologize and share with his client why he felt less useful than usual. But he decided against this so that he did not burden the client with his own problems. The session ended amicably enough, but the usual level of connectedness had not been achieved. The capacity of the client in the session had been significantly affected by the level of capacity of the mentor.

 How would you reflect on this session if you were Hal? What would you do as a result of your reflection? What principles do you use in order to decide whether to disclose personal details to clients?

> **Maya is an executive coach:** I have always been very interested in the dynamics of the coaching relationship and I use knowledge and insights from psychodynamics and from transactional analysis to help me to

understand what affects my level of connection and engagement with
my client. These insights help me to notice when I start to experience
something that has resonance with what the client has told me about
their relationships in the workplace. For example, a client was talking
about his boss wanting him to be more strategic in his leadership role
at work. As the session developed, I realized that I was feeling frustrated with him. He seemed to be flooding me with operational details,
and was reluctant to get to grips with a wider picture. As I became
aware of this, I decided to share with him what I was experiencing:
'Trevor, I want to share with you something I have noticed that is happening between us. You mentioned that your boss was not completely
happy about your ability to be strategic. Well, I have noticed that in the
session, whenever we get the opportunity to look at the wider picture
and strategic direction for your unit, we seem to trail back again to
discussing day-to-day operations. I have started to feel frustrated that
we don't seem to be able to move forward. I wonder if what I have been
experiencing here mirrors what happens between you and your boss?'

Maya has the knowledge and confidence to be aware of parallels
between what happens in the coaching relationship and what
happens in relationships at work. Rather than reflect on it later, she
is able to respond to this insight immediately and as a result the
level of engagement between the client and coach deepens. What
would help you to be able to spot and respond to such insights?

Mel's mentor was so competent that on this particular day the session
was transformed. It had started in a way that felt really heavy, yet it
finished on an upbeat note. This energized Mel, who arrived that
morning feeling pretty powerless, having been told that his job was to
go in the next round of cuts. Somehow, this loss had triggered the
memories of other losses, particularly the death of his father a couple
of years previously. Mel poured out his story of loss, anger and abandonment. His mentor was aware that he could get sucked into the
misery of all of this unless he kept his focus and energy directed at
Mel. This he did and it was his ability to pick up metaphors such as
'hit on the head with a hammer' and 'black void' that made Mel feel
that this mentor was completely alongside him. Gradually the trust
built between these two people who had met for the first time that
day. By the end of the session, there was a real sense of connection
and energy between the two of them and Mel's powerlessness was

transformed into the will to go back to work and actively secure the best possible deal to take him forward to his next job.

 What would you have to be conscious of in yourself if a client came with issues such as Mel's? Would there be any memories of personal experiences which could distract you? Any difficulties staying positive when others are in pain? How would you keep the balance of energy in the room, between yourself and a client facing such loss and abandonment?

Box 9.3 Some questions for reflection during your encounter with a client

- What does my client want and need from me today?
- What do I notice about my client?
- What do I do with what I notice?
- What will the client be noticing about me?
- What positive or negative thoughts and feelings have I got towards the client?
- Are these telling me anything about how the client is with others outside of the session?
- What do I do with this awareness, if anything, in this session?
- Am I being too directive, forceful, laid back, critical, colluding?
- What can I do about that?
- What is my energy level today? What about energy from the client?
- What am I missing?
- Am I keeping my eye on time, boundaries and outcomes?
- How am I ensuring that my client will be leaving this session with plans for action?
- How am I helping my client to leave this session feeling supported, affirmed and sustained?

Reflection on action: after the session

Schön (1983) contributed greatly to our ideas about reflective learning and draws attention to the distinction between *reflection-in-action* and *reflection-on-action*. In the previous section we focused on ways in which the coach or mentor reflects upon what is going on in the encounter with the client, in the here and now, by trying to be fully present. But that is not enough. After the session the coach or mentor needs to reflect 'on the action' of the session: involving the client, the coach or mentor, and the relationship between the two. This can be done alone, perhaps with the aid of a reflective practice log and workbook, or with peers or a colleague as part of what Hay (2007) calls 'intervision'. It could also be done, most profitably, with a supervisor. We will consider the role of supervision more fully in the next section.

It helps to set aside some time immediately after a session to reflect on what happened. Some coaches and mentors make audio recordings of sessions, but they do this with permission from the client and with the awareness of issues of confidentiality. The first thing to do is to allow yourself to reflect upon the session in a broad way, noticing what aspects come most easily to mind. Then use some prompts to see what else might have been going on. To do this, our mnemonic, REFLECT, can be very helpful (Box 9.4).

Box 9.4   Connor and Pokora's REFLECT mnemonic

Resources	*Competence, capability and capacity of both?*
Expectations	*What were the wants and needs of both?*
Flow	*What was going on in the relationship?*
Limitations	*What inhibits progress?*
Experience	*How was the session experienced by both?*
Content and context	*Was the session appropriate and manageable?*
Time, outcomes, action	*Were specific, valued, outcomes achieved?*

You may decide to use a more structured reflective practice log or brief. Box 9.5 gives an example of one used by some trainee coaches and mentors. Other examples of reflective practice logs and questionnaires can be found in resources such as Hay (2007).

At this point we shall look in more depth at the ways in which supervision closes the loop in our four-stage model of reflective practice. However insightful we are as coaches and mentors, we all have our blind spots and so reflective practice on our own will always be limited. We all need our resident 'internal supervisor' but we also need an external supervisor to ensure that our reflections lead to new learning with the help of different perspectives.

Supervision

Working as a coach or mentor can be stimulating, challenging and demanding. Supervision and support provide a confidential context for the coach or

---

Box 9.5   Example of a reflective practice log

Date of session: _____   **Length of session:** _____

1 What did the client want and need from you?
2 What did you want and need from the client?
3 How did you begin?
4 What approach were you using?
5 What skills and/or tools did you try to use?
6 How did you end the session?
7 What do you think that you did well? How did the other person benefit?
8 What, in retrospect, would you like to have done differently?
9 What do you need to practise, research or brush up on now?
10 Now that you have reflected on this session, how would you describe your coaching/mentoring style?

---

mentor to discuss their work and any problems associated with it. Importantly, the coach or mentor is the focus of the conversation, not the client. The European Mentoring and Coaching Council (EMCC 2016) have produced valuable guidelines for supervision, which list three functions and six competencies. These address important aspects of contracting and managing the supervisory relationship, support for both coach and client, maintenance of standards and good ethical practice. Hawkins and Smith (2010: 383) present three elements in coaching supervision:

1   Coaching the coach on their coaching.
2   Mentoring the coach on their development in the profession.
3   Providing an external perspective to ensure quality of practice.

They discuss supervision as *transformational* in the sense that the understanding which emerges from the process of sharing gives new insights and develops new perspectives on self, the client, self with client, work, and the context of work. The supervisor must be competent in enabling the coach or mentor in each of these areas. A knowledge of the psychology and dynamics of the coaching relationship is necessary, but so also is a knowledge of the organizational contexts, problems, issues and opportunities brought by the coach or mentor.

Not all writers assume that supervision is always beneficial. Jenny Rogers (2016: 275) argues that the jury is still out, because there has been so little research on coaching supervision to date. However, she discloses some of her own experience:

> I have worked with seven different supervisors in my coaching career. All have contributed something different to my own development but what they have in common is that their impact on me was to increase my feelings of *prudent confidence*. I have heard many other coaches describe the same thing and have heard it at first hand from my supervisees. But does a prudently confident coach do better work? We assume that this is so, but it is hard to prove.

Rogers draws attention to some of the problems of supervisors – for example, a supervisor with less knowledge, experience, wisdom or ability than the person they are supervising, or a supervisor with more blind spots, neediness, rigidity or blind adherence to particular coaching approaches than the person being supervised.

The alternative to individual supervision is peer co-supervision or group supervision. Terminology can be confusing, because the term 'supervision' is not used everywhere. Co-supervision and group supervision may be referred to as 'coach or mentor support'. However, they potentially offer the same benefits, helping mentors and coaches to work safely and effectively, to avoid burnout, to refer appropriately and to continue to develop skills and self-awareness.

The importance of supervision is well recognized in many helping professions, and it is mandatory in some. In coaching and mentoring, the AC & EMCC *Global Code of Ethics* (2016) requires that all members have regular supervision. The APECS *Ethical Guidelines* (see Appendix for websites) refer to ongoing and regular supervision. In practice, the definition of 'regular' varies according to the nature and amount of coaching or mentoring work undertaken.

Approaches to supervision

Just as there are a wide variety of approaches and theories in coaching and mentoring, so there are in supervision. In fact, the approaches to supervision often arise out of those that are used in coaching and mentoring. Some have more of a psychological base, whether more humanistic, as in the non-directive approaches, or with an emphasis on understanding the psychodynamics of the coaching and mentoring and supervisory relationship, as with Gestalt, neuro-linguistic programming (NLP) and transactional analysis (TA).

Others have more of an organizational and functional emphasis. But all approaches need to address the key competencies required by the professional and regulatory bodies for coaching and mentoring.

Perhaps one of the most widely used models is the 'seven-eyed process model' of Hawkins and Smith (2010: 159). For a very useful explanation of this model it is well worth referring directly to their work. They refer to 'seven modes' and these are illustrated as interconnecting circles:

1   *Client:* focus on the client and what and how they present.
2   *Supervisee:* exploration of strategies and interventions used.
3   *Relationship between client and supervisee:* conscious and unconscious.
4   *Supervisee:* focus on bringing self and client fully into awareness.
5   *Supervisory relationship:* focus on working alliance and parallel process.
6   *Supervisor:* focus on own process.
7   *Contexts:* focus on the wider contexts in which the work happens.

One way to approach supervision is to consider the main tasks required in order to help supervisees develop competence and confidence. These are listed in Box 9.6.

Box 9.6   Some tasks of supervision

- Clear contracting: safe boundaries and containment
- Providing supportive space for wide-ranging and deep reflection
- Working with the story
- Pushing the boundaries of the imagination
- Tapping into resources
- Developing the alliance
- Working with parallel processes
- Bringing the unconscious into awareness
- Challenging blind spots
- Offering new perspectives
- Using tools and techniques
- Working with 360-degree feedback
- Rehearsing new behaviours
- Supporting leaps of faith
- Transforming the capacity to function
- Learning about and learning from

The Association for Professional Executive Coaching & Supervision (APECS) refers to supervision as:

> the relationship between the coach and a qualified person who is not in any managerial relationship with the coach wherein the coaching work with particular clients may be discussed in strict confidence with the purpose of enhancing the quality of the coaching work and of ensuring client safety.
>
> (see www.apecs.org)

The Association for Coaching (AC) notes that while supervision is a formal arrangement for maintaining adequate standards of coaching provision, 'it is also a supportive process. Supervision has sometimes been called "Super Vision" as a way of demonstrating that it is not restrictive or prescriptive but rather a process for increasing creativity' (see www.associationforcoaching. com). Both these definitions draw attention to the formal nature of supervision, as a planned, purposeful activity and something more than a casual chat. The EMCC *Guidelines on Supervision* (2016) list seven criteria recommended for choosing a supervisor. Box 9.7 lists some questions in relation to making such a choice, derived from the EMCC criteria and adapted. Some of these questions may be more important to you than others, and this may give you some clues about who will be the right supervisor for you.

Box 9.7   Questions for choosing a supervisor

- Has the person been a coach, mentor or client?
- What coaching/mentoring framework do they use? Is this compatible with yours?
- Have they been supervised?
- How much/what type of experience do they have as a supervisor?
- Are they available for supervision at times/frequency to suit you?
- Have they been trained in supervision?
- What framework do they use for supervision?
- Do they communicate respect, empathy and genuineness to you?
- Can they be impartial as your supervisor (i.e. no conflicting roles)?
- Do they possess the qualities/skills which you are seeking in a supervisor?
- Do they subscribe to a code of ethics or belong to a professional body?
- Do they understand the context in which you work?

Julie works as a coach and mentor: I've known my supervisor for a long time. She taught on a coaching programme I attended, so I knew we both used the same coaching framework. I didn't think about asking which supervision framework she used. However, there was something about her quality of listening and attending that really impressed me even though she didn't know too much about the context in which I work. She just seemed like the right person and now that we have worked together I know that she is.

In a report published by the Association for Coaching (AC) (2007: 6), based on an online survey of members to which there were 300 responses, the main reasons given for choice of supervisor were: someone from whom the coach would receive honest feedback about strengths and areas for development; someone who was qualified and experienced; someone who was a member of a professional body; someone with experience within an organizational context. The respondents in this survey put five benefits of supervision in rank order:

1 Provides a basis to learn and develop (95 per cent).
2 Provides a place to discuss ethical issues/concerns (93 per cent).
3 Offers a trusting and open relationship (78 per cent).
4 Offers maintenance and stability of practice (76 per cent).
5 Offers opportunities to increase our creativity (74 per cent).

This result concurs with our own experience. However, we would say that in supervision, offering a trusting and open relationship is the foundation upon which learning and development take place. This is the direct parallel with coaching and mentoring. This relationship then enables the supervisee to feel safe, to address ethical issues and concerns honestly, and to face difficulties with courage. By their nature, ethical issues are never straightforward. There are no easy answers. (See Chapter 4 for a more thorough discussion of these matters.) What appears to be an ethical issue with a client often takes the coach or mentor back to an examination of their own values, beliefs and attitudes, both conscious and unconscious. In order for this to happen in a productive and transformative way, the supervisor has to be a safe, trustworthy and respected person.

Supervision has been described as fulfilling several roles: normative, formative, restorative and perspective (Inskipp and Proctor 1989; Bond 1993). Applying these headings to coaching and mentoring, supervision may:

• help the coach or mentor to work safely, ethically and legally (normative);
• help the coach or mentor to learn and develop skills and understanding (formative);

- support the coach or mentor in dealing with the demands and stresses of the role (restorative);
- help the coach or mentor to maintain an overview of their work, and connections with other ways of helping (perspective).

Box 9.8 provides a list of some of the benefits of supervision and support for the coach or mentor. How do they apply to you? Are some more important than others?

For more information on supervision, you may wish to refer to the guidelines produced by some of the professional bodies listed in the Appendix.

Box 9.8   Possible benefits of supervision and support

- Anticipating problems and avoiding/minimizing them
- Working as effectively as possible
- Responding to clients who are challenging
- Developing skills and confidence
- Getting support
- Maintaining perspective
- Staying connected with other approaches
- Maintaining boundaries and working ethically
- Developing self-insight
- Working fairly and valuing diversity
- Challenging assumptions about self and others
- Testing new ideas and keeping up-to-date

Two perspectives of supervision follow, in which there has been a good match between coach and supervisor. Leon is the coach and Ben is the supervisor.

Leon and Ben

My name is Leon and my supervisor is Ben. I run my own coaching business and I want to make the most of my supervision sessions, not least because I am paying for them myself. I always prepare for them by keeping a notebook of my work with clients. I don't write a lot, but I do like to pinpoint key things to bring to supervision, and I do this immediately after each session. Ben starts by asking what I want to talk about and I usually have three or four main things from two or three clients. We look at how to divide the time and then Ben keeps his eye on the clock so that we always have 10 minutes at the end to give each other feedback on the session. At the end of the session Ben asks me, 'What went well for you, what did you appreciate and what would you like me to have done differently or better?' At first, Ben seemed to find it difficult to know when to stop me in my tracks and when to let me just continue telling a rather lengthy story. As we have got to know one another, he seems more relaxed, realizing that I can actually do most of the work for myself, if he can just allow me the space to find the answers and solutions within me. What I have really valued in my supervision sessions is being helped to recognize when I have been vulnerable with a client in a way that I had not been able to admit before. He is so accepting that whatever thoughts and feelings get played out unwittingly with my clients, he will not only spot them, but do it in such a way that I am actually pleased to have realized what was really going on. That's what the books don't often tell you about supervision! That if you are using it properly, you lay yourself on the line and all sorts of things come to the surface. I have been surprised how often we talk about my current personal state, and patterns from my past, in relation to understanding me with my client. Ben works with the parallel processes he notices, things happening with us and between us, which seem to resonate with what I have told him about me and my clients. Those insights have helped me to be much sharper at noticing them when they happen with a client. I am even becoming skilled at how I then work with the insight in the here and now of a session.

As well as talking about work with clients, I get supervision on how I am managing the developments and changes in my business. You can't really do one without the other, because the whole context of my client work is the business. Ben doesn't want to advise me about it, but he helps me to see how relationships with business clients, fellow colleagues and sponsors impact on the resources I have and how they get allocated and distributed. Some of my 'clients' are groups or teams, and some are individuals. Often, I get supervision on how I can manage the confidentiality issues when coaching a team and then coaching them all individually as members of that team. Of course, another issue for me is when there has been a conflict of interest between the sponsor of a coaching intervention, and the individuals being coached.

My name is Ben and I supervise Leon. *Leon knows what he wants and usually arrives, notebook in hand, with important issues highlighted for discussion. He knows how much time we have, and I encourage him to tell me how we will use our time on the different issues. Sometimes it will be a couple of quite separate client issues, sometimes something about his own development, for example, further training needs. Sometimes there* *are personal issues which he has noticed are impacting on his ability to 'be' with clients, whether these are health issues or unfinished business from past significant relationships. Sometimes the personal issues are about confidence and self-esteem. Leon drives our agenda and I help him to navigate his own choppy waters! Sometimes he is causing the waves himself, and sometimes the turbulence of his clients is causing a lack of equilibrium. Sometimes we notice patterns among issues presented by his current clients, or patterns in the way they are dealing with them and this can lead to important 'aha' moments in the session. Sometimes we notice that what Leon says is happening with clients starts happening in the room, with us. I always try to notice when this is occurring, and give us time to reflect on what's going on and what we may learn from that.*

One of my issues as a supervisor is how much I should be intervening with someone who is so capable of learning from his own reflection. It feels like a balancing act most of the time, between allowing the space and encouraging focus. So at these moments when I'm not sure what to do, I say to myself, 'What would Leon benefit most from now?' Then I usually ask him! It sounds obvious doesn't it, but during a session as a supervisor I can get sucked into collusion with a supervisee without being conscious of what's going on, unless I stay really sharp and keep asking myself that key question, 'What is going on here?' If my supervisee is filling all the space with words so that I can't make a response, does that tell me how he or she is with clients? Are the words serving to keep a distance between us, or is it that my silence is unnerving him so he has to fill the space?

I have mentioned the importance of using my own 'internal supervisor' to reflect on the dynamics in the here and now of the supervision session, but we also do a number of more practical things as well. We talk about different approaches and tools that can be used with clients. We engage in role-play and rehearse client situations where I take the role of the client so that Leon can try out new approaches and techniques in a safe place. We spend time looking at his work with colleagues as well as with clients and we always have an eye on how the coaching business is developing. Some of the organizational issues we work on include how to manage conflicts of interest and confidentiality between organizations sponsoring the coaching and the individual clients whom Leon sees for coaching.

Accreditation

This section will be of particular interest to those who are working full-time as coaches or mentors and to those who may be considering purchasing coaching or mentoring services.

Competence, capability and capacity

The term 'competence' refers to the ability to perform to recognized standards. It implies successful performance against specific criteria – that, for example, a coach or mentor is 'fit for purpose'. While competence approaches have become popular in recent years, questions about their limitations have been raised. One of the issues highlighted by Burgoyne is 'whether performance can be divided into competencies and then re-integrated' (1990: 20), and the same question may be asked about coach and mentor competencies. The undoubted usefulness of competence frameworks in coaching and mentoring must be weighed against the risks of reductionism through the adoption of a 'tick box' approach to professional competence. One way of addressing this concern is to ensure that accreditation processes assess capability and capacity as well as competencies.

This is a challenge for coach and mentor training, and accreditation. Robust training and accreditation procedures should reflect not only competence at a given moment, but also capability, including the individual's willingness to monitor their own performance and development, and to be self-reflective. In addition to competencies and capability there is the importance of developing the *capacity* of each coach or mentor. This will vary according to individual resources at any given time. Supervision and support, alongside CPD, are the processes which enhance the ongoing capacity to learn, enabling the coach or mentor to maintain professional effectiveness.

Competence frameworks

In Chapter 2, there is a section called 'reflecting on competencies'. Our nine key principles for effective practice reflect these competencies. We give examples from two international professional bodies which have been at the forefront of developing competence frameworks alongside codes of ethical practice, as a basis for sound credentialing (the International Coach Federation, ICF) and accreditation (EMCC). The ICF has outlined four clusters of core competencies (see www.coachfederation.org): (1) setting the foundation; (2) co-creating the relationship; (3) communicating effectively; and (4) facilitating learning and results. The EMCC highlights eight coaching or mentoring competence categories (see www.emcccouncil.org) which include: understanding self, self-development, contracting, relationship building, enabling insight and learning, outcome and action, use of models and techniques, and evaluation.

There is currently considerable interest in the accreditation of coach and mentor training programmes, of individual coaches and mentors and of supervisors. This reflects a concern that those hiring or receiving coaching and mentoring services should know how to judge the competence and professionalism of the individual coach or mentor. In the UK, the CIPD has produced guidance for organizations wishing to develop coaching and mentoring and wanting to know what to look for when hiring coaches or mentors (CIPD 2015).

An example of training accreditation is the EMCC European Quality Award (EQA) (EMCC 2015) for coach and mentor training, which has four award categories. Capability indicators (CIs) are used to assess competence in each of the eight competencies listed in Chapter 2, and they are mapped against the four award categories, which are: foundation, practitioner, senior practitioner and master.

> The progression principles used are: at each 'higher' level, the CIs should describe the greater breadth and depth of knowledge; greater synthesis of ideas; ability to evoke more significant insights; working effectively with increasingly complex issues and contexts; and, at the higher levels, the creation of a coherent personal approach to coach/ mentoring.
>
> (EMCC 2009: 14)

The foundation level requires a minimum of 20 study hours, whereas the master practitioner level requires a minimum of 1,800 study hours and within this the coaching practice varies from 6 hours at foundation level to 252 hours at master practitioner level.

An example of individual accreditation is the ICF credentialing programme, with three designations: associate certified coach, professional certified coach and master certified coach. Each designation requires a set amount of coach-specific training, minimum coaching experience hours and minimum number of clients. These vary from 100 coaching hours at associate level to 2,500 coaching hours at master level. The number of clients required varies from at least 8 at associate level to at least 35 at master level (see www. coachfederation.org for more information).

The advantages of professional accreditation are not just in the outcome, but also in the learning that takes place during what can be quite a lengthy journey. Many people admit that their main reason for gaining accreditation is so that the stamp of approval will enhance their reputation and career prospects. It will be increasingly important to be accredited as purchasing organizations become more knowledgeable about the standards that can be expected from a coach or mentor, and as the number of available coaches and mentors increases. There is evidence that this is already happening. Our view is that the learning journey which will take you towards accreditation, though long and hard, can be a unique opportunity for CPD and networking.

Joss explains his experience of 'going-for-accreditation'

I had been a mentor for several years in my own organization and eventually I decided to go part-time so that I could do some training with a view to becoming a full-time coach and mentor. I chose the course carefully, it was one that was accredited academically by my local college but it was also accredited by the EMCC with the EQA. I was able to fit in the main workshops for the part-time course, but I did find it difficult at first to have enough clients for the mentoring practice sessions that we had to do and write up. I almost got panicky about this after the first few months but others on the course helped me to work out how to extend my hours of experience. We each had a course supervisor and we had to tape our sessions and play extracts back within an action learning set of four course members. I learnt so much from this. It was amazing to hear how other people mentor and coach, some so different from me.

We also had to keep a portfolio of all our learning. This was quite onerous to keep up to date. It included a reflective log of all practice sessions, both on and outside of the course. We were told that some of these could count towards individual accreditation hours, if we decided to go for that. When I read over my reflective practice log and journal I realize how difficult it all was at the beginning, and how I nearly gave up. But I stuck it out with plenty of support and guidance from my tutor and also from my wonderful action learning set. The theory of coaching was very interesting but I did find it hard doing the written assignments and I needed a lot of help with these. Well, after an unsuccessful first try at the certificate I resubmitted my supervised practice file and passed!

I am now enrolled on the diploma and I am working up my hours so that I can apply for individual accreditation soon after finishing the diploma. I wanted this so that my clients (individuals and organizations) would know that I am professionally qualified for the job. But, you know what, the reason I want it now is not so much to satisfy my clients as to satisfy me. It gives me some sort of assurance that what I am doing is on the right lines. Yes, I will make mistakes, but I know what to do and how best to proceed if things get difficult with a client. I have regular supervision, both group and individual. It is challenging, but very valuable. I am confident that I am up to date with developments in the profession of coaching and mentoring, and I have developed my own awareness to the point of being confident that I will be a 'good enough mentor'. I intend to move through the accreditation levels to master practitioner and I know that will take quite some time. But during that time I will be part of a stimulating, challenging and supportive network of coaches and mentors helping one another for the benefit of our clients.

Summary

In this chapter we have:

- Introduced aspects of coach and mentor development.

- Considered the value of learning from experience.

- Presented a four-stage model for reflective practice.

- Used several case examples to illustrate reflective practice.

- Discussed several aspects of supervision.

- Presented the perspectives of a supervisor and supervisee who work together.

- Discussed aspects of accreditation together with a case example.

10 How can I be reflective in practice?

> - Introduction
> - Your client: Paul
> - Session 1: Building the relationship and negotiating a working agreement
> - Session 2: Developing the relationship and managing the agenda
> - Session 3: Being resourceful and listening to your 'internal supervisor'
> - Summary

Introduction

This chapter is a case study to stimulate your thinking about some of the issues that arise when you are with a client. We hope it will help when you have to 'think on your feet', respond, and then reflect on your response both during the session and afterwards, perhaps in supervision. It is designed to help you to consider these questions:

- How do the key principles help me?
- What are some of the ethical and professional issues that may arise?
- What sorts of issues might I take to support and supervision?

Paul has asked you to be his mentor, and your first three sessions are explored in this chapter. You will have an introductory session with him and then two more sessions. There are interactive prompts and questions throughout the chapter, as well as explanations of how the principles of effective coaching and mentoring apply. You will find it useful to review the nine key principles for effective practice (see Chapter 1) before reading the case study. At various points you are asked to:

- reflect on what is happening;
- consider your response;
- decide how you will help the client.

Your client: Paul

Paul has recently completed his induction into the role of branch bank manager. This included a leadership development programme with coaching sessions. It has helped build his skills and confidence in working with his own staff, as well as with other managers. He has asked for some regular mentoring to support development in his new role. In particular, a challenge for Paul is how he can manage issues with one of the counter clerks. He also wants some help in managing the expectations of his own area manager. He has chosen you because you work for the same organization. He met you on the leadership course, and he respects you.

Key principles for effective practice

When working with Paul it will be useful to keep in mind the nine key principles for effective practice. They are shown in Figure 10.1. For an extended discussion of each of the principles, refer back to Chapter 1.

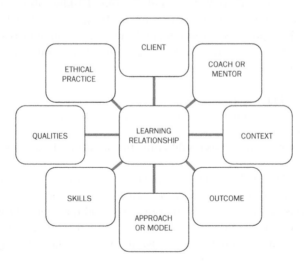

Figure 10.1   Nine key principles for effective practice

Session 1: Building the relationship and negotiating a working agreement

---

PRINCIPLES INTO PRACTICE

The context of the mentoring is Paul's development as a bank manager.

The agenda is his, and you facilitate the process.

You share **a model for change** and he decides whether to use it.

The outcome he wants is to become more skilful at managing and influencing in the organization.

The learning relationship is crucial because he has stated that he wants to learn from you as someone he respects.

The qualities of respect, empathy and honesty build rapport and trust.

The skills are active listening, appropriate sharing and negotiating.

Ethical issues include the possibility of blurring of boundaries because you work in the same organization.

 You are the mentor. What do you want to achieve in your first session with Paul?

How would you negotiate a working agreement? Refer to Chapter 2 for an example of a working agreement. Are there any areas that may be particularly important?

How will you decide if you can work together or not?

This is the first meeting with Paul. It is for both of you to find out if you can work together. You start by asking him how he would like you to help. This gives you valuable insight into his expectations. You are able to clarify what you can offer in terms of time, commitment, experience and knowledge. He says that he needs help with leading and managing colleagues. He would like to meet for two or three sessions initially. You agree to this. You suggest that you put time aside at the end of each session to review how you are working together. You give him a copy of the working agreement and allow him time to look over it and ask any questions. You explain your approach, and again ask if there are any questions.

Looking at the working agreement immediately raises the question of confidentiality, and Paul asks if everything in the sessions will be confidential.

 Here are some responses to Paul's question about confidentiality. Which would you make? Or is there a better one?

- Oh, yes, definitely.
- I have some ideas about what the limits are. Would it be useful to talk about these?
- The sessions are completely in confidence unless there are legal or professional limits placed upon our confidentiality. We would both be bound by these. You can choose what you wish to disclose to me. If I was concerned about having to share some information with another person, we would talk about it first, and I would help you, where possible, to take the initiative to disclose. How does that sound?

Another issue for clarification, because you work in the same organization, is about conflict of interest.

Paul: Can I just check? You're a senior manager in this bank. If I told you that I was having difficulty meeting various targets and objectives, what then? If I tell you that one of my staff is underperforming, what would you do?

 Would the response below adequately answer Paul's question. If not, what do you suggest?

Mentor: When the mentoring system was set up we agreed that my first responsibility is to you, the client. So be assured that your interest comes first. If there is a problem, I would be happy to help but I am not here, as a mentor, to get directly involved in managing your problems. I'm here to help you to do that!

Paul likes the fact that you have given him a working agreement for discussion. This echoes the transparency that he expects in his professional life. It makes him think that he can trust you. You agree to work together for another two sessions within the next month. Each session will be for two hours, with the final 15 minutes set aside for review. Paul is to set the agenda for each session and decide on relevant action between sessions.

ISSUES FOR REFLECTION AND SUPERVISION

What issues has this session raised for you in your work as a mentor?

- Reflecting on this session, what are your areas of strength and areas for development in an introductory session?

- Having negotiated the working agreement and introduced your approach, would you do anything differently in future? Would you want to include anything else?

- What might be potential ongoing issues concerning boundaries, confidentiality and conflict of interest in the relationship?

- Why do you think that Paul approached you to be his mentor?

- Where will you get supervision for your mentoring – will it be from inside or outside the organization? What are the advantages and disadvantages of each?

- What do you want and expect from your supervisor?

- How could you obtain copies of Codes of Ethics for Mentoring and for Supervision?

- What preparation do you need to do before the next session?

Session 2: Developing the relationship and managing the agenda

---

PRINCIPLES INTO PRACTICE

The **context** is Paul's role as a leader in dealing with staff, and the area manager.

The **mentoring objective** is to provide reflective space so that the story will unfold.

The mentor provides a balance of **support and challenge** so that new perspectives will develop and resources can be recognized and used. The first stage is to explore the story and find out which parts of it Paul would like to work on.

The **outcome** Paul wants is to be able to manage himself when dealing with difficult colleagues.

The **learning relationship** starts to develop and you use active and empathic listening to develop trust and rapport. Then the client asks if you would share your experiences.

The **qualities** that need to be communicated are respect for Paul, genuine interest in his story, empathic understanding and honest self-sharing. This will help to affirm and sustain him.

Ethical practice includes: responding appropriately to a request for shared experience; keeping to the time boundary; allowing enough time to end the session safely; and evaluation of the working relationship.

Before you start the session, you remind yourself that Paul will set the agenda for each session and so you ask him what he wants to work on today. Paul says that there have been a couple of very difficult situations in his leadership role with colleagues. You ask him how he would like to use the time. He wants to divide the time between the problem he is having with one of the counter clerks, and the problem he is having with his area manager. The final 15 minutes will be for review.

 You are aware that you need to keep an eye on the time if Paul is to deal with both the difficult situations. You also need to allow time for the review at the end of the session. How will you decide what to do next?

Paul starts to tell the story of his difficulties with the two colleagues. The first is a counter clerk. He is highly regarded by the customers, but he is often away. It falls increasingly to his colleagues to pick up his work. They are grumbling about this and some of them are unhappy about his dismissive attitude. An example of this is his reluctance to comply with recently introduced protocols for appraisal and personal development plans. Paul, as branch manager, has been asked to meet with this colleague and investigate.

After paraphrasing the story, you say, 'So you have been asked to meet with him?' and this repeating of key words helps Paul to continue.

> *Paul:* Yes, and I'm not looking forward to it. But how to handle it? That's the difficulty. If I'm going to do this job successfully, I need to keep people like him 'on board' and at the same time make it clear that some things will need to change. That brings me to my next problem, with my area manager, who keeps hounding me about reaching our financial targets. We won't reach them if I haven't got all the staff pulling together. I feel as if I am between a rock and a hard place. This job is already making me feel exposed and isolated.

 Paul has fairly quickly presented two difficult situations. You want to keep the focus on him, rather than spending too much time talking about the other people involved.

Reflect back to Paul what he seems to be thinking and feeling.

> *Mentor:* Let me check that I understand. You're not looking forward to the meeting with the clerk, but you know it has to be done in order to keep the staff 'pulling together' and so that the branch will achieve its financial targets. You're feeling 'between a rock and a hard place', exposed as well as isolated. Have I got that right? Is that how it is?

Now that you have paraphrased what you have heard and now that you have checked your understanding with Paul, he is encouraged to continue. He talks about how he enjoys a challenge and this is why he accepted the job. He knew that he would find being a branch manager rather difficult at first, but he hadn't realized how exposed and isolated he might feel, so soon into the job.

Paul is still telling his story, but you help him to clarify which part of it he wishes to pursue in this session. Your summary has identified that his feelings of isolation and powerlessness are an important part of the problem for him. You help him to focus, and prioritize an issue to take forward and work on. This may help him to move from feeling stuck to imagining how things could be better.

> *Mentor:* There is the clerk, there is the area manager, and there are your feelings about the job. Which of these should we look at first?
>
> *Paul:* I suppose that if I looked at how I react to these situations it would help. Have you any advice you could give me from your experience?

You know that Paul chose you as mentor partly because of your experience in the same organization. You want to respond to his request for advice, but you also want to keep the focus on Paul and his experiences so that he learns what is useful to him.

How do you feel when Paul asks for advice? How would you respond?

How could you share your experience in a way that opens up discussion and invites Paul's ideas, rather than offering your solutions?

You start by sharing some experiences of similar situations and you finish by saying: 'Those are examples of what worked for me. The same things may not work for you. Is there anything that seems useful to you in what I have shared?'

Having shared briefly some of your own experiences, you ask about Paul's reactions to his own situation. You help him to challenge himself by developing new perspectives. You do this by asking him to reflect upon times in the past when he dealt with feelings of exposure and isolation, and what or who helped then. You help him to consider what resources might be available: friends, family, other colleagues in the wider bank network? Finally, you help him to get some insight into the perspectives of both the counter clerk and the area manager by asking, 'If they were here now, what would they be saying about you? About what they would want from you?'

Time moves on, and you are nearing the end of the session. You encourage Paul to identify something that would move him forward with this issue. He says that the most pressing thing is to get more ideas about how to manage the meeting with the counter clerk.

Would you summarize what has been said, or would you ask Paul to summarize? What would you say in a concise but comprehensive summary?

How would you help him to find something to work on between now and the next session?

Paul decides that, in the next two weeks, he will make contact with the previous branch manager to talk over how he managed situations like these. He decides that he will postpone the meeting with the clerk until after the next mentoring session. At the next session he wants to look at specific strategies for handling both the meeting with the clerk, and the meeting with his area manager.

Finally, you review how you have worked together.

What might you include in the review of the session?

What do you think of the question below, as a starting-point?

You say: 'Could we finish by saying what it was like to work together today? What seemed to help or hinder? What did we appreciate and what would we like to be different next time?' The session concludes with both of you agreeing what Paul will do between now and next time. He writes down his action points. Finally, you check diaries for the date of the next session.

In this session Paul has articulated his problems with colleagues and developed insight into their perspectives as well as his own. He has identified valuable resources in himself and in others. There has been appropriate sharing from you, the mentor, with regard to relevant experiences in the organization.

ISSUES FOR REFLECTION AND SUPERVISION

- Did you deal adequately with Paul's feelings of exposure and isolation?

- How did you feel when Paul asked for your advice? How do you normally respond to such a request?

- Should you have offered to network for Paul?

- How can you prepare for working with him next time, on specific strategies for assertiveness with both colleagues: the clerk and the area manager?

- What were your strengths in this session?

- What would you like to have said or done differently?

- Which issues would you take forward to supervision?

Session 3: Being resourceful and listening to your 'internal supervisor'

PRINCIPLES INTO PRACTICE

The **context** is Paul's managerial role. He wants strategies for a meeting with a difficult colleague.

The **objective** is to develop his confidence by identifying a goal and planning realistic action.

The **outcome** is that Paul is arranging the meeting with the clerk after doing further preparation.

The **learning relationship** is tested twice in this session. First, when you, the mentor, experience 'resistance' from Paul in defining a specific goal. Second, when you need to manage a time issue.

You remain **facilitative** and client-centred even when planning action.

The **qualities** that are needed in the mentor are: affirmation of Paul; belief in his ability to make changes; and balance of support and challenge.

Ethical practice includes keeping time boundaries. As both you and Paul work in the same organization, it will be essential to maintain confidentiality. Contingency planning is necessary to support action.

Paul is returning for his third mentoring session, and you remember that he described how isolated he felt in his new role. You wonder how things are. You check the notes you made together:

1   Paul was to meet with the previous branch manager to find out how he managed difficult colleagues.
2   He wanted help with specific strategies that he could use when having meetings with both the clerk and the area manager.

How do you start the session?

Which of these introductions might you choose and why?

Would you have a better introduction?

- Hello, Paul. How are you today?
- Paul, I've looked at the notes we made last time. We listed two things, they were . . . shall we start with the meeting you had with the previous branch manager?
- Paul, I am wondering what you want to get out of the session today.

Paul says that things have moved on since last time. He tells you that he has met with the previous branch manager who informed him that there has been a history of difficulty with both the counter clerk and with the area manager. The meeting made Paul realize that he wants to be more direct than his predecessor. It also confirmed that Paul's feelings of exposure and isolation did seem to come with the job, and confirmed that it was a wise decision to find a mentor.

> *Paul:* So, can you help me with some strategies for not allowing myself to be overwhelmed, so that I can say in a meeting what needs to be said, even when I feel that the other person is 'drowning me out' with their version of what has been happening.

> *Mentor:* Well, let's start by looking at what you want to happen, in the ideal world. Let's take one of these colleagues, which should we work with first?

> *Paul:* The counter clerk.

> *Mentor:* Imagine the scenario now where you have asked him to come to see you about the absences and the complaints from colleagues Imagine your ideal meeting with him. Take a minute to visualize this and let me know when you have a picture in mind.

You guide Paul in brainstorming what he ideally wants and needs from such a meeting. You prompt him to describe what he would and would not be doing, thinking and feeling, and ideally what the clerk would and would not be doing, thinking and feeling. You ask about the ideal outcome from the meeting, and encourage him to go for some wild ideas. When he completes the brainstorm, you ask him to choose which of the possibilities seem most important to him. (For more information about this technique and useful prompts to use, refer to Chapters 7 and 8.)

> *Paul:* I saw myself sitting there, staying firm while a barrage of words was coming my way. I didn't raise my voice, but I said clearly what had to be said. That's what I want. I felt powerful then, and certainly not intimidated.

You ask him how he might turn that picture into something specific that he wants to do: that is, a goal.

> You notice that Paul is very energized and hopeful during the brainstorm. As he considers what he needs to do, he becomes more thoughtful, and he seems reluctant to specify a goal. How does this make you feel? What are you thinking? What will you do? How would you remain non-directive and facilitative even though you are guiding the process of change?

Despite his initial reluctance to be specific, you help Paul to shape up his goal and he decides that: 'I'll meet with the clerk next week and I'll achieve my objectives for the meeting without being overwhelmed by him.' You check with him whether this is realistic in the timeframe he has allowed himself, and how he will feel if he achieves this. He says that he will feel confident and reassured. You check with him the costs and benefits of being assertive. The personal costs almost outweigh the benefits, but Paul believes that the potential benefits for him as a leader are significant. If he can be assertive with this colleague, he will more confident in being assertive in other difficult situations, whether at meetings or with individuals.

Now that he has a specific goal, you help him to look at all the possible ways he might achieve it. You encourage him to think of as many as possible, whether realistic or not. This helps him to open his mind to as many possibilities as he can. Paul begins to brainstorm strategies, which include: listening to the clerk; understanding the clerk's concerns; preparing by rehearsing for the meeting beforehand; identifying his own 'bottom line position'; deciding what is negotiable and what is not; and trying out some arguments he might use with a friend as 'devil's advocate'. At this point you share with him some other strategies which he may not already be aware of: the CAN model of negotiation; using transactional analysis to examine his own reactions; doing some role reversal to rehearse how to end a negotiation with both him and the colleague committed to the outcome (see Chapter 8 for more information on these strategies). You also mention a couple of useful books.

> You are aware that you are more than halfway through the session. You are also concerned about leaving Paul with unfinished preparation for the meeting. You feel worried that you are mismanaging the timing as well as Paul's expectations of what can realistically be achieved in this session.

What would you do? Consider the five ethical principles when making your decision: what does least harm?; what does most good?; what safeguards Paul's autonomy?; what is fair?; what is in keeping with what has been promised? Would you choose one of the options below, or do something else?

- Cut him short in his planning, saying that there are only a few minutes left for this part of the session if you are to spend 15 minutes on review at the end?
- Decide to drop the review this time as there won't be enough time?
- Wait for a suitable moment, summarize your understanding of the session so far and mention that there is not much time left, asking Paul what he would like to do now?
- Do nothing and see what he says, letting him use all the time for this issue if he says nothing?

You can't decide, so you do nothing. Paul continues talking and you are getting increasingly worried but you feel that you can't interrupt him. A few more minutes pass and then he suddenly looks at his watch and says:

Paul: Oh! I didn't realize the time. We've only got 30 minutes left and I do need to be sure about what I'm going to do at this meeting.

You breathe a sigh of relief! Paul has solved the problem himself. But you are concerned that you hadn't been keeping a close eye on the clock. This could have led to Paul not achieving what he wanted from the session. In hindsight, you reflect that, whatever the problem or issue, the important thing is to have open discussion about it and allow Paul to be involved in any decisions about how to proceed. You now want to bring the discussion back to Paul's strategies for action and so you ask him to summarize the ones he mentioned before.

How will you now help Paul to firm up a strategy that would be 'best fit' for him?

How will you help him to explore what will help or hinder that strategy?

Of all the ideas mentioned, Paul decides that the most useful would be to read and to practise the CAN model of negotiation. He will then rehearse the negotiation with a friend who will take the role of the colleague. Paul will rehearse three things: trying to express his interests clearly; communicating that he understands where the colleague is coming from; and remaining calm and positive in the face of aggressive behaviour. You ask him what might help and what might hinder this strategy.

> *Mentor:* This idea of preparing your case and then rehearsing with a friend – what will help that strategy to succeed?
>
> *Paul:* The fact that I can trust my friend to be honest and supportive, and also that I really am keen on trying this out now. My friend will tell me directly what I need to change or do. Also, she knows what I'm up against!
>
> *Mentor:* And what might get in the way? What might stop it from working?
>
> *Paul:* If neither of us can get our diaries together. It's such a short time till the meeting. Or if I bottle out!

You have used some questions about what will help or hinder the strategy. These help Paul to identify untapped resources in himself or others and also anything that may sabotage his attempts at rehearsing the meeting. Now he moves to the practicalities of a manageable plan. He decides on a time when he can do his reading and preparation and also that tomorrow he will approach his friend so that they can firm up a date in their diaries, within the next week.

What would you include in discussion about a manageable action plan?

What contingency plan might be necessary?

What support might you offer?

What about links into the next session?

You have helped Paul to firm up his action plan and now you turn to ending the session. In this session you realize that Paul has moved from feeling stuck with his problems to the hope that came from realizing possibilities for different ways of thinking, feeling and acting. From this he, somewhat reluctantly at first, found the courage to choose a realistic goal for change. You notice that the session felt energetic and active and you used models and techniques to keep it moving. There was a hiccup halfway through when you realized that time was short, but in the end you felt it worked out, with Paul's objectives met. Now it is time to find out what Paul thinks as you evaluate how you have worked together. As this is the last of the agreed sessions with Paul, you also want to offer him the possibility of returning to review his progress.

> *Mentor:* I notice we have 15 minutes left. We've done quite a bit of active work together today and I'm wondering how you're feeling now?
>
> *Paul:* Exhausted! I didn't realize that mentoring was such hard work! It has given me plenty to think about, and to do. My most pressing problem is the meeting but I do feel more confident after our work today.
>
> *Mentor:* I'm pleased that you're feeling more confident. Is there anything that I could have done, or not done, that would have made the session better for you? And do you feel you would like to come back for another session to review your progress?
>
> *Paul:* Definitely. And maybe you need to make me keep more focused next time so that we cover more! I can ramble on a bit.
>
> *Mentor:* What would you like me to do, to help you keep more focused?
>
> *Paul:* Actually, I'd like you to be a bit more challenging.
>
> *Mentor:* That's fine by me. We can start next time by agreeing the focus at the beginning. Then we can review again at the end of the session to see if we achieved what you wanted. I've enjoyed working together today and have noticed your resourcefulness and determination. I admire your resilience in the face of challenge and I look forward to hearing what happens in your meeting! We seem to have achieved what you wanted. But can I ask you, when we got to stating a goal, did you feel I was pushing too much?
>
> *Paul:* Well, actually, I didn't really want to say something so definite as 'a goal' and I did feel myself pulling back at that stage. But you did give me enough space to decide for myself so, after my initial reluctance, I went for it.

You check if there is anything else that Paul wants to say, you ask him to summarize his action plan and how he feels at the end of the session.

ISSUES FOR REFLECTION AND SUPERVISION

You reflect on the three sessions. Then you decide which issues you would like to take to supervision. In particular, you want to use some supervision to reflect on your own development, including the way you use your approach, skills, tools and techniques, within the learning relationship. You want to explore how to keep the balance between support and challenge, and how to remain client-centred at the problem-solving and action stages of mentoring. You have heard about 'parallel process', where there is a resonance between issues the client brings to supervision and what the mentor experiences in the here-and-now relationship with the client. You are not sure whether that happened in these sessions, but you want to learn more about this, in supervision.

- What did you do well in this mentoring example?

- What would you now like to be able to do differently?

- Who will help you to develop as a coach or mentor?

Summary

In this chapter we have:

- Developed an interactive case study with Paul, over three sessions.

- Invited you to be the mentor during each session.

- Applied key principles for effective practice.

- Given extracts of dialogue so that you can reflect on what is happening in the session and choose appropriate responses.

- Highlighted, for reflection at the end of each session, some ethical and professional issues which could be taken to supervision.

11 What are frequently asked questions?

- What if someone is sent for coaching or mentoring?

- What if the client tells me something I can't keep confidential?

- What if coaching or mentoring doesn't seem to be working?

- Can I give advice?

- What if I am asked to coach or mentor by e-mail, phone or video?

- How do I balance the needs of client and sponsoring organization?

- What if the client asks for more than I can offer?

- Can I be the client's manager, assessor, appraiser?

- Can I coach or mentor a client that I meet socially?

- How important are supervision and accreditation?

In this chapter we have listed 10 frequently asked questions about coaching and mentoring, each of which also links to one or more of the chapters so far. The useful resources and contacts in the Appendix will enable you to explore these questions and many others in more depth in your own time.

What if someone is sent for coaching or mentoring?

It is not unusual for someone to be sent for coaching or mentoring – often with a view to 'fixing' a performance or personality problem. People who are sent may be: reluctant, seeing the encounter as punishment; unrealistic, imagining that everything will be magically fixed by you; seeing themselves as a victim and blaming everyone and everything for their difficulties; or perhaps a mixture of all of these. Sometimes, an unpromising start can be turned into a productive helping relationship. Begin with the premise that people can change if they choose. Avoid bending over backwards to help: you may be colluding with your client. Avoid the other extreme, a stance of 'I can't help you unless you want to be helped': this may become a fixed position. Try to establish a 'working alliance' so that your client sees themselves as a partner in a joint venture, with a payoff for them, rather than someone who is being 'done unto'.

The value of basic active listening skills and of communicating respect, empathy and genuineness cannot be overemphasized: some clients who are 'sent' have never had the chance to tell their story and to hear themselves without interruption, evaluation or advice. You can communicate empathy, not sympathy. You can empathically challenge the client to identify *their problem*, as distinct from *the problem*. If the client is able to own their problem and see a chink of light, something that they can work on, then perhaps progress can be made. It will help if you are clear and transparent from the outset about what information, if any, you will share with the organization which sent the client. Finally, stay realistic. These approaches do not work in every situation, and it is difficult to help someone who has decided not to be helped.

What if the client tells me something I can't keep confidential?

We want and need to offer our clients an assurance of confidentiality. However, no one can guarantee absolute confidentiality. We all work within organizational and/or professional guidelines, and so it is important to discuss boundaries and limits at the outset. Clarity about confidentiality is an essential part of negotiating a working agreement with the client. This is the opportunity to be explicit about what you can and cannot keep confidential. It is the opportunity to check the client's understanding of this, and so will benefit from time and space for discussion. If you have been clear about limits, and the client nevertheless tells you something that cannot be kept confidential, you can ask them why they have told you, and what they expect to happen now. What do they want or need from you? If they were in your shoes, what would they do? If action needs to be taken, it is best if you can agree this with the client. In rare circumstances, you may judge that the risk of harm outweighs considerations of client autonomy and you may decide to act unilaterally. In this case, you would normally tell the client.

When faced with an issue of something that cannot be kept confidential, it is best to seek support from supervision. Sometimes no action is better than hasty action.

What if coaching or mentoring doesn't seem to be working?

Sometimes we question whether we are helping a client. Do they really want to change? Are we the right helper? Do they need a different kind of help?

We may feel that we are working harder than the client which is often a sign that something is not quite right. Sometimes it is the client who feels that all is not well. Perhaps they see us as too challenging, or not challenging enough, or too structured, or lacking focus, or maybe just not on their wavelength. Establishing regular reviews to talk about how things are going is a powerful source of learning. Getting into the habit of reviewing is likely to make it easier to talk about any problems.

If the relationship does not seem to be working from your perspective, you may want to raise your concerns *in a non-judgemental way* with the client. Sometimes this can lead to a breakthrough that helps the client to move forward. Supervision can help you to look at your own part in any difficulties and to rehearse any conversation you might want to have with the client. When sharing concerns with clients, especially if you think that the client would benefit from referral elsewhere, it is important not to make the decision *for* the client. Decisions, as far as possible, should be arrived at *jointly*.

If it does not seem to be working from the client's perspective, remember that many clients find it difficult to 'criticize', and so regular reviews can encourage their feedback. To help this, you can ask questions that make the undiscussable more discussable. Good questions include 'What am I doing that is helping you?', 'What I am I doing that's getting in the way?' and 'If there was something that you could change in the way we work together, what would that be?' In addition, working agreements often include a 'no blame' clause that makes it clear that the client can end the relationship or request a change of coach or mentor at any time.

Can I give advice?

When we train people as coaches and mentors, we ask them to tell us, based on their own experience of being helped, what they consider to be the skills and qualities of effective helpers. Having trained many hundreds of people, we cannot recall a single instance where a group has agreed that 'giving advice' was an important skill of an effective helper. And yet, paradoxically, as soon as these same participants start to practise skills, they find themselves giving advice, often within minutes of a coaching or mentoring conversation! So although they know that advice is not helpful, the habit is hard to break. Giving advice is tempting, especially when many of us have a professional identity based upon our expert role. The teacher, doctor, dentist, nurse, lawyer, HR professional – each is expected to give sound advice. Clients often ask for advice. Sometimes they may demand it. Our guideline is *beware of giving advice*. It rarely works, because you are not the client, so you cannot know what is best for them. It can create dependence. Over time, it may diminish client resourcefulness and autonomy. And, as we all know, people often do not take advice, so you are likely to be wasting your time and theirs. And yet it is difficult to stop giving advice, when that's what you do in your day job.

So, if you are tempted to give advice, ask yourself:

- Am I concerned about this client or their proposed course of action? If so, can I share my concerns with them in a clear but non-judgemental manner? Or can I create the opportunity for them to check any blind spots?
- Would the client benefit from facts or information (as distinct from advice or opinion) that I have and they don't? Is there any downside to sharing that information? Or to telling the client where to find it?
- Does the client need advice or guidance? Perhaps they need something in addition to coaching or mentoring? Would they benefit from, for example, training, supervision, staff induction or some expert help?
- Would it be useful to share my experience with the client, perhaps of a similar situation to the one they are facing? Might I say, 'This is what I did and this is how it worked out for me, but it may not be the same for you'? We would caution against sharing your experience too often because this can easily become advice-giving in disguise.

What if I am asked to coach or mentor by e-mail, phone or video?

There is a growing interest in telephone, video or e-mail coaching and mentoring. Often, this is used to supplement face-to-face sessions, perhaps when a crisis at work has necessitated an unscheduled session, or when distance or weather have prevented a face-to-face meeting. Coaches have reported the value of telephone coaching with clients who have just been to an important interview or appraisal at work and who needed some immediate debriefing. With video, there is the advantage that non-verbal communication is still partly accessible, but with phone there is only voice, and with e-mail just the written word. However, whichever of these is used, provided the coach or mentor gives the same focused attention to the client, the process can work well. It probably works best when coach and client have already worked with one another. Before embarking on distance coaching or mentoring you need to think carefully through any concerns that either you or the client may have about confidentiality. This will include sessions being on record, for example, your e-mail replies. Will you be happy that they could be accessible to other persons or organizations you do not know? Another important issue for consideration is how you will deal with distress when you do not have the normal safeguards of a face-to-face encounter in place.

How do I balance the needs of client and sponsoring organization?

Your client is the person you are coaching or mentoring. Other interested parties may be involved, and have expectations which need to be negotiated, but they are not your client. As soon as you are approached to provide coaching or mentoring, you need to ascertain who the interested parties are and what their expectations are. Do they align with each other, or do they conflict in any way? We have mentioned the importance of clear working agreements. Where there may be conflicts of interest, it is even more important to explicitly agree terms of reference at the outset, preferably in writing. For example, a manager may have arranged coaching with an external provider, for a member of staff who is underperforming. The manager arranges payment out of a departmental budget and wants a successful outcome. They ask the coach for ongoing reports, submitted at the time of invoicing. In this case, the client should be made aware of this from the outset. A meeting could be arranged with all parties, before the coaching starts, to agree who will be involved in writing the reports, and what they will and will not contain. In some coaching and mentoring schemes within organizations, there is an expectation that both the coach or mentor and client will complete 'exit evaluation' forms to help in the further development of the service. The client needs to be assured that they are not being assessed for the way they perform in the sessions and that the content remains confidential. Always be transparent with your client, respect their autonomy, and involve them in any agreements pertaining to your work with them, preferably before you start. You may decide in some instances that you cannot agree to requests for information, from organizations or employers, because your view is that this will impede the relationship. If in doubt about compromising your work with a client, you may decide that it is better to turn down an assignment, rather than take on conflicting expectations.

What if the client asks for more than I can offer?

Perhaps this has happened because you were not clear about what you could and could not offer. It is always advisable to be clear about boundaries and limitations from the outset. Then, if difficulties arise, you have a point of reference for some ongoing review and negotiation. However, some clients may be more needy than others, some may find it difficult to operate within prescribed boundaries, some are more impulsive than others, or tend to leave things to the last minute and then hope that everyone else will adjust to that. In these situations, what is happening in the coaching or mentoring relationship may be telling you something valuable about a limiting pattern in the client's life generally. For example, a client tries to cancel a booked session at the last minute. You may respond on more than one level. It could be, 'You want to cancel our session tomorrow? Yes, I can do that but I had booked out that time for you and it's too late to fill that slot now so I will have to charge for it, as we arranged in our working agreement.' This level is straightforward and business-like and maintains clear boundaries. Then it may be followed up, when the client arrives for the next session, with 'I realized that this wasn't the first time you have asked to cancel sessions very close to the date when we were to meet.' This observation offers the opportunity to work on a pattern of procrastination and over-commitment.

Some clients want to contact you outside the agreed session times, or they ask for extra sessions, or they have a habit of going over the time allocated for the session. Such issues may be sorted out by clear working agreements or they may be indicative, as in the example above, of underlying patterns. Another example of a client asking for more than you can offer is when the client expects you to do all the work and come up with all the answers. This is where you will benefit from careful reflective practice and regular supervision. It will help you to work on your own reactions to clients expecting too much from you, as well as working on ways in which you can offer supportive challenge and immediacy to your client, in order to help both of you to move forward.

Can I be the client's manager, assessor, appraiser?

This is the problem of managing possible conflicts of interest. There is no right or wrong answer here. But ethical principles can inform your decision. What would do most good and least harm to your client? What would be most just and fair? What would empower the client most? What will enable you to keep to any promises you make to your client, or what may get in the way? Generally, we would not advise having a 'power' relationship with your client, such as managing them or assessing them. However, some clients positively choose their managers or assessors because they respect and admire their integrity. In other situations at work, coaching is being offered as part of a managerial or leadership role and mentoring is being offered by someone perhaps more senior or experienced in the same department or specialty. If this is the case, then it is the responsibility of the coach or mentor to raise possible conflicts of interest at an early stage in the relationship and to ensure that the client is able to give informed consent to the implications of sharing confidences, with someone who is in a position of influence and power.

Can I coach or mentor a client that I meet socially?

This question is about boundaries. The boundary of the coaching or mentoring session usually includes a timeframe and a clock, a specific location which is appropriate for the work that needs to be done, and an ambience that is conducive to the development of a sound and confidential working relationship. These boundaries provide safe containment for both client and coach or mentor. Once you step outside of these carefully constructed boundaries there is the possibility of uncertainty and apprehension in the way that you relate to one another. In the social situation you are not in the roles of client with coach or mentor, you are in the roles of friends, colleagues or acquaintances. Some people are easily able to adjust between roles and contexts. Others not so. Never assume that your client will be able to adjust because you can. If you are both aware that you may meet socially during the course of working together, do address the matter explicitly. Give space to discuss how each of you would wish to manage such a situation if it were to arise. There is a sense in which you can never be totally off-guard if you meet a client socially. You take with you the ethical responsibility to do no harm, particularly in regard to confidences that have been shared, and this responsibility lasts a lifetime, long after formal coaching and mentoring have concluded.

How important are supervision and accreditation?

If coaching or mentoring is your main work, then both supervision and accreditation are advised. They will help you and your clients to be assured of an ethical and professional service, where each of you is safeguarded because you will have regular opportunities for reflection on your work and you will have been assessed against specific competencies. We would also recommend membership of a national or international professional coaching or mentoring association to provide opportunities for updating, networking and renewal. If you are coaching and mentoring as part of another job you do at work, you will still benefit from getting into the habit of reflective practice. Depending on the extent of the coaching and mentoring you do, we would advise regular supervision either with a peer, a peer group, a qualified supervisor, or a supervision group facilitated by a qualified supervisor. If coaching and mentoring are a small part of your work, you may not wish to gain accreditation but may find it useful to keep up to date with the websites of major coaching and mentoring organizations, such as the ICF and the EMCC, in order to check your practice against their current codes of ethics, and their current requirements for accreditation.

12 Glimpses of coaches and mentors at work

This chapter is a collection of current experiences of those who are either coaching and mentoring, or developing coaching and mentoring schemes throughout the UK.

Each of the contributors summarizes key aspects of their work: their role, their coaching or mentoring approach; model and skills used; current issues or problems in their coaching and mentoring work; high points and rewards in their work; low points and lessons learned; ethical issues and supervision. They then share with you one tip, one piece of wisdom, one example of something that worked well; one example of something that did not work well, and finally they share a thought about their vision for the future of coaching and mentoring in their sector.

Context	*Contributor*
Executive and leadership coaching	*Martin Hill*
Developing a nationwide mentoring service: Housing Diversity Network	*Kam Urwin*
Coaching for health	*Arti Maini*
Developing a coaching culture in NHS Hospital Trust	*Sarah Montgomery*
UK mentoring scheme for doctors: AAGBI	*Nancy Redfern*
Executive coaching	*Wendy Briner*
Leadership and performance coaching	*Shaun Lincoln*
Management and leadership coaching	*Malcolm Hurrell*
Coaching and mentoring in education	*David Harrison*

Executive and leadership coaching

Martin Hill, Coaching, Supervision and Coach Training

I have a mixed practice in a range of different environments:

- Internal accredited Civil Service coach and executive coach for managers in various civil service departments.
- External practice that involves executive and leadership coaching with clients from SMEs (small and medium enterprises) and large organizations.
- Programme Director for ILM Level 7 Executive Coaching and Mentoring courses – this involves delivery within the UK and the Middle East.
- Qualified coaching supervisor.

Approach used/skills/model

- I use a solution-focused coaching approach, using the OSKAR, GROW and CLEAR models – adapting the models, tools and approach taken dependent upon the context and the client.
- The skills I use include contracting; silence; questioning; listening; challenging; feedback; and also the knowledge and experience gained from my practice and CPD learning.

Current issues/problems

- Current issues that I am dealing with include clients with issues relating to confidence/self-belief; leadership development and career development.
- Current problems that I encounter within my practice relate to dealing with the economic climate, when often training and development expenditure is reduced.

High points/rewards/what worked well/what helped

- High points relate to celebrating the successes and achievements of clients: promotion; successful completion of projects; or simply 'comfort within their own skin' having realized and recognized what it is they really want or what amounts to success for them.
- Rewards include recognition from clients and sponsors, thanks, unexpected tokens of appreciation, recommendations and referrals.
- What works well is going into a session with a flexible, adaptive approach – enjoying the pleasure of exploring something unknown and working with each client as an individual – adapting the style and

approach to suit their preference and/or strengths. Regularly reviewing sessions to clarify what worked well and what could be improved. This provides a strong basis for subsequent critical self-reflection.

- What helps is the knowledge and experience from researching a wide range of texts and journals, trying and adapting approaches and also striving to improve and develop.

Low points

More general problems relate to dealing with misapprehensions about what coaching is. Also, the mismatch of expectations within organizations, hence my focus on contracting and ensuring that there is a common understanding of coaching and agreed expectations for client, sponsor and any other stakeholder. This is done by forwarding an explanatory document to all in advance of a coaching intervention, setting out what coaching is and following this up with three-way (or more) contracting meetings to ensure ALL are committed to the agreed process.

What gets in the way, with regard to the above, are the internal politics of organizations. Also, there are the frequent misapprehensions, that coaching is to deal with performance management that should have been addressed by the line manager.

Ethical issues/supervision

Ethical issues that I frequently observe with my own students and supervisees relate to the pressure to deal with commercial demands (for example, trying to fit in a high number of clients within a single day). The coach fails to 'contract' for their own well-being and welfare to ensure that they can deliver the same focus and energy for the first client and the final client (as well as those in between).

My supervision approach is based on a variety of interventions:

- *Individual supervision* – in these 1:1 sessions I discuss the more involved or more 'confidentiality-critical' issues – this provides space for individual review, challenge and reflection.
- *Group supervision* – a chance to discuss more general areas of practice via a session facilitated by a supervisor – benefitting from the group knowledge and experience.
- *Peer supervision* – discussions with colleagues.

One tip I would like to share

Contracting for clarity – ensure that you discuss and mutually agree with client/sponsor/line manager, and that the contracting deals with all areas that may arise. Involving the client in this process also helps build rapport and trust.

One piece of wisdom

Develop your own approach to ensure that you have a process that supports critical self-reflection and continuous improvement – allow time after sessions to record your own reflections on the session and the skills and behaviours that you used as a coach – what went well?; what could have been improved?; what could have been done differently? Create a habit of seeking feedback and reflections from the client and then make a diary date on a regular basis to review your coaching practice and your own professional development plan.

My vision for the future of coaching and mentoring

Coaching and mentoring recognized and valued, as an intervention that supports the development and learning of individuals, and makes a critical difference to performance improvement.

* * *

Developing a nationwide mentoring service: Housing Diversity Network

Kam Unwin, Mentoring Manager, Housing Diversity Network

The Housing Diversity Network (HDN) is a social enterprise that aims to inspire and empower people, promoting equality, diversity and opportunity for all. We support organizations to improve how they address inequality, get the most from their staff and meet the needs of the communities they work with. HDN is the winner of the CIPD People Management Award for 'Best Coaching and Mentoring Initiative', 2016.

Overview

The Housing Diversity Network (HDN) mentoring programme has been running since 2005. It was established following research that identified that there were a range of barriers to progression for Black and Minority Ethnic (BME) staff in the housing sector. It was suggested that a mentoring programme would help in removing some of those barriers. Since then, the programme has expanded across the country. It is now no longer solely aimed at BME staff but our commitment to addressing inequality and enhancing diversity remains a key driver for the programme.

The objectives for the mentoring programme can be grouped into three broad areas:

- For the housing sector as a whole, it is about reducing inequality, improving diversity and sharing learning.
- For organizations, we hope to see them harness the talents of all of their staff.
- For individuals, they will achieve their objectives, become more confident and progress in their careers.

Mentors and mentees

Access is free to members of Housing Diversity Network. In the current year (2015/16) there are 235 mentees on the programme who have been matched with the same number of mentors. The programme involves:

- Applications from potential mentees which ask them to identify what they want to get from the programme.
- Matching mentees with a mentor from another organization.
- A combination of 1-1 meetings with their mentor and facilitated group sessions, in which mentees work towards their identified personal objectives.
- Themed group workshops focusing on development areas with experienced professionals from the housing sector and beyond.
- The HDN Annual Mentoring Conference.

Mentors are volunteers drawn from a wide range of housing organizations and are often at a senior level (senior manager, director or chief executive). We have mentors who have been on the programme since its inception. Mentors receive briefing and training to develop their own skills and knowledge on the programme as well. 'I feel better prepared to take on new challenges as being a mentor was something new to me' (Mentor).

Every year we have a celebratory conference that brings together the people from that year's programme. The stories people recount about how the programme has helped them is inspiring. 'Helped me learn about myself, my strengths and weaknesses which will really help me now, in the future and the organization I work for' (Mentee).

The outcomes for the programme are:

- For the housing sector as a whole, it is about making it a more attractive profession for all and to benefit from a more diverse workforce.

- For organizations, they increase staff satisfaction and retention.
- For individuals, they learn to be more confident and enjoy career advancement.

Challenges

Providing a national programme is a challenge. Until we receive applications we do not know the exact number of mentees. The programme has also grown significantly. Each year this means finding mentors willing to give their time and expertise to someone from a different organization. However, due to our reputation and networks, as well as the nature of the social housing sector, each year we are able to recruit enough high quality mentors.

Contribution

Not only have the mentees benefited, but so have the organizations they work for. The recent 2014/15 evaluation found that mentees reported the following outcomes as a direct result of participating in the mentoring programme:

Increased confidence – 87%
Networking opportunities – 76%
Training opportunities – 37%
Opportunities outside of work – 26%
Extra responsibility – 25%
Job shadowing – 18%
New job/role – 15%
Promotion – 14%

The programme has grown since its inception because it is a fantastic way to support staff, build confidence and overcome barriers and challenges. For us, the focus on diversity is critical, but we do not turn anyone away – we know that most people can benefit from a mentor. We have many mentees who in later years become mentors (and even one who has then gone on to join the Board of HDN).

We see mentoring as a vital tool in achieving our aim of inspiring and empowering people, promoting equality, diversity and opportunity for all.

* * *

Coaching for health

Arti Maini, GP and Clinical Teaching Fellow at Imperial College, London; Coach, Supervisor and Coach Trainer

Role

I use coaching approaches daily in my clinical work with patients.

Approach used/skills/model

Together with Jenny Rogers, an executive coach and trainer, I developed an approach to health coaching based on principles adapted from her original six principles of coaching (*Coaching for Health*, Rogers & Maini 2016):

1   Patients are resourceful.
2   The practitioner's role is to move from expert to enabler.
3   We take a whole life approach.
4   The patient brings the agenda for the consultation.
5   Practitioner and patient are equals in the consultation.
6   Coaching is about change and action.

To support this work, I draw upon a wide range of coaching-related approaches, including: The Skilled Helper (Egan 2010), TGROW and NLP.

Current issues/problems

The challenges of: funding constraints, staff morale, staff shortages and unsustainable workload. When clinicians are overworked and exhausted, it is difficult to maintain a coaching mind-set of curiosity, warmth, non-judgemental attitude and compassion because the clinicians themselves are in survival mode.

High points/rewards

Being able to make a meaningful difference to a patient's life as a result of using a coaching approach is incredibly rewarding. It puts the humanity back into medicine.

One example of what worked well/what helped

I saw a patient with several physical health problems and who was low in mood. It proved very useful to ask: 'What part of your problems do you have control over?'

This helped her to identify a specific area to work on. She set a goal to increase her level of exercise and successfully achieved this by regularly taking her grandchild for walks in the park. Her mood improved and her physical symptoms got better. She had less joint pains, less need for pain medication and more energy.

Low points

It can be challenging to empower patients when working within a healthcare system which itself can be experienced as disempowering, for example, through problems which patients encounter when trying to access and navigate the service.

One thing that did not work so well/what got in the way

Trying to use a coaching approach with a patient at the end of a particularly busy surgery was not a good idea! My own energy levels were depleted and it was very difficult to hold a coaching mind-set of genuine curiosity and openness.

My learning from this is about finding ways to recharge myself where possible, during busy surgeries, and this in turn impacts positively on my interaction with patients.

Ethical issues/supervision

It is important to practise within the framework of an ethical code of conduct. Doctors work within the General Medical Council (GMC) guidance. This guidance is relevant in a health coaching context.

One tip I would like to share

I have found it energizing and motivating to connect with other colleagues who use coaching approaches in their work, for example, through group supervision, refresher training events and social media. We learn from each other and continue to develop professionally.

One piece of wisdom

To coach effectively, the clinician needs to hold the right mind-set: non-judgemental, open, curious. For this to happen, we need to attend to our own well-being first!

My vision for the future of coaching and mentoring

My vision for the future of coaching and mentoring in the healthcare sector is that the ethos is present at all levels: patient, clinician, provider organizations, and commissioning. This would transform our approach to healthcare in the twenty-first century.

In the end the clinician role is more than just helping patients to survive, it is about the whole of life and quality of life; it is about well-being, autonomy, happiness and the power of choice. That is where coaching can add so much not just to patients but to the increased satisfaction that we, as clinicians, are likely to get from our work.

(Rogers & Maini 2016: 205)

* * *

Developing a coaching culture in an NHS Hospital Trust

Sarah Montgomery, Head of Learning and Organizational Development, Internal Coaching Faculty, Wrightington, Wigan and Leigh NHS Foundation Trust

Background

Wrightington, Wigan and Leigh NHS Foundation Trust is a major acute trust dedicated to providing the best possible healthcare for the local population. In 2015, the time was right for WWL to support our leaders to develop and embed a culture of coaching across the organization in order to do the following:

- improve performance;
- increase engagement at this time of uncertainty;
- encourage innovation and decision-making to support effective patient outcomes.

We wanted to establish a pool of coaches to support new managers and teams going through change. We also wanted to develop coaches to facilitate our organizational values-based 360-degree feedback tool.

Approach used/skills/model

The Trust held a launch event where we invited staff and managers from across the organization to learn more about coaching and how this can be used to support us in delivering an exceptional service to our patients.

As an accredited centre with the Chartered Management Institute we have a track record of success in delivering nationally accredited leadership programmes up to level 7 and we were able to build on this success by developing a bespoke range of accredited coaching programmes.

In partnership with Becci Martin (Director of Coaching from Boo Coaching and Consulting Limited, a recognized provider in coaching and mentoring), we delivered an assessment centre for people who were interested in developing their coaching skills and over 60 people attended this event. People were assessed through scenario-based practical sessions which assessed:

- intuitive listening
- skilful questioning
- empathy
- commitment to action.

From this we were able to allocate people to a relevant coaching pathway. We developed a range of accredited programmes linked to the nine dimensions of the Healthcare Leadership Model. The programme offers different levels of training and accreditation – level 5 or 7 of the Chartered Management Institute coaching and mentoring qualifications.

High points/rewards

- Seeing senior clinicians who were fairly cynical about coaching at the launch event, but who demonstrated potential for coaching, completing the course with flying colours and now being some of our top coaches!
- 100% of participants on the programme saw it as important to the organization and relevant to their roles and would recommend the programme to colleagues by the time they had completed it.
- The most recent NHS survey has also shown increased satisfaction with the way that appraisals are carried out, as well as witnessing improved communication with managers.
- This programme is set very much within a culture change agenda.

Low points

It was difficult to know when was the right time to launch the coaching programme. We wanted to develop our organizational pool of coaches to enable a coaching offer for staff and managers. However, our coaches needed to develop their skills and therefore needed to gain hands-on practical experience. So there was a point where we didn't have enough coaches for our coaches to develop their practical skills. This meant that we then decided to launch the coaching programme on a smaller scale and pilot it in certain areas so, for example, offering coaching to people on leadership courses or education pathways. We also offered it to new managers without going big bang across the whole organization.

Ethical issues/supervision

We established action learning sets/coaching circles and encourage senior coaches to facilitate these.

One tip I would like to share

Really ensure that senior leaders are fully on board with the coaching invest-ment and are prepared to share their own personal coaching journey, and be part of the process.

Quotes from staff who have been coached by one of our coaches

> I've had already three meetings and I am finding it very interesting, and very useful. I would recommend it to anyone. So far, it is meeting my objectives, it is making me see things in a different light.

> Prior to coaching I was already aware of my weaknesses which is why I asked about coaching. The sessions are helping me to take action to try and improve how I am. Very good indeed.

Our vision for the future of coaching and mentoring

Our philosophy is to ensure that coaching is embraced and helped people go from good to great and have a real impact on organizational and individual performance and behaviour.

The results we are seeing really demonstrate this and we are now working collaboratively with colleagues in local NHS organizations and councils, to take a shared approach to coaching across the health and social care system.

* * *

Developing a UK mentoring scheme for doctors: AAGBI

Nancy Redfern, Consultant Anaesthetist and the Honorary Membership Secretary of the Association of Anaesthetists of Great Britain and Ireland

My role on the AAGBI Council is to champion mentoring as a normal part of how we practise as doctors, through a training programme and matching scheme.

Approach used

I started working with the group who were likely to find mentoring most valuable, the trainees. At our annual conference, we offered a 'taster' mentoring session to anyone who wanted to try mentoring. This was received very positively. We were on our way.

One year later, the General Medical Council, advised doctors 'to find and take part in structured support opportunities (for example, mentoring), when you join an organisation and whenever your role changes significantly throughout your career'.

As a membership organization, the AAGBI could do this for its membership. It would take time to have mentoring available in every hospital or Trust, but we could start by offering it at our conferences and developing a training programme to grow the numbers of mentors.

Skills/model

Using a model or framework makes the difference between a conversation with a good listener and a skilled mentoring session. Egan's Skilled Helper model is the one I would recommend. Others such as GROW need the person to have a goal, whereas most doctors and dentists I talk to have a dilemma.

Current issues/problems

For the scheme, one big issue is how we grow it and embed it in all areas of the UK and Ireland. Doing this is a significant cultural change and needs plenty of local champions. This sounds like a busy extrovert role. In fact, I suspect it is achieved just as well by gentle persistence.

High points

Some of the feedback has been lovely. A highly respected consultant who was considering retiring early, wrote to say that following the mentoring session, she decided to carry on working. Another changed their role in management, and yet another got back to work successfully after two years away.

Rewards

- Seeing people achieve their full potential.
- Doctors who have had a mentoring session that broadened their horizons and gave them the confidence to have a go.
- The trainees who are setting up a mentoring scheme in Ireland.
- The trainee who got on to the National Committee.
- The person who passed an exam at the fifth attempt and whose article about the experience has inspired many other trainees to keep going.

One example of what worked well

Offering a taster mentoring session at our three big annual meetings has given many people the opportunity to try out mentoring confidentially. Sceptics have changed their views, people in real difficulty in their organizations have worked out a way of moving forward.

Low points

My low point came when I realized that the funding to continue the programme was in doubt.

One thing that did not work well

Securing the funding for the programme to become embedded was a real challenge. Somewhat naïvely, I assumed that, because we had just launched the matching website and the programme had received excellent feedback, that no-one would question its value.

One thing that did not work so well/what got in the way

Like many membership organizations, the financial climate was challenging. We got the programme through, but only with lots of hard work!

Ethical issues

One of the big ones for us, as clinicians, is avoiding conflicts of interest. Mentors are also consultants; senior trainees; educational supervisors; or colleagues of people whom mentees might discuss. When the conversation is about development, this is usually not a problem, but when there are real difficulties, this is tricky for both the mentor and mentee.

Supervision

We hold an annual refresher day and offer all mentors the opportunity to discuss the dilemmas they face, either individually or sometimes at a meeting at an annual conference.

Lessons learned

My lesson is to be more active in discussing dilemmas with mentors and with mentees. Doctors have a way of saying 'it will be OK' when really it won't.

One tip I would like to share

If you run a scheme, ensure the person who has first contact with those seeking a mentor, is a trained mentor. Attending a course with doctors who will also be mentors has many benefits. They hear doctors talking about our dilemmas, they grasp the vital importance of confidentiality and they see that many of the problems we face are similar to their own.

One piece of wisdom

It takes time to establish. Running one or two mentor development programmes is just the start. Those people have to spread the word, using mentoring for themselves and with their colleagues before it gets embedded.

My vision for the future of coaching and mentoring

Using mentors should become part of the way we think and practise medicine. Whenever we have a dilemma or opportunity, we should discuss this with a mentor. In this way, we would spend much less time worrying and much more in achieving a good outcome for all concerned.

*   *   *

Executive coaching

Wendy Briner, Leadership Coach and Researcher, Ashridge Executive Education at Hult International Business School

Approach used/skills/model

I draw from the following approaches:

- person-centred
- appreciative inquiry
- systemic and solution-focused
- social constructivist.

I try to build on 'what works' from 'what is'. The emphasis is on moving forward in a way that is useful for the person within their own systems.

I ask myself: 'What is the conversation that I am having, creating or co-creating with my client?'

Current issues/problems

Constant surprises. Change seems to be a constant, which can be unexpected to both client and coach.

High points/rewards

The real enthusiasm that clients can have, when they have internalized something as a result of a positive approach.

It has helped to work intensively with a client, for example, when doing appreciative inquiry interviews. It is a learning experience for both coach and client.

The stories told are sometimes very moving, whether positive or negative. It is very touching to hear the way that the human spirit can overcome adversity. For example, listening to the stories of immigrant workers who are trying to do what is worthwhile, and remain positive.

Low points

- When somehow the relationship does not get connected at the beginning.
- When it is not 'the right time' for the client and he or she is unwilling.
- When, for whatever reason, I am the wrong person in the wrong place. An example of this is when coaching has been offered as part of a training programme, but the client does not want to be coached.

Ethical issues/supervision

- From the outset, it is important to be clear about who 'the client' is.
- Being aware that there may be conflicts of interest between client, boss and coach or mentor.
- Using regular supervision as 'a place to go' to discuss such issues. Not waiting until things start falling apart. This known space is invaluable for review and reflection, as part of CPD (continuing professional development).

One tip I would like to share

When with the client, keep flexible, holding light your own assumptions and your own preferences.

One piece of wisdom

Look after yourself, to be fit for other human consumption.

My vision for the future of coaching and mentoring

- There is so much we now know about neuroplasticity, neuropsychology and mindfulness. This makes us aware that 'talking work' can only do part of what is necessary for people to change and grow. Working with mind, body and soul as they are connected.
- We need to help clients' patterns expand beyond the habitual patterns of discourse and conversation to bring about more constructive relationships.

- Two key questions for coaches, mentors and clients: (1) how could we relate to others in different ways?; and (2) where is it that you are trying to get to?

* * *

Leadership and performance coaching

Shaun Lincoln, Leadership and Performance Coach in the Further Education sector

Role

- Team development.
- Training in coaching skills.
- One-to-one coaching.

Approach used/skills/model

I use a solution-focused approach. In the education sector, the need for coaching has become stronger. This is because expectations of success have become greater at a time when resources are squeezed. In such a climate, it is easy for staff to focus on problems, rather than opportunities. As a leadership and performance coach I am asked to work with staff to develop more of a 'growth' mind-set.

I train staff in coaching skills in order to help them to focus on achieving outcomes that they 'want'. Instead of focusing on the current 'problem', I help them to focus on the desired 'outcome'. When they are clear about the desired outcome, they can begin to articulate the steps, immediate and small steps, that will be needed to get there. I use the OSKAR model to enable the client to be clear about where they want to get that would be 'future-perfect', recognizing where they currently are in relation to that goal.

Current issues/problems

Time is an issue for staff in the education sector.

People need help, in order to understand that the approach that culminated in them having a problem, is unlikely to help them to find the solution. They need a different kind of thinking. Solution-focused does not mean solution-forced.

One example of what worked well

A Further Education college asked me to work with them on culture change that would raise their OFSTED inspection grade from 'Good' to 'Outstanding'.

This was a whole College event. I used a solution-focused approach for three years. At the next inspection, The College achieved 'Outstanding' in all aspects. Some staff had initially been very cynical about the coaching approach and one returned later and said, 'You know what, it works!'

What worked well

- Not using jargon.
- Never doing one-off training.
- Making sure that clients can come back and tell you how things are going.

High points/rewards

Seeing people come up with their own solutions that you as a coach would never think of!

Low points/lessons learned

I was 'bought in' to do some training with middle leaders who were demoralized but still employed by the organization. This was difficult. What I learned was:

- Trust the process.
- If you feel that you are doing too much hard work as a coach, then you probably are!
- Let silence do the heavy lifting . . .

One thing that did not work so well/what got in the way

Finding the balance between support and challenge. Instinctively I am very supportive. Once I went into challenge because 'it seemed the right thing to do'. But right for who? Not right for the client because I had not contracted clearly enough, before I challenged.

Tips I would like to share

- People learn best from each other.
- If you want your client to realize the impact that they can have, then help them to focus upon: 'what you can work on and what you need to get rid of'.

One piece of wisdom

Recognize that the person coming to you for coaching is not you. Resist the number of times that they come to you to be 'their expert'.

My vision for the future of coaching and mentoring

I was in the College and one of the people trained by me said: 'We are going to bring-in coaching and mentoring.'

They have recognized:

- where they can focus;
- where they have an impact;
- what immediate, practical action will make a difference.

This is robust in two ways:

- it delivers results;
- they are sustainable.

* * *

Management and leadership coaching

Malcolm Hurrell, Leadership and Management Coach and Consultant

Approach used/skills/model

My early work was mainly informed by two models in which I had been trained: the GROW model and The Skilled Helper. Inevitably, over years of coaching experience, I have found myself using many other approaches that are available.

I encourage people to keep an open mind because it is surprising how some things prove useful, when they could too easily have been initially dismissed.

Many years ago, when working in an organization, I was feeling rather uncomfortable with some of the approaches in NLP. However, I decided to do my NLP practitioner qualification and now I am clear about what elements work well in my practice, and what elements of NLP I tend not to use.

Current issues/problems

I still regularly come across situations where I am asked, by a manager or human resources staff, to coach an individual who is struggling. What becomes evident is that the manager has not been doing their job in managing and supporting performance. I ask: 'How would you score the current performance of this individual? What would be happening if the investment in this person was realized? What is the timescale for expecting this?'

As a coach, I have a duty to challenge the organization thoroughly at the contracting meeting, to ensure that an open, realistic, contract is established.

High points/rewards

It is a huge privilege to be given the opportunity not only to go into many organizations, but also to be able to support individuals in their complex and fascinating work.

Rewards abound when I return to a client 6–12 months after completing my work with them. We meet for coffee, I hear their stories, and I help to re-stimulate them and inject new commitment. These are often the most rewarding times.

On a personal basis, I also know I learn from each contract. I have learnt to judge myself less and remain curious, even in difficult times, a behaviour change that has been helpful for me and others around me.

Ethical issues/supervision

I have never relied on one supervisor, but instead seek the views, wisdom and challenge of trusted contacts. Sometimes these people have relevant experience in the sector where I am working.

Building up a network of trusted and talented contacts is important to me.

Lessons learned

Coaching is best targeted at critical business strategy and projects. This approach justifies the costs of external coaching support. My work therefore needs to be about:

- developing key talent;
- supporting new incumbents in key critical roles;
- supporting teams who need to deliver important aspects of the strategy for the organization.

One tip I would like to share

The outcome of coaching is commitment to action by the client.

I always finish a client conversation with an open discussion about 'the three C's'. This acts as my test to see if our work is complete, and to ensure that any additional work adds value in a focused way:

- Do I hear clarity in the proposed actions?
- Do I hear confidence in the client's voice and in the words used?
- Do I hear commitment, indicating a desire to act?

In the event that any of these are not heard, then my job is to share that with them and ask what they want to do, that might lead to an increase in the three C's.

This is a great place to use a scale of 1–10 to score the answers to the three C's.

One piece of wisdom

Slow down, and model the use of reflection and space in conversations.

Follow this by asking the client to reflect on the pace of our own conversation. This allows him/her to consider how they may use this after the meeting. It is so helpful to make the coaching practice explicit and known, by talking about the experience they have just had.

My vision for the future of coaching and mentoring

Ideally my contribution to individuals and teams leads to embedding those skills into the organization. How wonderful it is to work in an environment where the core skills of coaching are used as the norm, leading to high quality conversations across the organization, where people are deeply challenged through supportive, probing questioning and listening.

* * *

Coaching and mentoring in education

David Harrison, National Leader in Education and Lead Headteacher, Polaris Teaching School Alliance

Role

- My role within the Teaching Alliance is to share good practice and develop outstanding teachers and future leaders in education.
- My role as Executive Headteacher is to identify areas of strength and areas for development in a group of schools in the primary sector and then to offer carefully targeted support and guidance.
- Mentoring is a means of encouraging learning and development through working alongside colleagues requiring guidance and support.
- Coaching is used to help with specific skills and performance targets.

Approach used

As a Teaching School we are part of a network, providing the opportunity for teachers to work collaboratively between schools and to become curriculum leaders across districts and regions. The ethos is one of shared leadership, support and collaboration. Mentoring and coaching are an integral part of 'the way we do things round here' through sharing knowledge and experience, supporting and valuing one another, so that each school in the Alliance is supported and challenged to become outstanding.

Skills/model

We are developing coaching and mentoring training for those in leadership roles. This training will give us an opportunity to get to know one another, to share our current issues and opportunities, to develop our coaching and mentoring skills, and then to share these with other staff in our own schools, so that a culture of coaching and mentoring can gradually be developed across the Teaching School Alliance.

Current issues/problems

For all staff, both teachers and leaders in education, the pace of change brings uncertainty. Currently there are political and government changes; changes to national assessments; changes in funding arrangements; changes in the role of local authorities. All this necessitates new partnerships, new boundaries, new forms of scrutiny. At such times there is a need for both mentoring and coaching at every level.

High points/rewards

Seeing staff develop and therefore seeing outstanding results for pupils. Getting an 'outstanding' rating from inspections and then seeing staff go from strength to strength because of the confidence shown in them. Trainee teachers graduate and get jobs, they then become NQTs (newly qualified teachers) and we continue to give them development opportunities at each stage of their career. The culture is one of support and challenge for constant development and change.

Low points/ethical issues

When there is resistance to change, this impacts upon pupils, who then suffer through underachievement. Some staff need support beyond what is routinely available. Confidentiality can be an issue when supporting staff in a small school, for example, balancing the perceptions of colleagues, at the same time as balancing the support and challenge needed to help a particular teacher in difficulty.

Lessons learned

Different people learn in different ways. My job is to find the strengths in each member of staff, and to nurture those strengths by building relationships with them. It is important to gain the professional respect of colleagues before trying to have difficult or challenging conversations with them. Respect and trust come before challenge.

One tip I would like to share

Rather than focusing coaching and mentoring resources on those who have difficulties, develop a mentoring and coaching culture, where all staff mentor and coach one another though working in teams that support and challenge.

One example of what worked well

Believing in people, and showing that you believe in them despite problems on the way! Not compromising and expecting 'good enough' but maintaining the right balance of supportive challenge to achieve outstanding results.

What did not work well/what got in the way

When a member of staff needs help, it will not work just because it is provided! Support and coaching can be put in place, but if the person is resistant to change, then the coaching does not work. Openness is needed. The time has to be right.

My vision for the future of coaching and mentoring

Leadership in education is all about collaboration: schools working together and challenging one another, for example, through regular reviews of aspects of curriculum and performance. In the ideal world, colleagues support one another to develop their knowledge and expertise, not by 'telling' but by 'sharing', whether this is a Headteacher with a member of staff, or whether it is a class teacher with a student. Sharing data and building strong support networks are two important ways in which a coaching and mentoring culture develops, at all levels and within all parts, of the school community.

* * *

How do you assess your organization?

If the benefits of coaching and mentoring at work are to be fully effective, then the culture of the organization will encourage, sustain, support and reward those who lead and manage these forms of learning and development. Clutterbuck and Megginson (2005: 96) identify four progressive stages on this journey: (1) *nascent*, where there is little commitment in evidence; (2) *tactical*, where the organization recognizes a need but does not show understanding about what will be necessary; (3) *strategic*, where managers are involved in coaching as part of everyday work and where this is rewarded; and (4) *embedded*, where coaching and mentoring are an integral part of learning and development and where all levels are involved in both the delivery and the receipt of coaching and mentoring.

The questions below in Box 12.1, reflect some of the factors which have been highlighted as significant when developing a coaching or mentoring culture. They may help you to reflect upon the development of a coaching and mentoring culture in your organization. The topics which they address include: the relationship between coaching and mentoring; developing a culture of learning, valuing and achievement; the link between individual development and organizational performance; the impact of coaching and mentoring on leadership and talent-management in the organization; team-working; resourcing and embedding coaching and mentoring. These topics throw light on the way in which values, structures, systems and processes contribute to organizational culture.

Summary

In this chapter we have:

- Shared the experiences of nine coaches and mentors, who work in a variety of sectors, both public and private, across the UK. Some of these are leading coaching and mentoring initiatives in their organizations, others are working independently, for example, as executive coaches.

- Offered 'glimpses' of their work under these headings:

  Approach used/skills/model
  Current issues/problems
  High points/rewards
  What worked well/what helped
  Low points
  Ethical issues/supervision
  One tip I would like to share
  One piece of wisdom
  My vision for the future of coaching and mentoring

- Concluded with a self-assessment questionnaire, based upon the experience of coaches and mentors, to help you to review the coaching and mentoring culture in your organization.

Box 12.1 Assessing the coaching and mentoring culture of your organization

---

1   Are both performance and development a strategic priority?
2   Does your organization link individual development to business performance?
3   Does senior management actively sponsor individual development? How?
4   What systems, procedures or processes support individual development? How well do these operate?
5   Are coaching and mentoring viewed as learning and development? If not, how are they viewed?
6   Are coaching and mentoring encouraged throughout the organization? If so, in what ways?
7   Do senior managers talk about using coaches and mentors themselves?
8   Do leaders and managers coach and mentor staff?
9   How would you describe the style of leadership in your organization? How does it fit with coaching and mentoring values?
10 In what ways are teamwork and participation encouraged and rewarded?
11 Is there a 'blame' culture anywhere in the organization?
12 Is there a culture where 'everything is a learning opportunity' operating anywhere in the organization?
13 Are there any forms of learning – for example, action learning and e-learning – that support coaching and mentoring?
14 Are coaching and mentoring non-hierarchical: downwards, upwards, peers?
15 Do managers embed coaching and mentoring in the way they work? How?
16 What resources are available for training and support of coaches and mentors?
17 Can you access both internal and external coaching and mentoring?
18 In what ways are coaching and mentoring used as part of talent management and developing potential?
19 How are the outcomes of coaching and mentoring reported?
20 What would be your main recommendations for your organization now that you have completed this questionnaire?

Appendix: useful contacts and websites

AC: Association for Coaching
www.associationforcoaching.com

APECS: Association for Professional Executive Coaching and Supervision
www.apecs.org

BACP Coaching: British Association for Counselling and Psychotherapy
www.bacpcoaching.co.uk

BPS: British Psychological Society
www.bps.org.uk

CIPD: Chartered Institute of Personnel and Development
www.cipd.co.uk

Coaching and Mentoring Network
www.new.coachingnetwork.org.uk

CUREE: Centre for the Use of Research and Evidence in Education
www.curee.co.uk

EMCC: European Mentoring and Coaching Council
www.emccouncil.org

ICF: International Coaching Federation
www.coachfederation.org

Mindtools
www.mindtools.com

Bibliography

AC (Association for Coaching) (2007) *Coaching Supervision: Analysis of Survey Findings*. Available at: www.associationforcoaching.com.

AC & EMCC (Association for Coaching and European Mentoring and Coaching Council) (2016) *Global Code of Ethics for Coaches and Mentors*. Available at: www.emccouncil. org/webimages/EMCC/Global_Code_of_Ethics.pdf (accessed 25 July 2016).

Adair, J. (1986) *Effective Teambuilding*. London: Pan.

Allan, J. and Whybrow, A. (2008) Gestalt coaching, in S. Palmer and A. Whybrow (eds) *Handbook of Coaching Psychology*. London: Routledge.

Asay, T.P. and Lambert, M.J. (1999) The empirical case for the common factors in therapy: quantitative findings, in M.A. Hubble, B.L. Duncan and S.D. Miller (eds) *The Heart and Soul of Change: What Works in Therapy*. Washington, DC: American Psychological Association.

BACP (British Association for Counselling and Psychotherapy) (2016) *Ethical Framework for the Counselling Professions*. Available at: www.bacp.co.uk/admin/structure/files/ pdf/15527_15470_ethical_framework.pdf (accessed 25 July 2016).

Bandura, A. (1969) *Principles of Behaviour Modification*. New York: Holt, Rinehart and Winston.

Barden, S. (2006) The team: the heart of executive coaching, *Coach and Mentor: The Journal of the Oxford School of Coaching and Mentoring*, 6: 6–7.

Bayne, R. (2004) *Psychological Types at Work: An MBTI Perspective*. London: Thomson.

Beck, A.T. (1976) *Cognitive Therapy and the Emotional Disorders*. New York: New American Library.

Belbin, M. (2000) *Beyond the Team*. London: Butterworth-Heinemann.

Belbin, M. (2003) *Team Roles at Work*, 2nd edn. London: Butterworth-Heinemann.

Bennett, M.J. (2004) Becoming interculturally competent, in J.S. Wurzel (ed.) *Toward Multiculturalism: A Reader in Multicultural Education*. Newton, MA: Intercultural Resource Corporation.

Berg, I. and Szabo, P. (2005) *Brief Coaching for Lasting Solutions*. London: Norton and Co.

Berglas, S. (2002) The very real dangers of executive coaching, *Harvard Business Review*, 80(6): 86–92.

Berne, E. (1972) *What Do You Say After You Say Hello?* London: Corgi.

Berne, E. (1976) *Beyond Games and Scripts*. New York: Ballantine.

Bion, W.R. (1961) *Experiences in Groups*. London: Tavistock.

Blanchard, K. (1994) *Leadership and the One-Minute Manager*. London: HarperCollins Business.

Blatner, A. (1996) *Acting-In: Practical Applications of Psychodramatic Methods*, 3rd edn. New York: Springer.

Blessingwhite (2009) *The Coaching Conundrum: Building a Coaching Culture that Drives Organisational Success*. Available at: www.blessingwhite.com.

Bluckert, P. (2006) *Psychological Dimensions of Executive Coaching*. Maidenhead: Open University Press.

Bluckert, P. (2010) The Gestalt approach to coaching, in E. Cox, T. Bachkirova and D. Clutterbuck (eds) *The Complete Handbook of Coaching*. London: Sage.

Bolles, R.N. (2002) *What Color is Your Parachute? A Practical Guide for Job Hunters and Career Changers*. Berkeley, CA: Ten Speed Press.

Bond, T. (1993) *Standards and Ethics for Counselling in Action*. London: Sage.

Boyatzis, R., Smith, M. and Blaize, N. (2006) Sustaining leadership effectiveness through coaching and compassion: it's not what you think, *Academy of Management Learning and Education*, 5(1): 8–24.

Brann, A. (2015) *Neuroscience for Coaches*. London: Kogan Page.

Burgoyne, J. (1990) Doubts about competence, in M. Devine (ed.) *The Photofit Manager*. London: Unwin Hyman.

Carroll, M. (2011) Ethical maturity: compasses for life and work decisions – Part I, *Psychotherapy in Australia*, 17(3): 12–23.

Cavanagh, M.J. and Grant, A.M. (2010) The solution-focused approach to coaching, in E. Cox, T. Bachkirova and D. Clutterbuck (eds) *The Complete Handbook of Coaching*. London: Sage.

CIPD (Chartered Institute of Personnel and Development) (2015a) *Coaching and Mentoring Factsheet*. London: CIPD.

CIPD (Chartered Institute of Personnel and Development) (2015b) *Learning and Development: Annual Survey Report*. London: CIPD.

Clutterbuck, D. (2001) *Everyone Needs a Mentor*. London: CIPD.

Clutterbuck, D. (2012) Understanding diversity mentoring, in D. Clutterbuck, K.M. Poulsen and F. Kochan (eds) *Developing Successful Diversity Mentoring Programmes: An International Casebook*. Maidenhead: Open University Press.

Clutterbuck, D. and Megginson, D. (2005) *Making Coaching Work*. London: CIPD.

Clutterbuck, D. and Megginson, D. (2010) Coach maturity: an emerging concept, *International Journal of Coaching and Mentoring*, 8(1): 4–12.

Clutterbuck, D. and Ragins, B.R. (2002) *Mentoring for Diversity*. London: Butterworth-Heinemann.

Connor, M. (1994) *Training the Counsellor*. London: Routledge.

Connor, M. (1997) *Mentoring for Medics*. York: University College of Ripon and York St John.

Connor, M. and Pokora, J. (2007) *Coaching and Mentoring at Work*. Maidenhead: Open University Press.

Connor, M., Bynoe, A.G., Redfern, N., Pokora, J. and Clarke, J. (2000) Developing senior doctors as mentors: a form of continuing professional development. Report of an initiative to develop a network of senior doctors as mentors, 1994–99, *Medical Education*, 34: 747–53.

Cooperrider, D.L. and Whitney, D. (1999) Appreciative enquiry: a positive revolution in change, in P. Holman and T. Davane (eds) *The Change Handbook: Group Methods for Shaping the Future*. San Francisco, CA: Berrett-Koehler.

Cooperrider, D., Whitney, D., Stavros, J. and Fry, R. (2003) *Appreciative Enquiry Handbook*. San Francisco, CA: Berrett-Koehler.

Covey, S.R. (1989) *The Seven Habits of Highly Effective People*. London: Simon & Schuster.

Creasy, J. and Paterson, F. (2005) *Leading Coaching in Schools*, Leading Practice Seminar Series, National College for School Leadership. Available at: www.ncsl.org.uk.

Critchley, B. (2009) Relational coaching: taking courage and making a difference, *International Journal of Mentoring and Coaching*, 7(2): 25–35.

CUREE online *National Framework for Mentoring and Coaching*. Available at: www.curee.co.uk/files/publication/1219925968/National-framework-for-mentoring-and-coaching.pdf (accessed 28 November 2016).

Davis, S., Clutterbuck, D. and Megginson, D. (eds) (2016) *Beyond Goals*. London: Routledge.

De Bono, E. (1992) *Serious Creativity*. New York: Harper Business.

de Shazer, S. (1991) *Putting Difference to Work*. New York: Norton.

Downey, M. (2003) *Effective Coaching: Lessons from the Coaches' Coach*, 2nd edn. London: Texere.

Earley, P.C. and Ang, S. (2003) *Cultural Intelligence*. Stanford, CA: Stanford University Press.

Easterby-Smith, M., Burgoyne, J. and Araujo, L. (eds) (1999) *Organisational Learning and the Learning Organisation*. London: Sage.

Eaton, J. and Johnson, R. (2001) *Coaching Successfully*. London: Dorling Kindersley.

Egan, G. (2002) *The Skilled Helper*, 7th edn. Belmont, CA: Thomson Brooks/Cole.

Egan, G. (2006) *Essentials of Skilled Helping*. Belmont, CA: Thomson Wadsworth.

Egan, G. (2010) *The Skilled Helper*, 9th edn. Belmont, CA: Brooks/Cole Cengage Learning.

Egan, G. (2013) *The Skilled Helper*, 10th edn. Belmont, CA: Brookes/Cole Cengage Learning.

Eglin, R. (2006) Building a more efficient society, *The Sunday Times*, 14 May, p. 6.

Ellis, A., Gordon, J., Neenan, M. and Palmer, S. (1997) *Stress Counseling: A Rational-Emotive Behavior Approach*. New York: Springer.

EMCC (European Mentoring and Coaching Council) (2004) *Guidelines on Supervision: An Interim Statement*. Available at: www.emccouncil.org.

EMCC (European Mentoring and Coaching Council) (2005) Press release EMCC19, December. Available at: www.emccouncil.org.

EMCC (European Mentoring and Coaching Council) (2009) *EQA Information Guide*. Available at: www.emccouncil.org.

EMCC (European Mentoring and Coaching Council) (2015) *EMCC Competency Framework V2*. Available at: www.emccouncil.org/webimages/EU/EQA/emcc-competence-framework-v2.pdf (accessed 25 July 2016).

EMCC (European Mentoring and Coaching Council) (2016) *Guidelines for Supervision*. Available at: www.emccouncil.org/src/ultimo/models/download/7.pdf (accessed 30 November 2016).

European Economic and Social Committee (2011) *The Professional Charter for Coaching and Mentoring*. European Coaching and Mentoring Council, International Coach Federation, Association for Coaching, Société Française de Coaching. Available at: www.eesc.europa.eu/self-and-Urpean coregulation/documents/codes/private/142-private-act.pdf (accessed 25 July 2016).

Fisher, R. and Ury, W. (1987) *Getting to Yes*. London: Arrow.

Flood, R.L. (1999) *Rethinking the Fifth Discipline*. Abingdon on Thames: Routledge.

Francis, D. (1994) *Managing Your Own Career*. London: HarperCollins.

Fraser, S. and Greenhalgh, T. (2001) Complexity science: coping with complexity, educating for capability, *British Medical Journal*, 323: 799–803.

Fritchie, R. and Leary, M. (1998) *Resolving Conflicts in Organisations*. London: Lemos and Crane.

Fritts, P.J. (1998) *The New Managerial Mentor*. Palo Alto, CA: Davies Black.

Gallwey, T. (2000) *The Inner Game of Work*. London: Orion.

Garret-Harris, R. and Garvey, B. (2005) *Towards a Framework for Mentoring in the NHS*, evaluation report on behalf of the NHS. Sheffield: Sheffield Hallam University.

Garvey, B. and Garret-Harris, R. (2005) *The Benefits of Mentoring: A Literature Review*, report for East Mentors Forum. Sheffield: Mentoring and Coaching Research Unit, Sheffield Hallam University.

General Medical Council (2013) *Good Medical Practice*. London: GMC.

Gergen, K.J. (2003) *An Invitation to Social Construction*. London: Sage.

Goldsmith, M., Lyons, L. and Freas, A. (eds) (2000) *Coaching for Leadership: How the World's Greatest Coaches Help Leaders Learn*. San Francisco, CA: Pfeiffer.

Goleman, D. (1998) *Working with Emotional Intelligence*. London: Bloomsbury.

Greene, J. (2003) *Solution Focused Coaching*. Ashland, OR: Momentum.

Grimley, B. (2010) The NLP approach to coaching, in E. Cox et al. (eds) *The Complete Handbook of Coaching*. London: Sage.

Hall, L. (2013) *Mindful Coaching*. London: Kogan Page.

Hardingham, A., Brearley, M., Moorhouse, A. and Ventner, B. (2004) *The Coach's Coach: Personal Development for Personal Developers*. London: Chartered Institute of Personnel Development.

Harris, A. and Harris, T. (1985) *Staying OK*. London: Pan.

Hawkins, P. and Shohet, R. (2000) *Supervision in the Helping Professions*. Buckingham: Open University Press.

Hawkins, P. and Smith, N. (2006) *Coaching, Mentoring and Organisational Consultancy*. Maidenhead: Open University Press.

Hawkins, P. and Smith, N. (2010) Coaching supervision, in E. Cox et al. (eds) *The Complete Handbook of Coaching.* London: Sage.

Hawkins, P. and Smith, N. (2013) *Coaching, Mentoring and Organizational Consultancy,* 2nd edn. Maidenhead: Open University Press.

Hay, J. (2007) *Reflective Practice and Supervision for Coaches.* Maidenhead: Open University Press.

Henley Business School (2016) *Corporate Learning Survey 2016 Using Learning and Development to Achieve Strategic Business Aims.* Available at: www.henley.ac. uk/files/pdf/exec-ed/Corporate_Learning_Survey_2016_report_final_WEB.pdf (accessed 16 August 2016).

Hilpern, K. (2006) Bringing law to order, *Coaching at Work,* 1(2): 42–5.

Hofstede, G. (2001) *Culture's Consequences: Comparing Values, Behaviours, Institutions and Organizations Across Nations,* 2nd edn. Thousand Oaks, CA: Sage.

Honey, P. and Mumford, A. (1992) *A Manual of Learning Styles.* Maidenhead: P. Honey Publications.

Honey, P. and Mumford, A. (2006) *The Learning Styles Questionnaire: 80 Item.* Maidenhead: P. Honey Publications.

Hutton-Taylor, S. (1999) Cultivating a coaching culture, *British Medical Journal,* 318: S2-7188.

ICF (International Coach Federation) (2016) *ICF Core Competencies.* Available at: www.coachfederation.org.uk/about-us/icf-core-competencies/ (accessed 25 July 2016).

Inskipp, F. and Proctor, P. (1989) *Skills for Supervising and Being Supervised.* St Leonards-on-Sea: Alexia Publications.

International Centre for Coaching and Mentoring Studies, Oxford Brookes University (2016) *What Is Coaching and Mentoring?* Available at: www.business.brookes. ac.uk/research/iccms/ (accessed 17 August 2016).

Iveson, C., George, E. and Ratner, H. (2012) *Brief Coaching: A Solution Focused Approach.* London: Routledge.

Jackson, P. (2002) *The Solutions Focus.* London: Nicholas Brealey.

Jackson, P. and McKergow, M. (2006) *The Solutions Focus: Making Coaching and Change SIMPLE.* Bristol: Nicholas Brealey.

Jacobs, M. (1989) *Psychodynamic Counselling in Action.* London: Sage.

James, M. and Jongeward, D. (1971) *Born to Win.* Reading, MA: Addison-Wesley.

Johnson, S. (1985) *Characterological Transformation.* New York: Norton.

Kabat-Zinn, J. (2015) Coming to our senses: healing ourselves and the world through mindfulness, in C. Pemberton, *Resilience, A Practical Guide for Coaches.* Maidenhead: Open University Press.

Karpman, S. (1968) Fairy tales and script drama analysis, *Transactional Analysis Bulletin,* 7(26): 39–43.

Katzenbach, J.R. and Smith, D.K. (1993) *The Wisdom of Teams: Creating the High-performance Organization.* Boston, MA: Harvard University Press.

Kauffman, C., Boniwell, I. and Silberman, J. (2010) The positive psychology approach to coaching, in E. Cox et al. (eds) *The Complete Handbook of Coaching.* London: Sage.

Kelly, G. (1963) *A Theory of Personality*. New York: W.W. Norton.

Kennedy, G. (1992) *The Perfect Negotiation*. London: Century.

Kirkpatrick, D.L. (1994) *Evaluating Training Programs: The Four Levels*. San Francisco, CA: Berrett-Koehler.

Kolb, D. (1984) *Experiential Learning*. Englewood Cliffs, NJ: Prentice Hall.

Kolb, D. and Fry, R. (1975) Towards an applied theory of experiential learning, in C.L. Cooper (ed.) *Theories of Group Processes*. London: Wiley.

Korzybski, A. (1994) *Science and Sanity: An Introduction to Non-Aristotelian Systems and General Semantics*, 5th edn. Brooklyn, NY: Institute of General Semantics.

Kotter, J.P. (1998) *What Leaders Really Do*. Boston, MA: Harvard Business School Press.

Lambert, M. (1992) Implications for outcome research for psychotherapy integration, in J. Norcross and M. Goldstein (eds) *Handbook of Psychotherapy Integration*. New York: Basic Books.

Launer, J. (2002) *Narrative-based Primary Care*. Oxford: Radcliffe.

Lewin, K. (1951) *Field Theory in Social Science: Selected Theoretical Papers*, ed. D. Cartwright. New York: Harper and Row.

Lord, P., Atkinson, M. and Mitchell, H. (2008) *Mentoring and Coaching for Professionals: A Study of the Research Evidence*. London; TDA.

Luft, J. (1969) *Of Human Interaction*. Palo Alto, CA: National Press.

Luft, J. (1970) *Group Processes: An Introduction to Group Dynamics*. Palo Alto, CA: National Press Books.

Maslow, A.H. (1970) *Motivation and Personality*, 2nd edn. New York: Harper and Row.

Matthews, G. (undated) *Summary of Recent Goals Research*. Dominican University of California. Available at: www.dominican.edu/dominicannews/study-backs-up-strategies-for-achieving-goals.html.

McKay, M., Davis, M. and Fanning, P. (1981) *Thoughts and Feelings*. Richmond, CA: New Harbinger Publications.

McKergow, M. and Clarke, J. (undated) *Coaching with OSKAR* (2 page information sheet). Available at: The Centre for Solutions Focus at Work, www.sfwork.com (accessed October 2016).

Mead, G.H. (1967) *Mind, Self and Society: From the Standpoint of a Social Behaviorist*, ed. C.W. Morris. Chicago, IL: University of Chicago Press.

Megginson, D., Clutterbuck, D., Garvey, B., Stokes, P. and Garret-Harris, R. (2006) *Mentoring in Action: A Practical Guide for Managers*. London: Kogan Page.

Myers, I. with Myers, P. (1980) *Gifts Differing*. Palo Alto, CA: Consulting Psychologists Press.

National College for Teaching and Leadership (2013) *Empowering Others: Coaching and Mentoring*. Available at: www.nationalcollege.org.uk/cm-mc-mccor-tp.pdf (accessed 17 August 2016).

Neenan, M. (2008) From Cognitive Behaviour Therapy (CBT) to Cognitive Behaviour Coaching (CBC), *Journal of Rational-Emotive and Cognitive-Behavioural Therapy*, 26(1): 3–15.

Neenan, M. and Dryden, W. (2002) *Life Coaching: A Cognitive Behavioural Approach.* London: Routledge.

Neenan, M. and Palmer, S. (2001) Cognitive behavioural coaching, *Stress News,* 13(3): 15–18.

Newton, T. and Napper, R. (2010) Transactional analysis and coaching, in E. Cox et al. (eds) *The Complete Handbook of Coaching.* London: Sage.

Page, N. and de Haan, E. (2014) Does executive coaching work?, *The Psychologist,* 27(8): 582–6.

Palmer, S. (2008) The PRACTICE model of coaching, *Coaching Psychology International,* 1(1): 4–8.

Palmer, S. and Szymanska, K. (2008) Cognitive-behavioural coaching: an integrative approach, in S. Palmer and A. Whybrow (eds) *Handbook of Coaching Psychology: A Guide for Practitioners.* London: Routledge.

Parsloe, E. (1992) *Coaching, Mentoring and Assessing: A Practical Guide to Developing Competence.* London: Kogan Page.

Parsloe, E. (1999) *The Manager as Coach and Mentor.* London: Institute of Personnel and Development.

Parsloe, E. and Wray, M. (2000) *Coaching and Mentoring: Practical Methods to Improve Learning.* London: Kogan Page.

Pask, R. and Joy, B. (2007) *Mentoring-Coaching: A Guide for Education Professionals.* Maidenhead: Open University Press.

Passmore, J. and Mortimer, L. (2011) Ethics in coaching, in L. Boyce and G. Hernez-Broome (eds) *Advancing Executive Coaching: Setting the Course for Successful Leadership Coaching.* San Francisco, CA: Jossey-Bass.

Pedler, M. and Aspinwall, K. (1996) *Perfect PLC?* Maidenhead: McGraw-Hill.

Pedler, M., Burgoyne, J. and Boydell, T. (1991) *The Learning Company: A Strategy for Sustainable Development.* Maidenhead: McGraw-Hill.

Pedler, M., Burgoyne, J. and Boydell, T. (1994) *A Manager's Guide to Self Development.* Maidenhead: McGraw-Hill.

Pemberton, C. (2015) *Resilience. A Practical Guide for Coaches.* Maidenhead: Open University Press.

Perls, F. (1951) *Gestalt Therapy: Excitement and Growth in the Human Personality.* New York: Julian.

Phillips, A. and Pokora, J. (2004) Diagnostic versus active listening, unpublished presentation to GP Leadership Programme, Northern Deanery.

Pokora, J. and Briner, W. (1999) Teams and the learning organisation, in R. Stewart (ed.) *Gower Handbook of Teamworking.* Aldershot: Gower.

Rawlinson, J.G. (1986) *Creative Thinking and Brainstorming.* Aldershot: Gower.

Revans, R. (1983) *ABC of Action Learning.* Bromley: Chartwell-Bratt.

Rich, J.R. (2003) *Brainstorm: Tap into Your Creativity to Generate Awesome Ideas and Tremendous Results.* Franklin Lakes, NJ: Career Press.

Rickards, T. (1997) *Creativity and Problem Solving at Work.* Aldershot: Gower.

Robbins, A. (1992) *Awaken the Giant Within.* Riverside, NJ: Simon and Schuster.

Rodenburg, P. (2007) *Presence.* London: Michael Joseph.

Rogers, C.R. (1961) *On Becoming a Person.* London: Constable.

Rogers, C.R. (1983) *Freedom to Learn in the 80s.* Columbus, OH: Charles Merrill.

Rogers, J. (2016) *Coaching Skills*, 4th edn. Maidenhead: Open University Press.

Rogers, J. and Maini, A. (2016) *Coaching for Health.* Maidenhead: Open University Press.

Rosinki, P. (2003) *Coaching Across Cultures: New Tools for Leveraging National, Corporate and Professional Differences.* London: Nicholas Brealey.

Schein, E. (1990) *Career Anchors: Discovering Your Real Values.* San Francisco, CA: Jossey-Bass/Pfeiffer.

Schön, D.A. (1983) *The Reflective Practitioner: How Professionals Think in Action.* London: Temple Smith.

Seligman, M. (2002) *Authentic Happiness.* New York: Free Press.

Seligman, M. (2011) *Flourish.* London: Nicholas Brealey.

Senge, P.M. (1992) *The Fifth Discipline.* London: Century Business.

Starr, J. (2003) *The Coaching Manual.* London: Pearson Education.

Steiner, C. (1974) *Scripts People Live.* New York: Bantam.

Steven, A., Oxley, J. and Fleming, W.G. (2008) Mentoring for NHS doctors: perceived benefits across the personal–professional interface, *Journal of the Royal Society of Medicine*, 101: 552–7.

Stone, D., Patton, B. and Heen, S. (1999) *Difficult Conversations: How to Discuss What Matters Most.* London: Michael Joseph.

Stone, F.M. (1999) *Coaching, Counselling and Mentoring.* New York: American Management Association.

Sulaiman, T. (2006) How to mentor: it's a shared experience, *The Times*, 11 May.

Trompenaars, F. and Hampden-Turner, C. (2012) *Riding the Waves of Culture: Understanding Diversity in Global Business.* 3rd edn. New York: McGraw-Hill.

Tuckman, R.W. (1965) Developmental sequences in small groups, *Psychological Bulletin*, 63: 384–99.

UK Coaching Bodies Roundtable (2008) *Statement of Shared Professional Values.* Available at: www.associationforcoaching.com/pages/resources/press-releases/major-breakthrough-uk-coaching-bodies-roundtable-produce-first-u/ (accessed 25 July 2016).

Van Dyne, L., Ang, S. and Livermore, D. (2010) Cultural intelligence: a pathway for leading in a rapidly globalizing world, in K.M. Hannum. B. McFeeters and L. Booysen (eds) *Leading across Differences.* San Francisco, CA: Pfeiffer.

Vickers, A. and Bavister, S. (2005) *Teach Yourself Coaching.* London: Hodder Arnold.

Viney, R. and Paice, E. (2010) *The First Five Hundred. A Report on London Deanery's Coaching and Mentoring Service 2008–2010.* Available at: www.londondeanery.ac.uk.

Whitmore, J. (2002) *Coaching for Performance: GROWing People, Performance and Purpose*, 3rd edn. London: Nicholas Brealey.

Whittington, J. (2012) *Systemic Coaching and Constellations.* London: Kogan Page.

Whitworth, L., Kimsey-House, H. and Sandahl, P. (1998) *Co-Active Coaching: New Skills for Coaching People Toward Success in Work and Life*. Mountain View, CA: Davies Black.

Williams, H., Edgerton, N. and Palmer, S. (2010) Cognitive behavioural coaching, in E. Cox et al. (eds) *The Complete Handbook of Coaching*. London: Sage.

Wilson, C. (2014) *Performance Coaching*, 2nd edn. London: Kogan Page.

Zdenek, M. (1983) *The Right Brain Experience*. London: Corgi Books.

Zeus, P. and Skiffington, S. (2000) *The Complete Guide to Coaching at Work*. North Ryde, NSW: McGraw-Hill.

Index